21

DOROTHY M. LOVE

Library of Congress Cataloging-in-Publication Data is available upon request.

ISBN (Print): 978-1-09837-707-6
ISBN (eBook): 978-1-09837-708-3

This book is the product of Love & Associates, LLC, produced as a mentoring and coaching resource. For more information, contact Dorothy M. Love, CEO, Love & Associates, LLC at email address: dlove21@gmail.com; 916-502-4725.

Dedication

To My family; My life; My legacy:

My sweet mother, Ethel and stepfather, Willie, and my biological father, Adell, all resting in heaven, and I am thankful for their love for and to me.

My children, my reasons to just keep moving:
Michelle, Larissa, Christine and Timothy, and his lovely wife, Nadiyah.

And my Grandchildren
LaQuesha, Jasmine, Marc, Dominique, Nicole, Naimah, Ajanae, (my) Elijah, Mekhi, Micah, Maryam, Isa, Joshua, Elias, Amirah, Timothy Jr. (2T), bonus granddaughter, Kweli

And Great Grandchildren
Bobby, Rico, the twins: Taz and Talia, Baby Tru, and those yet to come.....

To my extended family and friends who have encouraged and supported me with love and covered me with prayer, my heart smiles with gratitude.

Contents

Preface
The Vantage Point

It is my pleasure to introduce this book to you with great anticipation that you will be encouraged and find the freedom to begin to embrace your journey and eventually enjoy it. Whether you purchased this book or received it as a gift, know with certainty that, intentionally, it landed in your hands. Placed in your hand is half the journey; reading it is the other half. Let's get busy. Don't be a spectator. Get involved in your journey.

This book is an anthology, a string of short stories strung together like pearls with one theme: hope; one foundation: fear; and one turning point in each writer's life that I call the vantage point. The women are vastly different, from different locations and having different experiences, observing whatever is at the center of their attention, what it is they are striving to find. It matters not where they started; they all end connected at the vantage point. Most people look from the vantage point, but in these ladies' stories, the vantage point is looking at them. I challenge you to embrace each story. Should you find yourself within the pages, I pray you find hope. If you do not find yourself within the pages, be grateful for that. Maybe you dodged a bullet.

I have always dreamed of writing a book. I had the title and all the substance to write it from beginning to end, but it was not this book titled *21*. I could deal with writing a book about my journey, but to collaborate with twenty-one women telling their stories and penning them—well, that was not my desire. God wanted me on this journey to teach me about the characteristics of love and humility and the power of a story.

Unbeknownst to me, this book would come about when two friends and I traveled to Los Angeles to attend the 100-year celebration of the Azusa Street Revival. The revival was renowned for a few reasons. First, it ignited a strong desire in the hearts of people to return to God. In a time of racial segregation, it attracted Blacks and Whites worldwide and was led by an African American gentleman named William Seymour. Although it started somewhat racially united, it ended racially divided. Out of this revival came the birth of the Pentecostal faith giving us racially divided churches once again. For the Blacks, the Church of God in Christ. For the Whites, the Assemblies of God, and Church of God. But today we were a mixed multitude attending this memorable celebration.

Upon our arrival, we checked into our hotel, scheduled a time we would gather for dinner, and retreated to our rooms to make ourselves comfortable. My friend and dear sister Carol and I were well acquainted, but our other sister I only knew by face and name. Another friend had told us about her desire to attend the celebration and she wanted a traveling partner, so we connected. She was one of the sweetest people I could ever meet. Her name is Mulu.

I arrived at the hotel restaurant and found Mulu sitting alone, waiting for us. We greeted each other, and then the conversation ensued. I love meeting people, really meeting them. I sincerely want to know about the person and their interests, inspiration, and life ideology, not just the surface, passing the time in conversation. After we finished our introductions, we moved into deeper waters. I was curious enough to ask an openly bold question: I asked her to tell me her story.

I guessed she sensed my sincerity in knowing her better and began to share her story. The more she shared, the larger my eyes became and the wider my mouth fell open. I will not tell you her story; I will let you read it for yourself. The entire weekend we were together was an adventure. It was one glorious experience after another, and the more we shared, the more we knew about each other, all three of us. We became connected sisters.

Upon returning home, I couldn't wait to tell our Bible study director, Pastor Mary, about her story. I impressed upon her that it would be nice to share testimonies during our women's Bible study, starting with Mulu's story. After I told her Mulu's story, she agreed, and the journey began. I assisted Mulu in writing her testimony as concisely as possible to be shared in a short amount of time. The night came, and her testimony was the last item on the evening's agenda. Mulu stepped up to the podium, notes in hand, and began to tell her story. The audience was in awe, just as I had been the first time I heard her story. Because her story started when she was just a teenager of sixteen, the youth in the room could hardly believe it. Nonetheless, they were encouraged by her courage. Once she finished and stepped down, the audience bombarded her with questions and accolades.

As I was exiting the room, a young lady named Tina, whom I didn't know, got my attention. I knew she was an educator, but that was about all I knew. She asked me if I had written the testimony for Mulu to share. I hesitated to answer because it was Mulu's story, and I didn't want to distract from Mulu. I finally said yes, I had helped in composing it. She then looked at me and said, "I hear God saying, 'twenty-one'!"

I asked, "Twenty-one what?"

She replied, "Twenty-one, stories—testimonies!"

Suddenly, someone said that "twenty-one" was not a good number. I thought, *Praise God.* I was glad to hear that because I had no intention of writing twenty-one testimonies. And that is where I left the conversation. The problem was, the conversation never left me, and it would surface at the most awkward times.

I tried to get it off my mind by repeating what I had heard, that "twenty-one is not a good number." I didn't know what that meant, except it got me off the hook for writing a book titled *21.* I shared this occurrence with one of my pastors, and he said, "Twenty-one—wow, that is a good number. It is three times seven, and everyone knows that seven is God's number."

The dilemma in my head started again and worsened. I visited my friend Angela's home to celebrate her husband's birthday. One of the guests was her pastor, and as we were talking, he asked about what I was doing. By then, I had decided maybe I should reconsider the book. I told him that I was considering writing a book titled *21.* He quickly said, "That is a good number. It is God's number multiplied three times!" Done! I was convinced. I said yes to God: I would write the book.

Once I said yes, my next question to God was, "Who and where are the twenty-one women? And why women only?" It came with the revelation. Around that time, I attended a Sisters Retreat in the mountain, just us women having a fabulous time together in God's presence. While I was there, I started having conversations with other women. Once I said I was writing a book, I was surprised at the number of ladies interested. I left the retreat with the names of a few women who had shown an interest. Some of those ladies are in this book. I hadn't known them before this, just as I hadn't known Mulu, but they shared their stories with me.

The incident that sealed the deal and afforded me my last confirmation after I had committed to God to write this book occurred when I was seeking a location for our first writers' workshop. My dear friend Nancy was using a building called the Barn to conduct Bible studies. She offered to connect me with the owners. The owner and I finally connected, but the conversation was difficult because he had a bad cough. He said it was okay for me to use the Barn, but he insisted on telling me a story of a miracle that had happened a few years back. I offered to pray for him, and we could discuss it another time, but he insisted on telling me then. I listened. He told me about a young lady who had come to the Barn for a youth event her daughters were attending. She had been in a bad car accident and was having severe back pain and other physical problems. He said that the young man conducting the ministry for the event prayed for her, and God healed her back. Not only that, he said she had been shot twice in the face and had lost eyesight in one eye, and God restored her vision. When he said that, all I could think about was how I would love to meet this miracle, and it would be great to have this testimony in the book.

It was Friday, and I needed to get home to prepare to attend a church life group meeting later that evening. I offered to pray for him, he accepted, and we prayed and hung up. I was elated for the person whom God had blessed with the miracle of healings. That night, my daughter, her sons, and I went to the meeting and had a great deal of fun. We left refreshed after meeting so many friendly people. On Monday morning, I received a call from the life group hostess, Gloria, informing me that a young lady at the meeting wanted to meet me because she heard I was writing a book. We chatted, and I asked her to have the young lady call me. I thought, *Wow, God, You are making this happen. Thank You!*

Within a few days, the young lady called me. We talked small talk for a while, and she reminded me who she was at the meeting. I remembered her, her daughter, and her husband. Finally, I said, just as I had to Mulu, "What is your story?"

She said, "I was shot in the face twice!"

I did everything I could to keep from actually throwing the phone; I was speechless! It couldn't be true—no way. I was in the room with the miracle on the same evening the man had told me about the miracle, and now the miracle was calling me. She told me it would be an honor to share her story in the book, and my heart leaped with joy. God didn't have to do anything else to confirm the book; but He opened up the heavens.

We had our official writers' workshop at the Barn. I didn't have twenty-one women at the time, but I was over halfway there. Each lady introduced herself and told a portion of her story. We all marveled at the tidbits of information—a sneak preview into each lady's story. It was exciting, although many, if not all, were painful stories. The young lady whose vision God had restored shared her story, and we continued to the next person until the last person had shared. Then the miracle lady said she felt she needed to share more vital information with us. She said it was at this very place, the Barn, where she received the healing of her back and vision. And that wasn't all. She told us of how the young minister prayed over her for a long time, and during the prayer, he said to her that God said she would be back at the Barn, years from that date, and she would be writing a book with many women. Again, I felt the need to throw something; I couldn't take the way God was blowing my mind and confirming himself. I was already convinced and committed; now, I was fully persuaded.

Since our first meet and greet on January 24, 2018, it has been a journey. Many of the ladies who started with us were unable to finish for various personal reasons, but having their initial interest blessed me. Once I was convinced this was God's project, I never worried about the contributors; God was responsible for the twenty-one women, and He would find His replacements. We have had incidents where the enemy, satan, has sought to stop us, but to no avail. He may hinder us, but I will not stop because my commitment is to God, not myself. I have come to love more profoundly and to accept my sisters without a second opinion. We have cried together, prayed together, and hoped together. We celebrate each other for the boldness, mercy, and grace God has granted them to tell their story. And their stories are relatable because their struggles were real. They tell their stories because they are free—free enough to give the details and be transparent—and why? Because they want you to be free!

I fought within myself to complete this book and publish it in 2019 and then 2020, the year of COVID-19, and as you can see, that didn't happen. As I was beginning to feel a little defeated, slothful, distressed, and a few other words, *God caused me to pause.* He said it was me who wanted 2019 and 2020; it was always His will that this book titled 21 would be published in 2021. *The power of a pause!*

Enjoy this book but do more. Whatever healing you may need, receive it from God as you read the pages of each story. Twenty-one relatable women, twenty-one stories, and twenty-one miracles—each gets one, or maybe two or more, and you can get yours!

You own everything that happened to you. Tell your stories. If people wanted you to write warmly about them, they SHOULD HAVE BEHAVED BETTER.

Anne Lamott

My Journey as a Refugee

by Mulu Afework

Though I walk in the midst of trouble, you preserve my life. You stretch out your hand against the anger of my foes; with your right hand, you save me. (Psalms 138:7 NIV)

Why Do People Leave Their Homeland and Choose to Be Strangers in a Strange Land?

All around the world, large numbers of people leave behind their language, belief system, family, friends, and everything representing their culture and take major (sometimes unknown) risks to migrate to another country. Many are forced from their homes to become refugees because of political and religious persecution or ethnic genocides. Some flee from organized crime or human rights violations to seek a safer place, especially for their children, and a better living standard for their family as a whole. Here is my story.

Why I Left My Homeland at Age Sixteen and Became a Refugee

I was born in a small city located in the eastern part of Ethiopia. I had the privilege to be raised by a loving grandmother, my mom's mother. My grandmother owned a large plot of land, and there were multiple small, two-bedroom houses on the property that she rented to the locals, family members, and friends. She raised me to recognize and accept everyone around me as a relative, and uncle or auntie, or a friend. It was and still is quite common for many Ethiopian families and friends to live close to one another, so as you can imagine, everyone was like family.

I have the fondest memories of how some of the people in the compound loved me and treated me as their little girl. I would start my day with breakfast at my home. I would have lunch next door. And we ate dinner at whatever house all of us children just happened to be playing near at dinner time. That was and still is one of the many parts of the Ethiopian culture I love the most.

I remember my life as a young Ethiopian girl being remarkably comfortable and straightforward within the community that surrounded me. We had plenty to eat, and we could easily buy fresh meat, vegetables, fruits, and grains from the local market. Food was affordable, even for those considered underserved; here in America, we call them "the poor." The government did not provide social services; therefore, it was typical for the community to help our poor families and friends. Unbeknownst to me, my pleasant childhood life in

Ethiopia was about to turn into chaos, and fear like never before was about to be birthed in our country, sending us all into a panic.

During the early 1970s, tension among different economic classes and ethnic groups ignited in our country. At that time, we also learned about severe droughts that affected the northern part of Ethiopia. The drought greatly impacted those identified as peasants whose life depended on farming. The drought spread throughout parts of Ethiopia and caused major hunger crises. As millions faced starvation, the whole country grew restless. Antigovernment militants blamed the emperor at the time, Haile Selassie, and his administration for the trouble in the land.

Haile Selassie was the emperor of Ethiopia from 1930 to 1974; as you can imagine, it was a well-established system for decades. The Ethiopian emperor traced his dynasty back to Menilek, the first emperor of Ethiopia. The people believed that he was a Hebrew descendant who started the line of the Solomonic dynasty. You will find Ethiopia mentioned forty-four times in the Bible in the Old Testament. Many believe that one of the famous figures in the Bible, the Queen of Sheba, also known as Makeda by Ethiopians, was Ethiopian. They believe that upon her visit with King Solomon, their union produced a son named Menilek, thereby creating Jewish heirs among the Ethiopians. The Ethiopian Jews (Falashasak, aka Beta-Israel) link their ancestry settlement to the northern part of Ethiopia. Many of them migrated back to Israel between 1980 and 1992.

I remember when a Marxist-led military group overthrew Emperor Haile Selassie, who had reigned for over forty years. In 1974 the military dictator took over the country and turned it into a communist nation. The talk amongst the community was that during the takeover, they placed Emperor Haile Selassie under house arrest, and strangely, he died eleven months later. Between 1976 and 1978, the new Marxist government began rounding up and killing those suspected of being members of the opposing groups or resisting the change. Bodies were dumped in the street, mostly college students, but also children as young as thirteen years old, youths in general, government workers, and intellectuals. They sought to destroy anyone and everyone who appeared to be a possible threat to the new military regime. This era is known as the Red Terror. The new government killed approximately five hundred thousand of the country's citizens. To further drive the opposing groups from urban centers, the new government sent all high school, college, and university students and teachers who survived the chaos to rural areas for six months of service called Zemecha. Technically, I was a tenth-grade student, but I was recruited to attend a vocational school and sent to another province.

I have experienced significant moments, occurrences, and experiences in my life, and I call them "Wonders of My Wilderness."

I Was Given a Letter, a Pass

At age sixteen, they sent me to the remotest part of the country to work with students from different parts of the province to help locals, and I am still unsure what help we were providing. After serving almost four months, I was called into the office by one of the teachers, and he handed me a pass, in the form of a letter, allowing me to go home to visit my family.

I did not ask for this privilege but was happy to receive it. I often ask why I was given a pass by a teacher I barely knew. But on that day, he was my hero. I would see him again because I had to return to complete my time in service.

At that time, security was tight because the government had declared martial law, and students could not freely travel. They had to be in service (Zemecha), remain in school, or be given a pass. If caught traveling, they would go to jail and ultimately could lose their life. As fate would have it, I was caught at a bus stop while boarding my next bus to go home. A man in a military uniform started questioning me, and I showed him my pass, but he didn't care about it and ordered me to follow him. He took me to a hotel next to the bus stop, got a room, and ordered me to stay put. He told the hotel clerk to watch me until he returned within an hour or so. Ten minutes later, I ran out of that hotel as fast and discreetly as I could and mingled with the downtown crowd. I was familiar with the area. The campus I had attended for a two-year program was near downtown and only a few miles from the bus station. I knew the director and his wife, who lived on campus. The wife was from my hometown and would invite me over for tea. We had enjoyed a cup of tea together just before I was rounded up like the other youths and sent to serve for six months for Zemecha. I went to see her, and she was surprised to see me. She told me to stay at her house until she could arrange transportation home for me. She asked her husband to drive me to the next town to catch the overnight train home. I found safety on this campus with a lady who had befriended me months earlier. I knew the military man did not have any good plans for me.

Finally, I made it home, and I was incredibly happy to see my family, especially my grandmother. Soon afterward, a few days or more, people started talking about me, asking why and how I was allowed to come home without completing the service. They thought it could only happen if I had a connection with the new government. A conspiracy theory started in which I was suspected of being a spy for the new government. My friends, whom I grew up with, believed it. Sadly, even my half-brother began to act differently around me. I found out that the local police were questioning my status as well. I needed to leave town before the government or the opposing group killed me; I could even die at the hands of my brother.

My Mother Had a Dream

As a result of this threat to my life, I knew I had to run away as fast as possible. I decided to visit my mother, who lived about 150 miles away from my hometown. My grandmother had raised me, and I had little relationship with my biological mother. Only a few hours after I arrived, a police officer came to talk to my mom, asking her why I was not at school or providing service. She told them that I was tired and sleeping, and I would answer them the next day. When I heard what happened, I started planning my next escape. I knew I needed to leave this town the following day before the police returned.

The first problem I encountered was when my mother decided not to go to work early as she did every morning. My mother was a merchant; she owned several businesses, so she had to go to the market to make sure she opened her shops on time. She told me she'd had a dream about me. In the dream, she found out that I ran away, and she went out to look for me, calling out my name on a very dense and bushy road with high mountains left and right. Nervously, I cracked a smile and said to her, "That is crazy; I don't even know this town very well." My mother finally left the house around ten that morning. I immediately grabbed some of my clothes, put them in a bag, and placed the bag into the trash can to retrieve them later. I acted as though I was taking out the trash, but I encountered problem number two. My mom had a maid, and she did everything for her, which proved to be a problem. She insisted that it was her duty to take out the trash and began to pull the garbage bag out of my hands. I knew if she saw my clothes in the garbage, I was doomed, so I pushed her as hard as I could. She finally stopped pursuing me, and once she was out of sight, I grabbed my bags from the garbage and left on my journey to the unknown.

A Girl on a Woman's Journey

My mother's hometown in Ethiopia was small, and I could see the border while standing in the backyard. A few civilians lived there, but it was made up mostly of the military and police. They lived at the top of the hill and could see everything, keenly watching the border. I set my eyes on that border, but I had to make a stop first. There was an old church on a hilltop not far from my mom's house, and there I planned to change my clothing so I wouldn't look conspicuous but more like the people I was going to meet soon—Somalians!

I started walking, one step in front of the other. I could hear my heart pounding loudly, and it felt as though it would jump out of my chest. I was afraid, but the fear of staying and facing dire consequences was greater than the fear of at least attempting to escape and save my life. So I walked, and I kept walking. I walked up to the church, and thankfully, the door was unlocked, and I acted as though I had an open invitation. I walked in and changed my clothing—yes, right there in the sanctuary. After I finished dressing up somewhat like the local Somalis, I knelt and asked God and all the saints for protection for the rest of my journey. I had never read the Bible, and I knew nothing about this God of the Bible, but now I beseeched His help. I had gone to church, but I am afraid that was all I had done. Ethiopia was Christian based, and the church was our primary place of worship. We received everything from within the church: our political systems and process, culture, and teaching flowed into our social lives. That was the case until Haile Selassie was no longer the emperor; after that, everything had changed. However, Somalia, located on the "horn of Africa," has Islam as its primary religion. I walked toward Somalia.

On that day, I surrendered my overwhelming anxious emotions to Him that He might lead me in the right direction. I was about to embark upon a journey into strange territory, and everything was an unknown to me; this was frightening. And I was asking God, whom I was not intimate with, to lead me. I walked for hours, at least seven hours in the heat. I asked myself, *Why am I still walking?* After all, I could see the border from my mom's house just as I could see the church on the hill. *It cannot be that far from the house*—or so I thought. It is deceiving how something may seem close only because you can see it, when in reality it is farther than you imagine. But I had to begin my venture to find this out. The journey would teach me more than I wanted to learn. The journey was long, with few travelers. The few I saw looked at me as if they were trying to figure out who I was. I felt nervous because the Somalians hated the Ethiopians because of years of border contention. And now I, the Ethiopian, was venturing into my enemy country seeking refuge!

A Stranger's Sandals

It was getting late, the sun was setting, and I was still in the wilderness. Creatures come out at night, you know, and as I was getting more acquainted with God, I hoped that He would calm my fears again. Far away in the distance, I could see lights, and there appeared to be three different towns relatively close to each other. I remembered hearing in conversations in my homeland that the border had small cities with military bases. I guessed that was what I was seeing. It was getting darker, and I had no idea which light was for the right city—a safe, accepting city. I was in a quandary, and as I began to walk toward one of the city lights, I started panicking and crying, not knowing where I was going or what was going to happen to me. Suddenly, I saw a man riding a donkey. He stopped, and a conversation ensued.

I knew a few words in Somalian, and I managed to tell him I was a student and needed to leave the country. I asked him if he could give me his sandals because my walking shoes had blistered my feet. Can you believe it? He gave me his sandals and then walked me to the right town, a safe city, and placed me in the proper official's hands.

At the point of a major decision, this unknown man riding on a donkey became my hero, and I would never see him again.

The Unusual Favor

Although it was highly unusual for an Ethiopian citizen to be allowed into Somalia, they welcomed me and placed me in a nice hotel. On the third day, they transported me to another city. I stayed in that city for three months. They did not know what to do with me and transported me to the capital city. At that time, Ethiopia was at war with Somalia and the Eretria Liberation Party. A few Eritreans had fled to Somalia. The leader of the Liberation Party was passing through and heard about my story. He petitioned the Somali officials to meet me. After he met me, he immediately instructed his officials to place me with a family. Many prosperous Eritreans were taken to Somalia by Italians as soldiers during the era of the Scramble for Africa. It was also an unusual request for an Eritrean family to house an Ethiopian girl when they knew nothing about me. Soon after, I met a girl about my age, and she decided to take me home with her. She happened to be the daughter of one of the wealthiest Eritrean-Somalian families in Somalia. Her parents were on vacation at the time, but she told them about me over the phone.

After five months of living comfortably with this family, they offered to pay for me to go anywhere I desired to pursue an education or seek out employment. I decided to work, and they suggested I go to Jeddah, Saudi Arabia. I flew to Jeddah, and my adopted family arranged for another family member to pick me up at the airport and allow me to stay with them until I found employment. Unfortunately, due to miscommunication, no one showed up at the airport. The airline captain found it in his good grace to take me to his home. Overnight, he desperately tried to convince me that I could work as a hostess on his plane and earn good money, and he would arrange for me to have a nice place to live. By this time, I was immune to receiving proposals, and when he placed his proposal on the table, I wasn't surprised. I remember responding with a smile and never whispered a word. In my heart, I was saying, "No, sir, but thank you." I knew the motive behind every proposal, and it wasn't going to be a good outcome for me. I wondered in my mind what I would do if the family didn't show up to get me. I could feel my heart begin to beat faster, and panic was rising within me.

Someone Who Speaks my Language

Thank God, the family showed up the next day in the late afternoon and took me to their home. They welcomed me with open arms. The husband and wife showed me to my room, and I felt comfortable in my new surroundings. I immediately asked if I could shower and clean up. They understood, and I headed straight for the shower. While in the bathroom, I could distinctly hear another voice. Feeling refreshed with clean clothes, I noticed a handsome Eritrean man as I entered the living room area. I later learned that he had grown up in the capital city of Ethiopia, Addis Ababa. "Here's a girl from your country," the couple said to him.

We immediately clicked; after all, he was handsome, and he spoke my language. We had a friendly conversation. He agreed to come the next day to give me a tour of the city. After that, we spent each day together. It was refreshing to be with someone who was from my culture and appreciated me.

The family was so gracious to me, and I felt horrible because I couldn't financially contribute to the household. I was vigorously seeking employment, but nothing came my way. The inability to contribute started to make me feel uncomfortable, and I wanted to leave because I did not want to be a burden. I told my new male friend about how I was feeling, and he promised to find me a job—and he did.

Over time, my friend and I took our relationship to another level, and we got married and had two children. I loved the idea of having a family, but I did not plan to be a stay-at-home mom nor to deal with some of the treatment I was receiving. I had the ambition to pursue my education and be independent in every sense of the word. I felt trapped, confined, and held against my will. I hated my life but loved my children, and I kept pressing and praying for a better life. The status of my children and me in Saudi Arabia was that of diasporas from Ethiopia; however, I was there with a work visa and was given other papers by Somalia's government that allowed me to travel.

Leaving Saudi Arabia to start a new life terrified me, but I knew that I needed to move forward once again to have a better experience. I had no means or resources to get out of the country, but I was always planning and searching for any possibility that would come my way.

The Overheard Conversation

One day, my husband suggested we take a family vacation to Italy. He had extended family and friends who lived in all the major cities. I was excited because I loved that country. I heard many things about Italy in my Ethiopian history class, and I wanted to explore it. We packed for a month's vacation and decided to stay in Rome before visiting the rest of the cities. We rented a hotel close to restaurants and cafés for convenience with the children.

On the third day of our travel, we decided to tour Rome. After enjoying our day, we stopped to relax and have dinner at a beautiful café. A group of Ethiopian youngsters sat at the table next to us. We didn't acknowledge each other even though, in our culture, it is customary to greet one another immediately. But they were too busy laughing and having a good time. They spoke Italian and Ethiopian. I remember thinking about how they looked like those beautiful Ethiopian and Italian kids who had left for Italy because of the horrible condition in our homeland.

I listened intently to their conversation, trying to determine their origin. At the same time, my husband sat across from me, struggling to keep our son under control. Our boy eventually jumped off his father's lap and started running around, heading toward the main street. While my husband was chasing the baby, I overheard one of the Ethiopian youngsters talk about a new refugee office that had recently opened and was accepting all Ethiopian diaspora applications who had left the country due to the new regime change. My heart began to pound with excitement, and I needed to hear more. *Oh, my God*, I thought, *this is a program I could qualify for; I need to hear more; where is this place, where?* Before I could hear the location, my husband returned with the baby, and he was ready to leave for the hotel after that fiasco with our little boy. My heart sank because I needed to hear the location; it was a sign of hope.

The Unforgettable Phone Call to Freedom

As we walked into the hotel, the receptionist told my husband he had received an emergency phone call from Jeddah and gave him a piece of paper with a phone number. He called and had to go home immediately because a family member, who had borrowed his car, was involved in a bad car accident. He told me he needed to go home quickly to take care of the situation and would return shortly.

The next morning, he rushed back to Saudi Arabia and left the children and me in Rome. As soon as I knew he had reached the airport, I packed up my babies and decided I was going to the refugee office I had overheard about at the café. Although I had no idea where it was, I was determined to get there. I took the first bus I could find, not knowing which direction to go. It reminded me of my time in the wilderness wandering toward Somalia and not knowing which path to take. We remained on the bus stop after stop. I kept asking in my head, *Where is the building?* But I couldn't give up. As I looked at my children and thought of how badly I wanted to give them a new life, a prayer came up from my soul, and God implanted hope in my spirit.

I stayed on the bus. When the bus made its last stop, the driver made it clear that it was the last stop, and we needed to exit. Lost and afraid, I broke down in tears as we left the bus. Suddenly, a man walked up to me and asked me in Eritrean, "Where are you going with these children?" I told him I was looking for the refugee office. He immediately pointed to the building; it was just steps from where the bus had stopped—the last stop. There it was in front of us, the new refugee building recently open. As I gathered myself, beyond excited and filled with new hope, I marveled at how unbelievable this was and how it reminded me of the man on the donkey—what a significant moment.

This gentleman spoke my language, adding to my amazement. And like the man on the donkey, he escorted me to the proper Italian officer who conducted the interview. The officer asked my name and my children's names. He inquired why I left Ethiopia. I shared my entire story with him. As I was sharing, those buried emotions surfaced without warning, and I could no longer hold back the tears.

The flood gate opened, and I think I cried the entire interview, which lasted about thirty minutes. Later, he told me the good news—news that made my soul happy that I had held onto prayer and hope. He told me we could go to the United States within four months. Once again, I had my way of escape by a God I did not know. But I was getting to know Him.

My husband returned from Saudi Arabia as planned, and we continued touring Italy. I didn't murmur a word about my plan and pretended all was well. After our tour, we went back to Rome and started packing to return home to Saudi Arabia. I had to tell him that I had no plans to go back. I attained his undivided attention and told him, in detail, the story of what had happened. He had the shock of his life and stood there in disbelief. We went together to the refugee office and spoke to the manager. He looked at my file and confirmed that my destination had been Houston, Texas, but was changed to Los Angeles, California. My husband couldn't believe that I could have accomplish this feat. But he did not fight against my wish.

At the end of my bus ride, this unknown man became my hero, and I would never see him again.

On New Soil, the United States of America

Two months later, I was in Los Angeles, California, with my children. Look at us—we had made it—we were in AMERICA! All arrangements had been made for us by an agency. I was going with the flow, filled with excitement. A gentleman whom I did not know picked us up, and he took us to his home. He told me he was a priest at a church. He showed me his kitchen, the refrigerator, the bathroom, and a room for me and my kids. I didn't feel welcome to eat his food. He would leave for days at a time. Three days had passed, and we had not seen him. My kids and I were eating crackers I had packed, and we ate some of his bread and drank his milk. We were all craving real food, but the man worked all day and came home late at night; seldom did we see him. Finally, Sunday came, and he asked me if I wanted to go to church. I got my kids ready, and we went to church with him. To my surprise, the church was full of our kin, African Americans, but no refugees from Africa. I was hoping to meet some Ethiopian families so we wouldn't have to go back to the priest's house. My kids were starving!

From the Beginning to the Ending

One gentleman at the service was Ethiopian. He announced that he had heard a new sister with two young kids recently arrived in the country. I knew he had to be talking about me, and he was asking the church to help me with all my needs. Well, that would make two Ethiopians in the church, not counting my children. When I heard his announcement, I looked up and saw his face; I starred at his face as though I was in a trance. I begin crying, but it was more like sobbing. When others asked me why I was crying, I couldn't answer; I was choked with tears. I finally whispered an answer and said, "I know him, I know him; I know the speaker." After the service, he came out to meet me, and he was shocked when he saw my face. Remember, at the very beginning of my story, when I told you about a teacher who gave me a pass to go home? Well, here he was in living color, like a pot of gold at the end of my rainbow. I told him my situation at the priest's home, and being saddened by my story, he took me to his house; we cooked and fed the kids. We both couldn't believe how we had met again. Years later, on a different continent, here I was, with a teacher I barely knew, preparing a meal together. I couldn't help but think that he had a divine assignment in my life to send me off on my long journey, and here again to receive me at the end of my journey. What a joy—my children and me now in the United States of America. It was beyond significant; it was incredible. No, it was a miracle!

A lady who saw me at church called him later that day and told him that she couldn't stop thinking about me. She said she had plenty of room at her place and was willing to house my children and me. Sure enough, this lady helped me with everything a newcomer needs in this country. She welcomed us and allowed us to stay at her home for months until I could move out and get an apartment.

Remember the church on the hilltop as I was exiting Ethiopia, and how I prayed to God? I had gone to church all my life, but I always wondered why there didn't seem to be any focus on God Himself. At least for me, I had never heard or saw God in our midst as I was seeing Him walk with me now. It was because I had religion, and it seemed to me that our God was untouchable. I later relocated to Sacramento, California, and while driving to work, I came across a Christian radio station that broadcasted a question-and-answer forum about the Bible. Afterward, I started to read the Bible, and soon after that I decided to seek out a church home. I found Harvest Church of Elk Grove, California. Attending Harvest Church has been a blessing in my life because of the friendly people, various Bible studies, and hearing the preaching of the Word of God that has penetrated my soul. The God I was not genuinely acquainted with and had prayed to at that hilltop church became more and more known to me. I can and do look back over my journey and begin to see Him making a way for me time after time, again and again.

Getting to know God intimately reminded me of a scripture David wrote when he was in the wilderness of Judah. It seemed fitting for me and the situation I was in, having experiences with God I had never before known. I was becoming intimate with Him—so different, so needful!

You, God, are my God, earnestly I seek you; I thirst for you,
my whole being longs for you, in a dry and parched land
where there is no water. I have seen you in the sanctuary
and beheld your power and your glory. Because your love is
better than life, my lips will glorify you. I will praise you as
long as I live, and in your name I will lift up my hands.
I will be fully satisfied as with the richest of foods; with
singing lips my mouth will praise you. On my bed I remem-
ber you; I think of you through the watches of the night.
Because you are my help, I sing in the shadow of your wings.
I cling to you;
your right hand upholds me. (Psalms 63:1–8 NIV)

I had never prayed and cried so much as I did on this wilderness crossing. I had never before experienced fear in this manner—the manner of walking into the enemy camp and hoping they treat me as a friend, too scared to turn around and too afraid to not keep walking. I prayed, I wept, and God heard me.

Come near to God and he will come near to you. Wash your
hands, you sinners, and purify your hearts, you double-
minded. Grieve, mourn and wail. Change your laughter to
mourning and your joy to gloom. Humble yourselves before
the Lord, and he will lift you up. (James 4:8–10 NIV)

Finally, I rested upon this scripture, which speaks out loud my conclusion to the matter!

"I have heard of You (God) by the hearing of the ear,
But now my eye sees You." (Job 42:5 NKJV)

Back to the Homeland

I have visited my homeland, Ethiopia, a few times, but home was not the same. After I ran away, my mother thought the military police had come and arrested me. She was terrified and upset and demanded they tell her what they had done with me. I was long gone by then. A year after I left my country, a war broke out between Somalia and Ethiopia. My grandmother had raised me as an infant. She was my anchor, a godly woman, and a beautiful soul who lost all her hard-earned properties to the government takeover. But thankfully, she survived it all. we remained in contact by letter writing and she was happy that me and my children were safe. I was able to be a financial blessing to the woman who had given me everything. She passed away about seven years after I had escaped to America. In her final days, God had blessed me to be a blessing to her. I loved my grandmother!

My mother lived in a region called Ogaden, different and distant from my grandmother. After days of intense battle, the Somali government took over the area. Ethiopians, including women and children, were taken to the capital city and placed in a concentration camp. My mother and a younger brother became political prisoners for over ten years. Afterward, they were released and returned home, but my mother had lost everything she had worked hard to establish. God blessed me to see my mother and brother again. My mother passed away a few years ago due to natural causes, but she had a broken heart. This is why I say home was never the same.

But I recently went with friends and took my ten-year-old grand-daughter and her best friend to show them the country and to experience the culture. I was six years older than her when I started my journey to freedom. My granddaughter was born and grew up in the United States and only speaks English. The same goes for her best friend, and it was great they had each other on this trip. I noticed that everywhere we went, upon meeting girls or boys their age or older, they didn't know what to say or how to act. They didn't even attempt to relate; neither did the Ethiopian kids. I can honestly say these two girls were strangers in a strange land—just how I felt living in different countries and exposed to different cultures. But the educational value one receives for being exposed and experiencing other cultures is priceless.

I must confess that after the changes that had taken place in my country that forced me to run for my life, and after the significant amount of time that had passed, I felt like a stranger in my homeland as well. There is a saying that "you can never go home again." I understand that now because I could still speak the language, but many decades had passed. There was a gap, and I had to get reacquainted with my homeland.

The Refugee

As I have settled in and taken an in-depth look into my journey, I have thought of how it felt to me personally to be a refugee fighting for my life, for my very existence. Also, I have recalled how many people felt about me as a refugee. Many were optimistic, but others were pessimistic. I understand there are many reasons people migrate, most of them because of human rights abuses, armed conflicts, persecution, and drought, all of which were my issues. I understand there are international laws in place for such reasons. The rule of laws is there to protect other human beings just because they are members of humanity. This does not negate countries' laws concerning their borders. The laws ensure that even if there is a violation of the law, the immigrant receives humane treatment.

Because I was getting to know my God personally, I turned to the Bible to see how God describes immigrants and their treatment.

As a Christian, I believe in biblical principles, and I found several scriptures on how we should treat our refugees or immigrants (referred to as "foreigners").

"Also you shall not oppress a stranger, for you know the heart of a stranger, because you were strangers in the land of Egypt." (Exodus 23:9 NKJV)

"When you reap the harvest of your land, you shall not wholly reap the corners of your field, nor shall you gather the gleanings of your harvest. And you shall not glean your vineyard, nor shall you gather every grape of your vineyard; you shall leave them for the poor and the stranger: I am the LORD your God." (Leviticus 19:9–10 NKJV)

"And if a stranger dwell with you in your land, you shall not mistreat him. The stranger who dwells among you shall be to you as one born among you, and you shall love him as yourself; for you were strangers in the land of Egypt: I am the LORD your God." (Leviticus 19:33–34 NKJV)

He administers justice for the fatherless and the widow, and loves the stranger, giving him food and clothing. Therefore love the stranger, for you were strangers in the land of Egypt. (Deuteronomy 10:18–19 NKJV)

(But no sojourner had to lodge in the street, For I have opened my doors to the traveler) (Job 31:32 NKJV)

Then the King will say to those on His right hand, "Come, you blessed of My Father, inherit the kingdom prepared for you from the foundation of the world: for I was hungry and you gave Me food; I was thirsty and you gave Me drink; I was a stranger and you took Me in; I was naked and you clothed Me; I was sick and you visited Me; I was in prison and you came to Me." (Matthew 25:34–36 NKJV)

I encourage us all not to judge all immigrants the same. All who dare to cross our borders are not criminals. *You don't know their story; it may just be another Mulu.*

I am forever indebted to the individuals who have touched my life and to this country, the United States of America, that took in my children and me.

Finally, a Safe Place to Call Home

More than thirty-eight years ago, my family relocated to this great country. I came as a young refugee, a single mother with two children. I can honestly and gratefully say that coming to America spared my life and my children's lives.

I have lived and continue to live the American dream, experiencing good times and bad times. I had the opportunity to educate myself, which enabled me to have a better life. I have experienced owning businesses, successful and not so successful. I strived and persevered to stand tall and be independent in every sense of the word—emotionally, mentally, financially, and spiritually. I am truly free to explore what I want in life. At the end of my journey escaping from Ethiopia, I am sincerely happy and proud to say that my family and I are citizens of this beautiful country that we call HOME, the United States of America.

May God continue to bless this great Country!

I am an author, and I have told my full story in a book titled *Coincidence or Divine Intervention? You Be the Judge.* You will read the many stories of the twist and turns, the near misses, and the "Oh God, get me out of here" moments. You can purchase my book on Amazon. com or directly from me by emailing me at divinec2018@gmail.com or contacting me by phone or text at (916) 708-8306.

The Process and the Purpose

by Angelique Bailey

I have chosen to share a short story about a portion of my life's story with great anticipation that you will enjoy the tale and gain enrichment. Love and compassion have prompted me to share this, hoping that it will empower you and bring hope where you may have lost all hope. We often forget that life is a *process*. Learning the process is the most crucial aspect of life because we live life; life doesn't live us. It shows every experience that we've endured to become who we are presently. And, if we like who we are, then it should give us hope for tomorrow. I will share my process. It has been a bumpy ride and has taken many detours. It has also been a complete leap of faith.

Writing this short story within my life's process has been the most challenging endeavor. But the struggle to birth this story speaks loudly and is itself a declaration to share for the glory of God.

Helping others is my signature, a characteristic I received from my mother. As a child, I watched my mother closely and observed how she cared for everyone, including animals. If she saw someone on the side of the road with a sign asking for help, as soon as I could blink, that person would be in our van. We had a large white family van to transport us four children, mom's adopted children, cousins, and whoever could fit. My mother would make it work. She didn't only give people rides; she would allow them to stay at our home, provide them meals, and help them find jobs. I watched as she helped others without asking for anything in return. I can honestly say I am my mother's child.

Helping is one of my many gifts. When our friend asked my husband and me to help at youth camp, I said, "Yes!" They held the camp at a place called the Barn. This location will be of great significance as I continue with my story.

On the first day of the event, I was lying on my back in intense pain. I couldn't escape the pain. I asked my husband to attend the event without me, and I would come the following day. I needed time to "get my body together." The next day I was still in pain, but I didn't want to let the youth or my friend down. More importantly, I didn't want to show my daughters that giving up was an option. I managed to get out of bed, pushing back the pain. Slowly and painfully, I put on my clothes. The final item I had to put on was a smile on my face; I call it my "suck it up" smile, which I learned how to do at a young age. Making the hard decision to get out of bed was the start of my journey.

The Day of Camp

I was excited to attend the camp and help with mentorship. I'd had a rough childhood, but many mentors came into my life and were a blessing because they believed in me. I always wanted to pay it forward to other youths. When I was a teenager, I strongly desired to open a teen center that would be a safe haven and provide at-risk teens resources. Due to unforeseen circumstances, I was not able to make that goal a reality. My heart hurt because I couldn't help those teens. But life is a process.

I grew more anxious as I was driving to the camp because my daughters were there, and we are incredibly close. I became a mother at a young age, and I worked hard to create a bond that would be strong. I wanted a strong relationship with them that would never crumble, break, or fall apart. Frequently, I hear people say, "You can't be your child's friend!" I disagree with that statement. My daughters are my best friends. I have found that the best approach for me to raise my children is to listen and provide a safe space for them to tell me anything and everything. It may be scary at times, but they need me, and they need to feel safe. If they don't have a safe space with their dad and me, they will seek it elsewhere.

Upon arriving at the event, I prayed and prayed and prayed. Did I mention I prayed? Everyone who knows me knows my personality and how extremely blunt I am, and that is how I talk to God. God knows me; He understands me. On that day, I prayed this prayer: "Lord, I am tired. I'm tired of being in pain, and I need You. I need You to come through for me. I am tired of being tired. Lord, I am done!" I'm not sure if you have ever been sick and tired of being sick and tired, but that is where I was. I didn't know what was coming my way. I just knew I had to surrender everything, and I mean everything, to God. I didn't want to live any longer with the pain thwarting my progress. I wanted to be free from pain, free from bondage. I wanted to be free to live out my purpose the way God intended me to live.

I was determined to be a blessing on this day, but I also believed a blessing was coming my way. I did tell you that I prayed, right? God wanted me to realize that I needed Him. And I needed to stop trying to fix things on my own. I had to stop acting as if I was God. No more trying to control things; just be done. I cannot explain the freedom I felt when I was no longer in control, done with trying to play God. On that day, God placed a real smile in my heart, replacing the fake smile on my face. I prayed for others, knowing I needed prayer myself. I had learned I didn't have to beg God; I just needed to trust Him.

"Trust in the LORD with all your heart and lean not on your own understanding; in all your ways submit to him, and he will make your paths straight." (Proverbs 3:5–6 NIV)

What Caused the Pain?

Years prior, I was in a horrible car accident, and the injuries I incurred left my body twisted and in pain. I didn't understand the severity of the crash until I received an MRI. My doctor suggested physical therapy, but when that didn't work, he referred me to a neurosurgeon. I have high pain tolerance, and sometimes that has become my god complex, tolerating when I should be finding real answers. For example, I was in labor pain for thirty-six hours without pain medication while giving birth to my oldest daughter. Imagine being in labor with no pain medication for that long; well, maybe you shouldn't imagine that! But I shouldn't have taken the pain caused by my accident lightly. Perhaps I made it worse by delaying care. The pain limited me to the point that I couldn't brush my hair, vacuum, or perform simple daily routines. The slightest of movement required considerable effort and almost bought me to tears.

My amazing husband would brush my hair. Picture that! It was a mess, but a sweet mess. Now, that's love. Speaking of my husband, I remember praying for him before I knew him. God wrapped everything I prayed for as a gift in him. Does this mean things are perfect? Heck, no! But it does mean that God answers prayers, and I get to partner with Him in the perfecting of our marriage. He never said it would be easy, but it is so worth it. It is incredible how God works. I went to high school with my husband. He was in front of me the entire time. I allowed other things to overshadow his presence, but God had other plans. No one and nothing can stop what God has already ordained, but we can delay it. Life is a process.

As the pain continued, it became intolerable and was affecting my daily life. Once again, I wasn't respecting the pain that was trying to tell me something. I finally made an appointment to see a neurosurgeon. I intentionally went alone to the appointment. I didn't want anyone going with me because I felt in my heart that I would receive bad news. Once again, I put a smile on my face and quietly spoke to my spirit, "Suck it up!" My smile was my shield, but it was a lie; nevertheless, this shield was my protection.

The neurosurgeon reviewed my MRI and suggested surgery, removing a disc and replacing it with an artificial disc. The other option was not to have surgery, and the pain would increase, and the damage to the discs would be severe. I didn't want surgery, I didn't want an artificial disc, and yet, I didn't want to continue to live in anguish. I left the doctor's office with my smile intact, but as soon as I walked out, heading for the elevator, I started crying; I couldn't hide the pain anymore. I allowed a few seconds of grief, just a few seconds, and I quickly wiped away the tears and kept telling myself, "Suck it up, Angelique!" Soon after, a young man entered the elevator, and we got off on the same floor to exit the hospital. I tried my best to avoid eye contact. He said, "Excuse me, I don't know what you are going through, but those bad days will soon be over." I thanked him, and the tears poured out from my eyes even more. God used a stranger to comfort me at a time such as this. The truth is, God will bring people into our lives at the perfect time. God loves me more than I could ever comprehend. I went to my appointment thinking I was alone, but God covered me in my darkest hour.

Earlier in my life, having taught myself how to "suck it up," I unknowingly entered an abusive relationship with the same mentality. I taught myself how to be brave while holding everything in, not allowing my abuser to see me cry. If I showed fear, that would appear to be weakness. I thought I was winning by being emotionless and not showing the pain. Growing up, I had witnessed a family member being abusive toward their partner. I saw the abuse, and I told myself I would never allow anyone to put their hands on me. To my detriment, these words would forever haunt me. Honestly, I never imagined my life taking the turn it did. I had met a young man, and our relationship was so romantic; I believed he truly liked me, maybe even loved me. If I had only known what I know now, I wouldn't have indulged in such a relationship. I didn't notice the isolation, the extreme controlling behavior, or even the stalking behavior. I just saw him and didn't see any of the big red flags and flashing red lights warning me to run. My eyes weren't trained to see danger, and my heart hadn't learned true love. I foolishly believed his love for me was real. Life is a process.

As the relationship grew closer—the correct words are "more controlling"—the abuse grew worse. I was in my last year of high school and camouflaged the abuse as love. Violence doesn't care about age, and when others observed the abuse, it went unreported. I managed to graduate a year early, but who would have thought the girl who graduated a year early with scholarships, who had goals and aspirations in life to become a psychologist and an artist, would become sidetracked and lost in an abusive relationship? I dreamed of showcasing my artwork in my office for my patients. I was that girl with ambitions to attend a historic black college, who had received honors and was nominated prom queen. This girl was involved in community service and was president of the student body government. Who would have thought this girl would be in an abusive relationship? Not this girl—not even I, the girl herself, could imagine such a life. But abuse doesn't care about potential or status.

Outside versus Inside

From the outside, our relationship looked perfect, but the appearance was deceiving. As time passed and I accepted the abuse, it became normal. I didn't realize that love shouldn't hurt. He became my "ride or die," and I believed I was his "ride or die." I felt I could lean on him and believed we only had each other. That is what he wanted me to believe. One particular night while I was home relaxing, he called and asked to borrow my car. I had no problem with that and said yes. Although things weren't perfect with us, and although he had anger issues, stalking issues, controlling issues, and loved isolating me, I still felt there was hope; I was still his ride or die. I had convinced myself that he would change and that I had the power to change him, and we would be happy together. Amazingly, I didn't realize that it was me who had been changed by him. Blinders were on—the real dark ones!

I awoke the next morning, ready to start my day, when I noticed that he hadn't returned my car. Through my grapevine of friends, I found out where he was. I had errands to run and borrowed my cousin's car. My intent was not to run my errands, however, but to go get my car. I felt anger because that same grapevine told me the possibility of him being with someone else. I felt anxious and somewhat fearful;

it was a feeling I had never had. Maybe I was being warned, but unfortunately, my heart wasn't trained to sense danger. After all, he was my ride or die. I continued convincing myself I had a right to get my car, ignoring what I was experiencing. Upon arriving, I noticed my car parked in the driveway. I boldly exited the car, walked to the door, and knocked like I was the police. He opened the door and stepped outside; I asked him for my keys, but he refused to give them to me. I wanted to get my car, leave my cousin's car parked on the street, and return later to get her car. But he told me to go; after all, I may have embarrassed him since he was with his other girl.

I am sure he made it clear to her that he tames people well, including me. But on that day, I stepped outside the boundaries. He was shocked and saw my boldness in tracking him down, knocking on the door, and asking for my keys as an attack on him. How dare I claim what was mine at his expense? I was not a stranger to his anger, and I knew what it felt like to be on the other side of it. Seeing this was a lost cause, I returned to my cousin's car and sat down to make a phone call. I didn't look back and believed that he had entered the house, but then I felt a strange presence. I remember slowly looking up, and there he was, standing in front of the car. He was staring at me down the barrel of a gun aimed at my head. I felt lifeless. I knew I couldn't change his mind or talk him out of it. I knew if I made one move, he would instantly shoot me. Where do you run when you have nowhere to go? I knew my life was in grave danger, and it flashed before my eyes. Why hadn't I listened to the feeling that was impressed upon me? But no sooner had the thought of losing my life taken over my brain than I heard a horrible loud sound. It was the sound of death coming for me. The sound of shots fired!

Time converted to slow motion, a second-by-second play. He fired two shots. I remember the bullets piercing the windshield, but I didn't know immediately if they had hit me. I didn't know where the bullets had gone. I didn't know what had happened to me. I immediately started to pray. My prayer was, "Please, LORD, don't let me die," I cried out again and again, "Please, LORD, don't let me die." While I was praying that God wouldn't allow me to die, I started to get out of the vehicle. At this point, I knew he had shot me, but I didn't know where. I couldn't see out my right eye, and once I got out of the vehicle, I started to walk toward him, asking, "Why did you do this to me?" I began to slip away. The world around me became dark, and my body started to tingle and become numb. The last thing I remembered was his silhouette walking toward me and the sound of him crying and saying he loved me. I passed out. Amazingly, I described myself as his ride or die, and it appeared that I was about to die by his hand. Maybe these words were only code words for unhealthy, dangerous relationships. Life is a process.

My mother received the call that no parent wants to get. The hospital called and told her she needed to get to the hospital because I had been shot and would most likely not survive, and if I did, there was a high possibility I would be paralyzed. My mother called my aunt, who was at her church, Harvest, in Elk Grove, California. The pastor was made aware of my condition and stopped the service to pray for me. The entire church stopped and prayed for me.

I remember waking up while in surgery to a bright light. I then remember fully waking up and hearing the horrific sound of the doctors sawing into my skull. I remember the nurses and doctors panicking and yelling, "She's alive!" I found out later that I had been pronounced dead. Another childhood friend of mine told me that they were waiting for my body at the morgue.

Now listen, you who say, "Today or tomorrow we will go to this or that city, spend a year there, carry on business and make money." Why, you do not even know what will happen tomorrow. What is your life? You are a mist that appears for a little while and then vanishes. (James 4: 13–14 NIV)

After being in surgery for hours, I awakened surrounded by my family. What a beautiful sight! My head was the size of a large watermelon. I didn't know how many days had passed; I didn't know anything. I just knew I was alive, and my family was there with me. My cousin, who had loaned me her car was there and she was traumatized. She told me they were told my boyfriend called 911. Days later, the nurse wheeled me into a huge hospital shower, and as the water was flowing over my body from head to toe, I saw an unbelievable amount of blood covering the floor; it was as if someone had died. But I did die. My life and how God spared it is clear and present evidence of the power of prayer.

I later learned I was shot twice, and the bullets had entered my right eye, splitting it, and exited the top of my head as quickly as they had entered. The doctors removed a blood clot from my brain and the fragments from the bullets. My doctor told me there are a few certainties; one is that gravity doesn't change. He said the bullets should have continued to travel through my eye, through my brain, and exit the back of my head, killing me. God changed the direction of the bullets before he fired a shot and before I prayed. That day the course of my life shifted. I suffered! I had more pain than I can explain. I had fifty staples in my head, and my right eye was stitched together. The doctors weren't sure if I would walk, but I was thankful, so thankful, that I was alive.

A few days before this incident, a childhood friend of mine had called me. She was going to purchase a ticket for me to come to Alabama, where she was attending college. She didn't know the full extent of what was going on with me or how severe and deadly my relationship was, but somehow she knew she had to try to get me out. I spoke with her briefly, and we ended our conversation, knowing I would soon be safe with her. I never got the chance to get on that bus. God has given us all free will. Therefore, there are choices for us to make. Yes, I could have paid attention to the uneasy feeling I was experiencing while retrieving my car. I could have decided to take advantage of the opportunity extended to me by my dear friend to get out of the madness right away—to get on the bus and never look back. But I didn't. Please know this is not victim-blaming; this is the training of my heart to sense and know danger. I never thought our relationship could or would become deadly.

I could never forget that day. I remember it vividly as if it was yesterday, forever etched in my mind and heart. If you are in a dangerous relationship, I want to encourage you to tell someone you trust and get out of it as quickly as possible because your "ride or die" philosophy can cost you your life. Life is a process.

Even though I walk through the valley of the shadow of death, I will fear no evil, for you are with me; your rod and your staff, they comfort me. (Psalms 23:4 NIV)

As I stated, the Barn would be a significant place for me after I was shot twice in my right eye and the bullets penetrated my skull, I was in a horrible car accident, and was confronted by many other obstacles. I have had plenty of "why me, Lord?" moments, but I have never given up, by His grace. He gave me faith and hope, and I believed He had a bigger purpose for my life.

The gunshots left me partially blind in my right eye, and I suffered severe migraines and was prescribed seizure medication. The migraines are another portion of my pain that my body experiences from time to time, not to mention the scars on my face or how part of my skull is missing. More severe are the invisible scars. But I began to seek God with my whole heart. The perpetrator was arrested and served time in prison. I decided that I didn't want to imprison myself, so I chose to forgive. I chose to live in love for God and self and not in hate of life and him. I came to understand that forgiveness was not for the person who had wronged me but for me. You may want to try this if you find yourself stuck in unforgiveness, hating, and full of bitterness. God got my full attention after I had this experience, and He forgave me and gave me life, both physically and spiritually. God alone saved my life! .

Healing

Arriving at the Barn to help at the camp, as I previously stated, I knew I was going to receive something from God in the depth of my soul. I came with great expectations to be a blessing and to receive a blessing. I was tired. I wanted to live my life to its full potential with God as my center and without pain. I needed Him to help me live out His purpose for my life. I continued to mentor the youth at the camp. On the final day, I repeated the struggle to make it to the camp. We always started the day out with prayer and worship; I prayed with both my girls. A young man named Caleb was part of the worship team; he started praying over everyone in the sanctuary. He prayed a specific prayer, and it stood out to me because he prayed for young women who had experienced a difficult pregnancy, and God was addressing those residual issues.

I had faced many difficulties during pregnancies, with horrible sickness. Coincidentally, my cousin and I were pregnant simultaneously; she could eat whatever she wanted, while I was throwing up everything. I had infusion therapy. Did I mention I've been through a lot? After Caleb was praying, I approached him, thanking him. I thought, *Well, God, if this is what you wanted me to receive, I receive it, and thank you.* I wasn't upset. I was beyond thankful that God loved me so much, to speak encouragement to me through Caleb.

Caleb asked if he could pray for me, and without hesitation, I said yes. I'm cautious with who I allow to lay hands on me to pray. I've always been this way. But I felt safe with him. I had never met this young man before, and he knew nothing about me or my many struggles. He placed his hands over my head and asked another man to pray with us. He started to prophesy over me. He mentioned things that no one would or could have known but God. God used him and orchestrated the power of healing. That day God healed me from pain. God healed me from the blindness in my right eye and severe migraines that directly resulted from being shot in the head. Yes, God healed me! Caleb prayed and prophesied over me for almost two hours. As I put God in a small box and was okay with just a word regarding my pregnancies, God had complete healing for my whole body.

The Process

Life is a process if we allow ourselves to keep moving forward. However, many times, we choose a season in our life and set up camp there, and then life becomes a cycle—the same old thing, just different days. The truth about life is that it's a process, a thread of events streaming in our lives. It intends to get us to our purpose. Often, we forget about the process. My process turned my pain into power. We look at people where they are now, not appreciating their journey. We look at ourselves the same way. My process to get here took time. God is still writing my story. I knew who I was, and I didn't like who I was, but I didn't think I could be different. But then God revealed Himself to me.

> *You, dear children, are from God and have overcome them, because the one who is in you is greater than the one who is in the world. (1 John 4:4 NIV)*

My process may seem familiar to you as you are reading this. If so, don't give up. The process is the most valuable part of your testimony.

My Purpose

If someone had told the younger Angelique that she would work with women, I would have laughed in their face. I had lost that dream a long time ago. When God has called you to do something, no one can take it away. It may take some time due to our free will or the many detours along the way, but it is still His divine purpose and plan. Therefore, we ought not to allow the world to dictate our purpose. The world did not make us, but if we give it permission, it will break us.

When I think of purpose, I ask the question, Why am I on planet Earth? We all have probably asked that question. I defined my purpose when I was with my abuser as my responsibility to love and change him. I was to make him happy at my expense. When I did ask why I was on planet Earth, I had to ask the backup question, Who created and placed me here? That was the million-dollar question that I couldn't answer for a long time. It stands to reason that whoever created me was the one who knew my purpose. I soon realized my purpose came before my birth and was embedded within my life. It was not for me to define because I did not create me, God did, and with that understanding, it changed my very core. In the second lesson, I was to love myself—game changer!

When I was a young girl, my dream was to help young people—children who found themselves in trouble, mostly not of their choosing but what others thrust upon them. As I look back over my life and through a different viewfinder, I can see how God raised this little girl and grew her into a woman. Now, the grown-up Angelique can speak to the broken little girl in every woman she meets. I found out He brings beauty out of ashes.

To console those who mourn in Zion, To give them beauty for ashes, The oil of joy for mourning, The garment of praise for the spirit of heaviness; That they may be called trees of righteousness, The planting of the LORD, that He may be glorified. (Isaiah 61:3 NKJV)

I wasn't a fan of females growing up—it was a trust issue—but now, they are my heartbeat. Although I experienced something that could have killed me, God saved me and gave me a new life. There is no rational explanation for why the bullets did not continue their straight path through my brain and kill me. Gravity doesn't change, my doctor said. There isn't any scientific explanation but God. Therefore, whatever you are facing, God can turn it around, just as He changed the bullets' direction that was supposed to kill me; instead, he changed my life.

"For I know the plans I have for you," declares the LORD,
"plans to prosper you and not to harm you, plans to give
you hope and a future." (Jeremiah 29:11 NIV)

My purpose is beyond comprehension, but I must move my feet, and that is what I am doing by helping other women know their worth. Maybe you are that person—woman, man, young lady, or whomever— God loves you. In case you didn't know this, you were born with eternity embedded within you; you are a living soul!

He has made everything beautiful in its time. Also, He has
*put **eternity** in their hearts, except that no one can find out*
the work that God does from beginning to end. (Ecclesiastes
3:11 NIV)

We have all sinned and come short of the glory of God. In other words, we have shunned His purpose for our lives, and we have gone our own way because many of us don't know the love of God. But this is what God did for all of us, and at the same time, He gives us choices:

For God so loved the world that he gave his one and only
Son, that whoever believes in him shall not perish but have
eternal life. For God did not send his Son into the world
to condemn the world, but to save the world through him.
Whoever believes in him is not condemned, but whoever
does not believe stands condemned already because they
have not believed in the name of God's one and only Son.
(John 3:16–18 NIV)

I was medically at eternity's door, pronounced dead, but God granted me mercy I did not deserve. Being a good person is not a qualifier. Jesus spoke on the subject of eternity in the scriptures below:

Then Jesus went through the towns and villages, teaching as he made his way to Jerusalem. Someone asked him, "Lord, are only a few people going to be saved?" He said to them, "Make every effort to <u>enter through the narrow door</u>, because many, I tell you, will try to enter and will not be able to. Once the owner of the house gets up and closes the door, you will stand outside knocking and pleading, 'Sir, open the door for us.' But he will answer, 'I don't know you or where you come from.'" (Luke 13:22–25 NIV)

Jesus is the door:

Then Jesus said to them again, "Most assuredly, I say to you, <u>I am the door</u> of the sheep. All who ever came before Me are thieves and robbers, but the sheep did not hear them. I am the door. If anyone enters by Me, he will be saved, and will go in and out and find pasture." (John 10:7–9 NKJV)

I formed a nonprofit to bring healing and restoration. If you know your worth and truly understand who you are and who God created you to be, no one can take that away from you. The view is much better from how God sees you, as opposed to this world. I'm priceless in God's eyes, and no man can shatter that. I decided not to give up, and I declared victory over my life. I am not a victim; I am victorious. I seek to be a voice for the voiceless. I have found my purpose because my Creator found me. Now, when I encounter storms, hills, and valleys, I rest on this scripture:

We are hard pressed on every side, but not crushed; perplexed, but not in despair; persecuted, but not abandoned; struck down, but not destroyed. (2 Corinthians 4:8–9 NIV)

It may be surprising to know that today, many of our youth suffer from domestic violence, child abuse at their parents' hands, and other relatives. Many are onlookers of one parent abusing the other, and they suffer in silence. They may experience domestic violence at the hands of boyfriends and girlfriends. Yes—news flash—some males suffer from domestic violence from their girlfriends, partners, or wives, but they seldom report it. I encourage you, if you are in a violent domestic relationship, get help, and get out! You are valuable.

Finally, I must share the last portion of the prophecy Caleb prophesied over me. He said God told him that I would be back at the Barn in years to come, writing a book with "many women." This book—yes, the one you are holding in your hand—is titled *21* because twenty-one women are telling their stories to the glory of God, and I am one of them. I would say that twenty-one women qualify as "many women," and guess what: we held our first writers' workshop at the Barn, unbeknown to the author. It was the only place she could find suitable. God designed it, just like He said.

I established an organization called Flourishing Wings, a Christian Ministry. My website is: Flourishingwings.org, email: Angelique.flourishingwings@gmail.com, and phone number is: 916-582-0379

Church Hurts

by Glory Hope

Many of us have probably gone through some "church hurt," big or small. Many of us carry unforgiveness, bitterness, anger buried in our souls. Or maybe we go through life numb and harboring the disappointments like a designer backpack that we carry around everywhere we go. This is my story; this is my life's song.

Where It All Began

My name is Glory Hope, and that is a story in itself. I was born and raised in good old sunny California, and I have three younger brothers. As far as I can remember, my parents were Christians, and they took us to church all the time. However, when I was five, I found out what church hurt was when parents wouldn't let their kids hang out with me because I was different from the rest. You may ask how I knew I was different. It seemed since I became aware of being alive, I had a strong desire to know God, and I would talk about Him a lot. I guess I talked about God too much for most parents, and it sounded strange to them that a young girl would have such a topic on her lips. As a matter of fact, at six years old, I remember going to school early one morning to pass out Bibles to my teachers. My parents encouraged and catered to my passion and provided me with small Bibles to give away. My parents told me stories that when I was a baby, on several occasions, I had freak accidents where I almost died, and strangely, they only seemed to happen when I was alone. I guess they always knew they needed to shelter and protect me. Maybe this story can add some understanding of my attachment to God at a young age. My parents told me the story of how they took me to a Billy Graham crusade and how a stranger prayed for me and asked for God's anointing to cover me. I remember dreaming so vividly that it felt as though I was still living out the dream when I awoke. This may sound strange to some, but it may sound familiar to others. Maybe some of you understand this better than most because this is your experience as well.

We had neighbors, a married couple, who were friends with my parents although there was not much socializing between them. However, I could visit them whenever I pleased, which I liked to do because the wife would cook me exceptional food; I was spoiled and hung out at their home frequently. But I began to notice pictures on the garage wall that today I know as pornography; they were just "nasty pictures" to me at that age. They caused a disturbance in my little spirit to the point that I would talk to the husband, visit after visit, about how he needed to take down those pictures. I knew in my mind that they did not honor God, and I said so. Now I know they did not honor him or his wife. I am sure my parents had never been in his garage.

It was that kind of passion and boldness that set me apart from other children my age.

Finally, we moved, and one day that neighbor called our home. I answered the phone, and he told me he had taken down all his posters, praise the Lord! He said that he had found God through what I had said to him. I guess hearing this from a child weighed heavily on his heart. I know one thing: I praised God for his new life!

Of course, once we moved, along with finding the right house, we had to find the right church. I grew up in legalistic churches for half of my life. By that, I mean churches with lots of rules without the spirit of love or grace, just do's and don'ts. Our home environment was warm and loving, unlike the environment I experienced at church. We had slim picking finding a church that matched us. Now, at the ripe old age of nine, I found my family changing churches to a nondenominational church, and I didn't fit in. Nondenominational churches distance themselves from the mainstream Christian faiths, with somewhat independent thinkers and rulers. At my young age, I observed that men ran these churches, and I noticed it appeared they were manipulative when it came to women and children. As a result, my parents moved from church to church, trying to find somewhere I could feel like I belonged and have friends. They were comfortable with their faith and could tolerate those differences, but they were concerned about my development with God and socially. I appreciate my parents' heart for me.

At this same age, while I was struggling within the church to find my place in God, I was also being bullied in elementary school. It had gotten so bad that all I could do when I came home was eat, go to my room, and cry myself to sleep every night. I camouflaged it with my parents as just being tired or complained about how boring the other children were. Honestly, depression had set in, and I was in deep despair. Imagine how lousy bullying made me feel in my elementary school days, and now fast-forward and see what it is doing in this day and time. Today, the number of suicides as a result of a child bullied is astronomical and growing. Some students are making suicide packs, so they won't be alone while experiencing the process of dying. The darkness thickens. It was and is a diabolic plot!

I thought that by the time I got to high school, this depression stuff would be a thing of the past. I would be all grown up and could handle small talk, but it didn't get much better. Nonetheless, I continued to share my faith and met many students. You might say I was a social butterfly, even if the school or other students didn't necessarily like me sharing my faith. All I had was my faith and my family, and I was not going to let go of either. It paid off when I later saw a student with whom I had shared my faith working as a waiter at a restaurant I visited. We had known each other since middle school. It was so incredible that he remembered me talking about Christ with him. I love being recognized as the one who shared her faith, building people up and not tearing them down.

At the new church, I decided to brave up and join the youth group. I was trying to increase my social network among my Christian church family. But, once again, I was talked about by people who didn't have a clue as to who I was. Sadly, as I went to church and as I sat in my youth group, I went into depression again. I felt rejected as they defined me as too churchy and talking about God far too much. I resorted back to going to my room and watching television. The church people hurt me more than people who weren't Christian. It was because of my expectations. I truly believed that I should find God in His house—that same loving God I experienced when alone with Him or enjoying my family. I expected the church to be excited with me about my passion for my faith. And I expected that talking about God would be appropriate, but I was wrong. My passion was too expressive for them. Once again, I left that church to find my own, and I did. I was beginning to learn that there is a difference between going to church and being a Christian.

I struggled through high school and finally decided to join the college-aged group at my new church. I expected mature conversations with this group and more substance, with well-thought-out points of view. However, a young man I had considered very friendly within the group shocked me to my core. Somehow the conversation came up regarding domestic violence against women—a bleak discussion that only got darker. Unexpectedly, it became a heated discussion. I was connected again to a church that viewed women and children as sideshows, property, and powerless. And the young man I was having a discussion with on the subject believed that a woman needed to be kept in her place, even if forcibly.

I vehemently disagreed, and he kindled his anger against me. Without warning, he pinned me to the church wall so fast I could barely catch my breath or blink my eyes. He raised his fist, threatening to hit me in the church because I disagreed with violence toward women. Imagine that: he was about to hit me because he believed it was perfectly normal to hit a woman! When this came to the church leadership's attention, no one would listen to me; they said it was my fault because I had made him angry. I guess the inference was if a man gets mad at a woman, he has the right to hit her, shut her down, and remind her where her place is, to be seen and not heard. That day I would have been black and blue if he had carried out his threat while in the church. Church hurts! God pity his wife if he ever gets married and doesn't change this ideology.

My whole world came crashing down at that moment. The leadership told me I needed to attend the college group, and I needed to apologize to the guy who threatened to hit me. They informed me that they were trying to get young adults in our church to attend the college group, and as a result, couples would emerge, and then marriages would take place. Also, they wanted the young adults to attract other young people and bring them into the church. Ironically, the person they wanted me to be with and to marry was the guy who had threatened to hit me. They then handed out my potential punishment if I failed to apologize and connect with this violent guy. I would be restricted from participating in any church activity or ministry. Their weapons were to isolate and destroy; I would be seen but never heard. Needless to say, I left this church in a hurry, not looking back; I was off and running. God, please help me find the right church!

God blessed me to find a new church, and at my new church, I was beginning to be healed from the majority of the pain I had suffered up to my young adulthood. I remember that one of the guys in the college group apologized on behalf of all the men who had ever hurt me mentally inside the church walls. God lifted a thousand pounds off my shoulders, and I knew that I was free. I was no longer holding on to the guilt, shame, and fear. I felt like I had found the right church for me. I always believed that God had a church for me where I could learn, grow, and serve. This church had three core values that rang my bell. One, they believed in personal identity. How long I had waited to be accepted for me? Two, they believed in building a community. I often sought social connection, but this church encouraged community, being a family beyond the church's walls. They intentionally built relationships based on honor and respect. Amazing! Lastly, they tossed in one of my true loves, mission, serving locally and globally, showcasing God's kingdom. Finally, I found a church HOME!

Then we received the bad news that my father had been diagnosed with acute myeloid leukemia, and he desired that I attend church with the family. I had no problem pleasing my beloved father. He needed to feel surrounded by the love of his family at all times. Although I made this change to please my father, I had a pit-like feeling in my stomach, screaming that I did not belong back in one of the churches I had left. But for my dad, I would tolerate it. Before I had left the church, someone had told me that I was too spirit-filled for the church, and I would never fit in. I made up my mind that for my dad, I would tolerate this. After all, I had finally tasted the goodness of God, and this was only for a season.

God showed me at that moment that I was not to fit in, because Jesus didn't fit in with his people; they would not accept Him. He told me that I was His daughter, and my faith would cause mountains to move and dry bones to live. He told me how I would be part of a revival and how I am not defined by what people say to me or about me. After all, they only knew me for a short time; God knew me my entire life, including time in the womb. Paul said:

Am I now trying to win the approval of human beings, or of God? Or am I trying to please people? If I were still trying to please people, I would not be a servant of Christ. (Galatians 1:10 NIV)

God made this so clear to me that this was just a bump in the road. God began to form the big picture with the small puzzle pieces of my life. I knew I could not look at what was before me, but I had to look beyond and see what He had in store.

"For many are invited, but few are chosen." (Matthew 22:14 NIV)

"But you will receive power when the Holy Spirit comes on you; and you will be my witnesses in Jerusalem, and in all Judea and Samaria, and to the ends of the earth." (Acts 1:8 NIV)

God encouraged me concerning my future and made me know that I would war for those who cannot war for themselves. And knowing that fear would attack me, He reminded me of this scripture:

"So do not fear, for I am with you; do not be dismayed, for I am your God. I will strengthen you and help you; I will uphold you with my righteous right hand." (Isaiah 41:10 NIV)

I must share with you that today, my father is in remission, and as a family, we are so happy to have him as the head of this family, and it is such a wonderful family. I am thriving in my faith, and yes, I have a church home where I can learn, grow, and serve. God is good, and God is faithful!

The Storm of Yesteryear

by Jana Brewer

If we were to have this conversation about my yesteryear in my home, I would welcome you warmly and offer you a cup of something sweet to drink. My voice would get soft, and my body language would possibly exhibit that I was beginning to feel a little vulnerable as I prepared to share my story. The caption of my story would read something like this: "Here sits a survivor!"

I share my story with you because I want for you what I have received. It is called freedom—freedom from bondages put in place by family members. Once upon a time, I had no hope for my present or future; I was hopeless. I was beginning to believe that what has been will always be. My world's prospective stopped at the mountain; I couldn't see into the horizon. After I was in pain for so long, my coping mechanism was to shut down any hope, get comfortable in my environment, and wait for death. I once believed that lie, and if that is the place my story finds you, then I challenge you to dare hope again. God has a plan!

Hello to the woman who wants to break the generational curse and declare no longer to allow abuse to be your best-kept secret; you have the strength to kick open that door and expose the dark secrets that lurk inside. To the girl who doesn't see an end in sight because the court is taking forever to prosecute the abusers: please trust the system, endure the process, and know that God is in the waiting. To the woman who hasn't dealt with the abuse she has suffered while she helps others who deal with their storm of abuse: breathe, and let God fill you with peace and wisdom, and know that you can do this, for yourself and others like you. You may fit one of those scenarios, but I know a woman who has dealt with the pain of being abused, helped her daughter face her accuser, and continues to experience inner healing. That woman is me!

Domestic violence and other forms of abuse were common in the small town where I was born and raised. Elementary classes required discussions on the subject, and teachers would ask us if we were experiencing any form of abuse. How can a child answer that question honestly? You are so afraid, so you shrink into the background and hope that nobody notices you. I speak from experience. My abuser paid close attention to me, and if I appeared getting close to another adult, I would be reprimanded and no longer permitted to be in the presence of that person. Therefore, I hid and always denied any abuse happening at home. I have heard him cuss out the entire pastoral staff at church because someone had called our home. He didn't want anyone getting close, and he didn't want me to go to church. He kept people away from me and me away from people. From the age of four until I was sixteen, I suffered abuse in every possible way you can imagine, and probably some ways you could not begin to imagine. I kept this a secret, buried deep inside my heart from everyone in my life.

My story began when I was four years old when my mother married my stepfather. She met him at church and thought he was the answer to her prayers. I knew something wasn't quite right in my young heart, and I refused to be the flower girl and walk down the aisle at their wedding. I threw the biggest crying fit—so much so that my mamaw, my nickname for Grandmother, carried me down the aisle. Honestly, I can't remember the exact moment the abuse began. All I know is that my life was scary and filled with terrifying moments for the twelve years they were married.

My earliest memory of the physical abuse was around six, and my parents had been in a fight. My stepdad had beaten my mother while she was holding her newborn, my younger brother. My mom had gone to church to seek help to get away from my stepdad. I saw him as my dad, the only one I had ever known. I was a typical six-year-old and liked to talk back; I challenged things. One time, my stepdad had wiped grease on my leg, so I returned the favor. My reward was a slap across my face and being grounded for a month. In that month, my toys were boxed up and taken away. For the next twelve years, every six months, I received physical beatings. The reasons my stepdad would hit me were always different. When I was six to eleven years old, he would hit me for any reason, like interrupting a conversation, or no reason, leaving me to think that he was mad at me. As a child, I was a people pleaser, and I wanted everyone to be happy, so I would honestly try to make everyone happy. Of course, I understand why I adopted that personality trait; if I could make him happy, he wouldn't hit me.

As I got older, I began to shut down. I wouldn't throw fits or interrupt my parents. I shrank down as far as I could, trying to become invisible. That did not work; he then began hitting me for any reason that sounded good to him. I remember one time, I asked to visit my mamaw. He said that I could, and I was so excited! He then changed his mind for reasons I will never know, and I was so mad that I yelled back at him. As I was walking by him, he punched me in the stomach hard and told me to go to my room. I ran to my room as fast as I could; I was terrified. He followed me quickly with a broomstick. He broke the broomstick and struck me against my back and my wrists. He finally stopped because I was screaming, and he told me to shut up.

I thought that he would leave and I would be fine, but he then went to the kitchen and picked up a butcher knife. He came back in and told me if I said a word that he would cut my heart out. I had visible bruises from that attack. I covered them up with a sweatshirt. I saw the bruises as a reminder to keep my mouth shut. I told myself, *You need to learn to shut up and stay out of the way.* I started spending a lot of time in my room, which kept me out of the danger zone for about a year.

The next time he beat me was while gathering for dinner. He had made turkey sandwiches. I chose a sandwich, not knowing that it had more meat on it than the others; it was a special sandwich unbeknownst to me. He was angry that I chose that one. Even worse, I had taken a bite, but I kindly and apologetically offered it to him. He refused it. I was sitting on the floor next to him. The next thing I remember, my head was being slammed against the arm of the couch. He screamed that I should have known which one was his. My injuries were never visible to anyone other than myself. He would slap me so hard it left his handprint on my face. Those slaps would usually happen at night; I would hope the handprint would disappear before school.

Honestly, the sexual abuse began around age four; it started with simple touching until the result was sex. He would physically and sexually abuse me. I knew whenever my mother left the house, I would be having sex. It became my norm. If she left, he would quickly do it. He would tell me that if I told anyone, he would make my life miserable.

He threatened to kill me if I said a word. He said if I got pregnant, he would throw me down a flight of stairs or punch me in the stomach. Thankfully, that never happened. In my mind, this was normal. I never cried; I just lay there, inhaling the stinky cigarette smell, and waited for it to be over. To this day, every time I smell cigarette smoke, I cringe inwardly.

In addition to all of the physical abuse, the emotional abuse was never-ending. Daily I was told how ugly or stupid I was. Sadly to say, even my mother chimed in on that. I can remember her saying to me, "I wish you were blonde and as pretty as you were at four." I got this from all along the spectrum, from family to foe. I was only allowed to take baths once a week. With that being my life, I was frequently made fun of at school due to body odor. In the fifth grade, I started my period. During that time, I was only allowed to use two pads a day. My stepfather reasoned that they were expensive. In sixth grade, I was finally allowed to wear deodorant. Because of the abuse I suffered in my home and being made fun of at school, I became withdrawn and unable to have a conversation with anyone; fear had stolen my voice. My mother noticed that I was becoming an introvert and that it was starting to affect my life. I guess she correlated it to him and the home environment; after all, he was beating her also. Somehow she found the courage to leave. I instantly felt like I could breathe; however, I always looked over my shoulder because I was worried he would kill my mother or me. So I never told my mother what had happened. I never said to her that her husband had sexually abused me during their entire marriage. I also thought she might hate me for sleeping with her husband. Imagine that: the abused becomes the criminal; the twelve-year-old had become the other woman. So I kept it a secret from everyone.

From the age of sixteen to twenty-seven, I fell in love with two different men. I met my oldest daughter's father while we were living at a domestic violence shelter. My mom had made her grand escape. We met because his mother was staying there as well. As I said, abuse was routine in my small town. He was friendly and cute. So within two months of dating, we started having sex. I think my interpretation of showing love was to have sex. I wonder where I learned that! Unfortunately, the relationship only lasted a few months, but it changed my life forever. The outcome of the relationship was pregnancy. I was so scared of my life changing that I kept my pregnancy a secret from everyone. I was a month overdue with my daughter. Thankfully, even without the proper care, my beautiful daughter was born healthy. I was so scared and ecstatic at the same time. I made her a promise that I would always keep her safe and protect her. My other promise was that she would never suffer abuse as I had.

A year later, I met my future husband, whom I thought was terrific. And once again, I had sex before marriage, but we did get married. My thought was that this is how I show love; I couldn't seem to unlearn this bad habit. He was everything that my stepfather wasn't. He loved my daughter as his own. During our marriage, we had two beautiful daughters. When I became pregnant with my younger daughter, I proudly made it known. My mother wasn't too happy to know that I had three children while I was seventeen to twenty-one years old. We had been married for seven years when he decided that he had found someone else that he loved more. At the end of the marriage, he told me that he had never loved me.

Again the person I loved left me feeling unloved. From the age of sixteen to twenty-seven, I tried to find love. My mind seared with twisted thoughts. The lies about love and keeping secrets branded me and left me confused. I kept the abuse by my stepfather and my first pregnancy a secret—sealed lips but a weeping heart. Thankfully, my ex continued to be the loving dad he had been to my oldest as well as our children together. Whenever people asked him how many children he had, he always said he had three girls. The inner child in me leaped because my daughters would never have to feel the pain of being unloved by their parents.

Suddenly, my world was shattered and turned upside down. The news hit my heart like a bomb. Molestation had invaded my home and afflicted my oldest daughter. My initial thoughts were, *I should have seen it. How did I let this happen?* I was protective of her around my abuser, but I didn't see the man who molested her as being a threat. When this came to the forefront, I was going through a divorce and living with my grandmother and several other family members, one being my uncle. The man I did not see as a threat, my uncle, was my daughter's abuser. In her elementary class, she did the opposite of what her mother had done. She did not shrink into the background, fearful of saying a word. No, thank God, she was brave enough to stand up and speak up. Her teacher proceeded to call social services. *I should have known the signs*, I told myself over and over again. However, I cannot begin to tell you the pride I felt in my heart because my daughter said something. She wouldn't have to go through what I had endured. I still didn't tell anyone my story. I was determined to fiercely take care of my daughter and allow my abuse to hang in the shadows. My brave daughter faced her abuse head-on.

The police began an investigation, and they requested that I remain living in the house with my grandmother to avoid tipping off the abuser. Immediately, I told my mother what had happened with my child. She questioned if her statement was true and whether it really happened. I asked her why she would not believe her granddaughter. She replied, "He is my brother!" To which I replied, "She is my daughter and your granddaughter!" Finally, they arrested my uncle. The process and wait time were long, and the stress almost unbearable. I rejoiced with my daughter that law enforcement had arrested her abuser. However, after three months of being in jail, he was bailed out. I found out that my mother had signed the paper to bail him out. The momma bear in me was outraged that anyone would willingly allow him back on the streets. The inner abused child in me said, *See? If you had spoken up about your abuse then, she would've believed you now.*

During the three months when he was out on bail, he would yell and scream at me while in a drunken state, saying, "Your daughter is ruining my life!" It was emotionally draining. He spent much of his time drunk, and once while in a drunken state, he came to my church looking for me. He wanted to talk but was utterly belligerent. He thought that if he threatened me, I would back down. I wouldn't, and I didn't. It was the strangest thing because my family was angry that my daughter had spoken up for herself. My family never wanted to believe that he could and would do that. Thankfully, my daughter, for her protection, moved to live with her father, and she didn't have to endure the wrath of my family. In the end, my uncle chose to take a plea bargain offered to him because the evidence against him was overwhelming. He never admitted guilt. He was accused of more than twenty-seven counts of aggravated sexual abuse of a minor but convicted and found guilty on six counts. The court process was long. It took two years for them to charge him and go through the system. After this was all said and done, a cousin admitted this had happened to her as well.

While dealing with my daughter and her abuser, I never admitted what had happened to me. Finally, one day, my adopted sister asked the question I had been dreading. "Did it happen to you?" I finally broke down and told the truth. I said yes. She thought I would say my abuser was my uncle. I began to share that my abuse was not from my uncle but my stepdad. She was the only person who knew about my abuse for over four years. I processed a lot during the situation with my daughter. But my thoughts became so complicated, more than ever before. The wicked one, we call him the devil, would speak loudly in my mind and tell me that if my family didn't believe my daughter, surely they would not believe me. I had so much rage in my heart that it spilled over. My abuser was still in my mother's life, and he dared to express outrage over my child, pointing out her abuser; I had to control the urge to curse him out and punch him right in the mouth. It took everything in my spirit not to take out all the rage I had carried in my heart against him. How dare he make comments about my child when he had done the very same and even worse to me!

God works in unique ways. He allowed me to meet an extraordinary family who allowed me to heal in a place of freedom and honestly deal with the abuse I had held in my heart for so long. They took me in as their own and stood with me as I shared my struggles of abuse. I finally felt like I was able to come out on the other side. They helped me realize that nothing that happened was my fault. I was only a child at the time, but I had felt so strongly that I somehow deserved the abuse. In addition to these beautiful people, my daughter inspired me and helped me realize that I took the enemy's control away from him by finally standing up and saying what had happened to me.

Fear is no longer a tactic of the enemy when you are willing to turn, face it, and yell right back!

I have heard many different stories of abuse. In some, the abuse becomes a way of life, and the abused individual wants to give up. I am so thankful that I have an amazing God who heals and restores what the enemy has stolen.

God is our refuge and strength, A very present help in trouble. Therefore we will not fear, Even though the earth be removed, And though the mountains be carried into the midst of the sea; Though its waters roar and be troubled, Though the mountains shake with its swelling. Selah. (Psalms 46:1–3 NKJV)

I never knew that God was right there with me during all the different stages. There were times I had doubted God saw me or heard me. I doubted that God cared about me. Even when I didn't think He was there, I later realized that He was with me. He was for me, whether it was keeping me safe and alive or sending the friend who had turned into a sister, who helped me finally gather my voice and speak boldly and confidently about what had happened to me.

My story is a story full of redemption, not making light of the abuse but realizing I didn't have to remain a prisoner wrapped up in chains; God is a chain breaker. He was breaking chains off my life, my daughter's life, and into our future for generations. It is about the restoration of a little girl who grew up into a woman who would not look people in the eye or get too close to anyone because she was afraid they might know the signs of abuse and ask the question she was too scared to answer. It is about healing a heart broken into a thousand pieces. As you read my story, may you be encouraged to allow God to break the chain of the vicious cycle of abuse visited upon you or upon someone you love or know. Abuse comes in all flavors: mental, physical, sexual, or emotional. My prayer is that you will realize that your past and your family bloodline doesn't define who you are. With God's help, you can be an overcomer, standing in truth and for truth.

In the last ten years, I have come to realize God was my refuge during my childhood. I did not see it at the time, and I had no idea.

Often, other people's stories sounded worse than mine, and I imagined that my story and my voice weren't valuable or needed in this generation. I started to wonder if I should share because I was unsure if it would make a difference. It was easy for me to get caught up comparing myself to others; I had done it all my life. But now I know that these are tactics of the enemy. I realized that God had and still has a bigger plan for my life. Sometimes the things I encountered provoked questions in my mind. Some of mine were: What if the abuse had never happened? Would I be so overly protective of my daughter? If I had been brave and spoken out, could it have saved my daughter from her pain? Why didn't I protect her better? To me, these are justifiable questions, and they would run circles in my mind. But then I realized the things I have endured weren't only for me. They empowered and enabled me to be very vocal in defense of my daughter. She was ten when she spoke up, and I had to be a strong voice on her behalf. Many people in my family accused her of lying. I never doubted in my mind that she was telling the truth. It took bravery and guts for my daughter to speak up, and to this day, I am so proud of her.

The healing from the abuse didn't happen overnight. I overcame the fear and shame by telling someone close to me about what happened. Once I said it, the enemy lost control. It could no longer hide in the dark places of my heart. If you are suffering from abuse, bring it to the light. Tell a sister, a friend, a pastor, a teacher—tell someone. The enemy loses his grip on your heart. I allowed the healing love of Jesus to begin to saturate my heart in a way I had never felt before. The first time I told my story, I couldn't look my sister in the eye. I felt ashamed, embarrassed, afraid she wouldn't believe me or would judge me. She helped me share my story in several small group settings. There is freedom in standing together, and we are overcomers.

I also encourage you to praise God every time you get a chance. God always made sure I was protected. He kept me safe, whether it was a neighbor dropping by or a telephone call. I praise Him for that. There is power in the praise you bring before the Lord. Shout unto the Lord, and walls will fall; ask Joshua in the Bible about those Jericho walls! I remember one time at an altar call during church; the pastor asked people to come forward who needed to forgive others. I went up because I felt a tug on my heart; it was time to forgive my stepdad, it was time to forgive my uncle, it was time to forgive everyone who had ever hurt me, and it was time to forgive myself. He asked us to imagine the person you need to forgive sitting in a white chair. In my mind, there were several rows of white chairs in front of several doors. As soon as I proclaimed "I forgive you," the chairs were knocked down and turned to red. The doors flew open. That is when I knew I had finally forgiven the abusers and myself. All I could do was praise God for the love and freedom that filled my heart that day. I haven't been the same since.

I hope you understand the power of true forgiveness. Forgiveness is not for the abuser's benefit, but yours. Once you forgive, the enemy loses his hold on you, releases you to move forward with your life, and allows God to continue working on your heart. Unforgiveness steals every last bit of your joy. It can turn very quickly to bitterness and hatred stored up like a brick in your heart. Together, we can stand up and say, "Not today!" We can choose to love, choose to forgive, and choose to walk in the joy that comes only from walking in the freedom that God has for us. Walking in a forgiving life is fantastic; please join this walk of forgiveness.

People who don't know or have never experienced abuse may not understand why we should tell a safe person. They may not know why it is essential to share our story, but what they will understand is

God's grace. If my daughter had never spoken up, my uncle might have abused our younger cousins. I also would still be carrying the weight of my own secret story that I had held so tightly. My mother did eventually find out what happened to me. She got to experience firsthand the anger I had felt for years. She immediately told my stepdad that she knew what happened. Of course, he denied it, but she knew I would never lie about something like that after all that had happened with my daughter. When my brother found out, his immediate response was that he wanted to beat him up; he had wanted to do the same thing to my uncle before finding this out. My stepdad, my sexual and physical abuser, passed away two years ago. He died alone with no one to care for him. My mother feels a lot of guilt—the same regret that I felt with my daughter. I have been through those emotions, so I try to help her understand that it wasn't her fault. I share with her about how I didn't tell anyone, so she couldn't have known. I have a unique understanding of both sides of this particular story and try to allow God to use me however He wants.

God gave me amazing people who showed me His unconditional love. They showed me grace and kindness. They helped me understand that bad things do happen, but I could choose my attitude once I understood the cross's power and who I wanted to be. I decided not to be a victim and carry a victim mentality. I am victorious and stand with my head held high. I join the proud group of overcomers. Being victorious is merely admitting and proclaiming, "This happened to me, but look where I am today." I am healed, loved, beautiful; I am the opposite of everything my abuser said I was. I am not broken but whole; not scared but brave; not ugly but beautifully and wondrously made.

Most importantly, the "abuser" thoughts no longer dictate my life or my view of myself. I reject and throw off the banners he spoke over me; God's banner over me is love. I cling with all my might to what the Bible says.

For I know the thoughts that I think toward you, says the LORD, *thoughts of peace and not of evil, to give you a future and a hope. (Jeremiah 29:11 NKJV)*

The longer you keep silent, the more control your abuser and the devil will have over you. Bad things happen, but you can overcome them. I asked my daughter, "If you had to do this thing over again, would you do it?" She told me, "Absolutely."

Please let me share a word of prayer with you.

Dear Heavenly Father, I pray for people who just read my story that they will know that You have a plan for their lives. That they will know that they can choose to walk in Your victory with their head held high because You are fighting on their behalf. I pray they will know the freedom and joy that comes by walking in the plan and calling You have for them. I pray for the women, girls, men, and boys who are reading this to feel encouraged to report their abuse and share their stories. I pray for those who may not have surrendered their lives to You to do so now by accepting Your Son, Jesus Christ, as their Savior and Lord, by repenting of their sins, and today, they will become Your children. I pray, God, that You would reveal to all of us more of Your heart for us and continue to show us Your goodness. God, I am thankful from the core of my being for the chance and opportunity to share the story You have given me with whoever is willing to listen, and thank You for redeeming my life and giving me a new heart. Thank You for protecting me in those dark moments and for rejoicing with me in the moments of freedom and truth. Do likewise for those who are reading this story—this book. Thank You for Your goodness that is on display for all in Jesus's name!

Shout it from the mountain top: No more secrets. No more bondage. FREEDOM!

An Army of Angels

by Ramona Crossley

He who dwells in the secret place of the Most High shall abide under the shadow of the Almighty. I will say of the LORD, "He is my refuge and my fortress; My God, in Him I will trust." (Psalms 91:1–2)

It was a late afternoon in the spring of 1990. I was running late picking up my son and his two friends from a church league softball practice. My mother and two teenage daughters were with me. I always endeavored to pick him up on time because the park nearby was known to be a hangout for gangs in the city of Stockton, California. But on this particular bright sunny day, I wasn't on time, and I cannot remember why. I assumed the coach would wait with the boys until I picked them up. I didn't have any means to contact them to let them know I would be late. The year was 1990, and although the first cell phone had been manufactured and sold to the public, we couldn't afford to pay the cost for such a toy. I was fifteen minutes late, and those fifteen minutes changed my life and the life of these young men forever.

My spirit was high, and I was feeling rather good. The week was a fantastic "God" week, as I like to say. I had spent much time in prayer and devotion, and my faith was at an all-time high. It was a day when I felt like I was on top of the world. Have you ever felt that way?

I drove into the park and could see the baseball diamonds, but I didn't see the boys or their coach. I began to feel concerned and defaulted to praying in my mind, "Lord, help me find these boys." Although the boys were old enough to be left alone, the area's gang activity dictated differently. As I continued to drive around the park, I saw what looked like four or five gang members in hot pursuit of my son's two friends with baseball bats. I did not see my son, only his two friends. I stopped in the middle of the street and didn't take the time to park my van. Before I could exit the van, the gang members were surrounding both boys. I jumped out and started running toward the boys and screaming at the top of my voice for those guys to leave them alone. My mother was shouting for me to stop, but that was not an option. I could hear their chasers taunting them, saying, "You think you're bad? Come on! Let's see what you can do!" They were laughing and jeering, waving the baseball bats in their hands.

I immediately began praying earnestly, asking God, "Lord, I need an army of angels right now. Please send an army! Let them see an army surrounding them just as Elisha did in the Bible after Elijah prayed for his eyes to be open."

So he answered, "Do not fear, for those who are with us are
more than those who are with them." And Elisha prayed,
*and said, "L*ORD*, I pray, open his eyes that he may see."*
*Then the L*ORD *opened the eyes of the young man, and*
he saw. And behold, the mountain was full of horses and
chariots of fire (i.e., an army) all around Elisha. (2 Kings
6:16–17 NKJV)

. . . And it was so . . .

"Please, Lord, I know You can do this; I am asking for a hedge
of protection around these boys and that no harm shall come to them.
Lord, protect me as I enter the battlefield and let them see a mighty
God that protects his children!" Immediately, I felt a boldness come
over me, and I was not fearful of what they would do to me. I knew that
my God was going to protect us, and we would walk away. As Elijah
said in 2 Kings 6:16, "Fear not: for they that be with us are more than
they that be with them."

I walked rather swiftly and in an authoritative manner amid the
gang! About twenty gang members started to surround me. Thoughts
began to flood my mind, and I realized that I could be in danger
because the odds were against me. But I rebuked those thoughts and
began quoting scriptures. I quoted 1 John 4:4 (NIV):

You, dear children, are from God and have overcome them,
because the one who is in you is greater than the one who is
in the world.

I also quoted Psalms 18:2–3 (NIV):

The LORD is my rock, my fortress and my deliverer; my God is my rock, in whom I take refuge, my shield and the horn of my salvation, my stronghold. I called to the LORD, who is worthy of praise, and I have been saved from my enemies.

I recalled David and Goliath's story and asked the Lord to help me conquer Goliath for his glory. All this happened in a matter of minutes.

What Faith Can Do—Divine Intervention

The gang members continued to surround and close in upon me. But I felt confident that God was with us. I could no longer hear their voices. As they continued to step forward toward me, suddenly, they began walking backward away from me. I recall a number of their facial expressions looking at me with anger and malice, with the intent of hurting me, but then their facial expressions changed to surprise and apprehension in approaching me. I think they saw more than a protective mother courageously rescuing her children! In my mind, I began praising God for the army. Although I never saw the army with my physical eyes, I knew in my spirit, my heart of hearts, angels were present! God had answered my prayer, and everything about their expressions and behavior confirmed it.

Now, what to do about the boys? How will they be set free? A boldness came over me, and I said to the gang member who appeared to be the leader, "Let the boys go now!" Then, I looked at the two boys and said, "Go! Get in the car." I looked at the gang members that were surrounding the boys and said, "Let them go!"

I am small in stature, all of four feet, eleven inches tall, and at that time, I didn't weigh more than a hundred pounds. I was not holding any weapon in my hands, and believe me, I am as feminine as they come; I am a girly girl.

The gang members surrounding the boys backed away so the boys could leave. I asked one of the boys where my son was, and he pointed and said that other gang members had chased him across the street into the backyard of a person's home. The boys ran to the van. By this time, the gang members all stood there staring at me, some with evil expressions that led me to believe that if they could do something to me, they would. Others had had the look of total surprise, and still others had compliant, respectful expressions, as if I was the gang's king or ruler. By this time, I was sure we were safe, and the Lord would not allow anything to happen to us. What an awesome God we serve!

Suddenly, I heard sounds that horrified me. The sounds were coming from the house the boys had pointed out. I ran to the backyard, the gate was open, and I ran in. I saw gang members surrounding my son and beating him with boards and bats. I yelled at them and said, "Get away from him now!" They immediately stopped hitting him and stood still, as though frozen in place. They gave me a glaring stare. Again, I saw an expression on these guys' faces as if they saw an army of angels! Is it possible they saw a group of police officers, a U.S. Army soldier, a SWAT team, or maybe actual angels? I don't know what they saw, but that day, I knew we had the hand of God on our side. I approached my son, helped him to his feet, and led him to the van. The gang members did not try to stop us, and they were looking at me as they spoke back and forth to each other. They were astonished that I had the boldness to dare challenge them, but my son's life was at stake; nothing was going to stop me from defending his life with my life.

We made it! All were safe in the van, which was still parked in the street! My mom and daughters were happy that we made it back safely. As I was shutting the van's side door, one of the boys said, "Oh, wait! My baseball gear is still out there!" All three boys' baseball bags were in gang territory, and they were staring and pointing at our van as they were talking amongst themselves.

I thought, "Okay, Lord, one more time, protect me, please! I know you will not let them harm a hair on my head! You are the creator of all earth, and all power is in your hands." I calmly walked to the three bags amid the gang members who were giving me evil looks, picked up the gear, walked at a normal pace with my back toward them back to the van, loaded the equipment into the van, hopped into the driver seat, and calmly drove away as if nothing had happened.

Now I had to make sure the boys were okay. There was much chatter about what happened and what a miracle it was. My son's two friends didn't suffer any physical harm, but they were in great fear for their lives. They had beaten my son with boards and bats, and he said he was a little sore but felt okay. There were a few scratches on his arms, and he had bruises on his torso. I drove directly to the hospital to have him checked out. Thank God, he only had bruised ribs. The hospital called the police to talk to us. The police told us that we were "lucky" as this gang was well known to be a violent gang. But we knew it wasn't luck; it was a miracle!

I learned that day about the power of God and the power of faith in God. Call on the Lord, and he will answer. That is what He did that day. My mother explained that it was indeed a remarkable sight to watch. Although she did not see a visible army either, she said she watched the gang members charge me and then abruptly stop and walk backward, as if they were afraid to approach. When I told her what I had prayed for, she also believed they saw an army of angels! What an awesome God we serve.

The boys had indicated to me that the "gang attack" started because one of the boys had a T-shirt on that had a picture of Jesus weightlifting the cross and said, "Bench press this. Not by might, nor by strength, but by my spirit, sayeth the Lord." A gang member had approached the boy and said, "Hey, you think you're bad? I'll show you bad!" and the attack began. Wow! I realized it was a spiritual battle from the beginning, but there was no way they would win. Our God is awesome. He loves us so much and will go to the ends of the earth to help us.

Often, we hear about "free will" and the fact that God doesn't interfere with one's free will. These gang members had the freedom and the power to do what they wanted to us, and the Lord would not interfere with human nature. But I also realized that I was not asking God to stop them from imposing their free will to hurt us; no, I asked for the forces with us to be greater than the forces that were with them so they would be afraid. The Lord didn't have to interfere with their free will, but He gave them an option to fight this army even though they could not win.

I have thought about this drama many times since that day. I realized that the most effective way to pray and not interfere with free will is to request God to fight for me. It is mind-boggling when you think about it.

Fast-forward eighteen years later: my son works with troubled individuals every day. I pray for protection for him daily. One day, I felt impressed to remind him how the Lord protected us from the gang and that I was praying that same protection over him daily. "Mom," he said, "it is so weird that you should bring this up." My son looks much different today. Back then, he was a skinny, scrawny boy. Because of that event, he began a bodybuilding regimen. Today he is a muscular and well-built man. He doesn't look like the same person at all. But remember what got that incident started—a T-shirt that declared: "Bench press this. Not by might, nor by strength, but by my spirit, sayeth the Lord." Thank God that my son is healthy and physically strong today, but this remains true: our strength is not by our might.

I have forgiven and pray for those gang members that they would find God in a real and powerful way and commit their hearts to Him. Maybe they will realize that on that day, God got involved. One day, they will see it as an extraordinary event that will bring them face to face with their creator. Our youth and adults who commit violent crimes have filled jails and prisons to the brim. It would be awesome to have a revival sweep through our prison system, in which joining the Lord's Gang would become the "in" thing to do rather than joining a violent gang. It could happen!

I believe in the power of God. I believe that whatever I ask for that is aligned with God's will, and asked for in faith without wavering, will be done! Our God loves us so much! He delights in answering our prayers.

I encourage you to read Psalms 91, which speaks of he who dwells in the secret place of the Most High. That is where I was on that day, *in the secret place, and angels were with me.*

The Tie That Binds

by Kristin Rich

We met at a high school football game. I was cold, and he offered to keep me warm. We were in the same circle of friends, but I had never looked at him "like that." Little did I know that night would be a major turning point in the course of my life. Soon after, we became boyfriend and girlfriend, and young love commenced. I was fifteen. He gave me butterflies, and it wasn't long before we became inseparable. We wrote letters, held hands in the quad, spent our lunches together, and called each other every night. On the weekends, we would hang out with friends. He was always on my mind; it sounds like a familiar song. Life was good; I felt real joy and happiness. He was everything to me.

I soon found myself in conflict with my parents over the relationship. For anonymity's sake, let's call my boyfriend Mr. D. He was Black, and I am White. My parents didn't know how to take their daughter in an interracial relationship, and they were not supportive. It was tough for me to understand their lack of acceptance because growing up, my parents taught me to love everyone and treat people with love and respect, not with conditions. I didn't see color when I looked at him or see race as a dividing line between human beings, and to me, he was an exceptional human being. It was evident I had strong feelings for him; I'd even go as far as to call it love. But what is love when you're fifteen? It was like the movie starring Sidney Poitier and Katharine Houghton, *Guess Who's Coming to Dinner.* Maybe it wasn't a color thing after all; perhaps they didn't want me to blaze this unpopular trail and feared it would cause me significant pain. These are assumptions, just guesses, because we never had that full conversation. I could have assured them that it was none of the above, just love.

I remember my mom telling me as I was growing up that I could come to her with anything and tell her anything. I learned quickly that if I actually did that, I needed to be prepared to get in trouble. Not wanting trouble, I learned to lie and be sneaky, even though I was terrible at it. I desperately sought their approval and acceptance of the relationship, and when they didn't offer that, I became rebellious.

After nine months of dating, one day out of the blue, he broke up with me with no warning. Later, I found out that he had started talking to another girl at the church; she would visit him while he was working at the local community center. As soon as he broke up with me, he was with her. I was heartbroken. I came home, went to my room, and cried. My mom asked me why I was crying; I told her that Mr. D had broken up with me. Her response at that moment was pivotal; I will never forget it. Standing in the doorway to my room, she said, "You'll get over it!" At that moment, I needed my mom to comfort me—to tell me that she loved me and that everything would be okay. That's not what happened. I often look back at that moment and wonder how my life may have been different had I had the comfort and affirmation that I needed at that time. We all have these sudden moments in our lives that become defining moments.

Right away, I noticed that I was not ready, willing, or able to let go of this relationship because I hadn't seen the breakup coming. Therefore, we continued to engage both emotionally and sexually, or so I thought. In fact, I was the only one making the emotional deposits. I was so tied up and entangled with him that I couldn't even see that I was wrong. I was now the "side chick." Although he wasn't committed to me or choosing me, I still felt like he was my guy. I was devoted to him, loyal, and even lied to protect him. His family loved and welcomed me whenever I was around; they knew what was going on and accepted it. When his other girlfriend was over, they treated her the same. Being the "side chick" wasn't pretty, and I was even in physical fights over this guy. I looked so foolish to my friends and family. I didn't care either; I wanted what I wanted.

Eventually, the other girlfriend and I knew about each other, and at that point, she didn't care either. We disliked each other, but neither of us wanted to let him go. This relationship was toxic, dramatic, and tumultuous, but I was addicted and refused to stop fighting for him to choose me. These shenanigans went on for over a decade. He would be with me, her, or whoever his current girlfriend was at the time, sleeping with and being intimate with all of us. In my twenties, I started to see other people and attempted to move on, but my heart was still loyal to him.

Then I met someone else; he was a coworker. I noticed him noticing me in the break room one evening. He was sitting with a girl, but I assumed she was a friend. Their interaction seemed more friendly than romantic (I found out later that she was his girlfriend). There was a fiery spark between us in that exchanged glance; within the week, we had made plans to hang out. That spark led to a few sexual encounters, and then things ended abruptly. He said he had been on a break from his girlfriend, but they were getting back together, so we couldn't "hang out" anymore. It was an in-between decision kind of thing. I respected him for being honest with me but felt the sting of rejection once again. To spite him, I wrote his girlfriend a letter and told her everything that had happened between us. He denied it, of course, and she believed him, of course. Shocking? No. Sadly, it was typical; believing their man was a normal reaction. I had seen it many times in different relationships. When he abruptly stopped working there, I figured that was the end of it. Well, little did I know that was just the beginning for us. I guess he wasn't that committed to his girlfriend. For anonymity, let's just call him Mr. L.

During my time with Mr. L, I felt incredibly guilty and disloyal to Mr. D, who had already had about three other girlfriends since our breakup. Go figure that out, but my heart still belonged to him. I knew it hurt Mr. D that I had been intimate with other people, even though he wouldn't admit it. At least, that is what I wanted to believe. Besides, he had no problem repeatedly choosing others over me, so he shouldn't care, right? You could see that he wanted to remain number one in my life. He didn't want to lose me, but he didn't want to commit to me either. We were comfortable in our dysfunction. It was almost as if I enjoyed being hurt and playing the victim. I was addicted to the drama, creating it and talking about it. I was living in a continuous cycle of rejection.

A few months after Mr. L and I lost contact, I received a call from him on the way home from work. He asked to see me, and I was willing. The spark was still there. He convinced me that he had placed the ex-girlfriend and their relationship in the past. He also said that the drama of our past was in the archives. I knew from the beginning that he was emotionally unavailable, and although I craved to learn more about him, his mystery attracted me. It was an easy "friends with benefits" sexual relationship. I knew he desired me, and that's what kept me excited. As with Mr. D, it didn't matter what had happened before; he kept coming back for more. The craziness fed my ego; I got off on it. I felt a sense of power and confidence. Being desired sexually was enough. At least, that's what I kept telling myself until I started to "catch feelings." In case you haven't heard the term, it is what my generation describes as the feelings you develop from a "no strings attached" relationship to an attached one. We hung out for several months after that.

I would go between the two of them. When I wasn't with one, I was with the other. Soon I stopped hearing from Mr. L; he fell off, and I didn't mind much because Mr. D was still number one to me. Mr. L and I lost touch, and I moved on with my life, but this was not the end of our story.

Over the next five years, Mr. D had his first child; it devastated me that he had his child with someone else. It was a reality I had to face, but I resented it. I found out about it through someone else, not him, which was even more hurtful. The icing on the cake was having to work with the woman who was carrying his child. It was hard for me, but it didn't change much between us. We continued to see each other after the baby was born. He had started to see someone new—same story, different girl. While with the new girl, he got his baby's mother pregnant again. Even though she was about to have his second child and he was still hanging out with me, he decided to marry his current girlfriend.

It was bad enough to be the side chick, but I didn't want to be the mistress. As far as I was concerned, we had something special, but once he chose someone he was willing to commit to—to marry—it was a game changer. This news had broken me to the point of no return. I knew I needed to stop fighting because I was boxing with the wind. I put some distance between us. We maintained our friendship, but out of respect for his marriage, I thought it would be best to put Mr. D in the past. Occasionally, we would talk on the phone or meet to catch up on life, but the sexual relationship was over.

Around the same time that all this was happening, I bought a home and moved about an hour north. I had reconnected with Mr. L a few months prior, and now there was less physical distance between us. He caught me up on everything that had happened after we lost touch. He told me he had met someone, gotten married, and was now going through a divorce. He also shared that his soon-to-be ex-wife was pregnant and that he had a baby on the way—but that wasn't all. He told me that he was in a new relationship and that this woman was also pregnant, and that both women were due in the same month.

That should have sent me running for the hills, but since he and I were never really emotionally attached, it was easy to disassociate myself from his circumstances. Maybe I was tempted because he told me he was "getting a divorce" and was not that serious with the girl-friend. I tried not to let my heart get involved, but eventually, it did. Remember "catching feelings"? I was a follow-your-heart type of girl; I didn't know then just how wicked the heart really could be. I ignored all the red flags; I guess you could say I ran toward them. It seemed like he was finally vulnerable emotionally with me, and of course, I started to feel something the more we were together. We were always sneaking around because he was still with his baby's mother. He asked to borrow money from me to pay a bill. It started small, so it seemed like no big deal. He eventually got his own place, and we would see each other occasionally. I was beginning to see that he didn't stay in one place very long; he would move throughout the state, and there were plenty of times I'd make the long drive to visit him, or he would come to see me.

After going back and forth and traveling to see each other, on one of his trips to visit me, we decided to make it official: we were together now, and he decided he wanted to stay, so I let him move in with me. He began to settle in and started looking for a job, but it didn't take long for things to get rocky. One day I found his phone on the couch. He was sleeping, and something told me to pick it up and take a look. That something was called "I don't trust you!" His phone was locked, but I figured out his code. A stone hacker! When I looked at his messages, I saw that he had reached out to a friend with whom he had previously been romantically involved. She asked him where he was staying, and his response threw me into a rage. He told her that he was staying with "this chick" until he could get on his feet! At that moment, I realized that he was just using me and had no intentions of sticking around long term. I was so livid that I grabbed the phone, went upstairs where he was peacefully sleeping in MY bed, woke him up, and threw the phone at him. I told him to leave, and I would help him pack. I was so upset that I started throwing his clothes over the banister. I was so angry. To have someone fake everything just for a place to stay? That broke me. We talked through it, and although I couldn't trust him anymore, I allowed him to stay. He wasn't there long, maybe a couple of months. I can't recall why we finally broke up or when he left, but we were toxic for each other. Perhaps we hadn't talked anything through, but instead he had talked me out of being angry.

Things got dark for a while after that. I was so angry with God. I didn't understand why I was alone, why neither of the men I had chosen chose me. I had worked so hard to prove myself worthy of their love that it just didn't seem fair that they got to walk away and move on and leave me with emotional wreckage. I began to isolate myself; getting to work every day became a challenge for me. I was in full-fledged depression; I was drowning emotionally, financially, and physically; I just felt sick. My thoughts were overwhelming, my energy was negative, and my anxiety was out of control. I would spend days at home watching TV, unable to get out of bed, shower, get dressed, and go to work. I would cry out to God to just take me out. I didn't want to live anymore. Life was not going the way I had expected, and although I had friends and family who loved me and all the essential things to thrive, I was missing something that I yearned for the most: a family of my own.

I began to see a psychiatrist; I remember her asking me about my childhood. I explained it as great. I said I was a bit spoiled, but I had a wonderful upbringing overall. My parents were married young, right out of high school. I was the firstborn. They didn't know if I would be a boy or a girl, but my mother said when they told her I was a girl, she was thrilled. My parents didn't have a specific name picked out for me, but at the time, the hit TV series *Dallas* was in the headlines, and everyone was trying to determine who shot JR. Well, it was Kristin, and that's how I got my name. Maybe this explained my love of soap operas from a young age and my dramatic teenage years. My one and only brother was born fourteen months later.

I grew up in the country in a small farming community where everyone knew each other, and neighbors were family. My upbringing was unique because my maternal grandparents lived next door; the only thing between us was a couple of almond orchards and a canal. Growing up, extended families regularly surrounded me on both sides. To outsiders, it almost seemed strange how close we all were. There has always been so much love, laughter, and great memories. So when she asked me about my upbringing, it just didn't make sense to me that maybe something in my happy childhood could be the cause of so much distress in my adulthood. I became defensive when she told me that the patterns and issues we have as adults directly reflect our childhood experiences. Yes, my teenage years and early twenties were a bit tumultuous, and my parents and I didn't always see eye to eye, but my childhood was amazing.

My mom put me in singing lessons at the age of eleven. I began performing all over my local area, and when I was fourteen, my parents took me to Nashville to record an independent album. I spent my youth attempting to get discovered, and although I loved to sing, it started to feel like a job. As a teenager, all I wanted to do was hang out with my friends in high school. I kept it up for ten years, and my parents were right there supporting me through it all. My mom would sit in the back, smiling at me and letting me know how the sound was, and my dad was there to make sure the equipment was set up correctly. They had my back; they were proud of me when I was on stage. They believed in me, but even back then, I didn't believe in myself.

I would see my psychiatrist regularly, and we would talk about how I was feeling. I couldn't believe that I was about to enter my thirties, and all I could focus on was how life was passing right by me. It sounds like another familiar song with the words "isn't it funny how life just slips right on away." I focused on everything that was wrong with my life. My head felt stuck in a hole so deep that I was suffocating. I was desperate to have this fairytale life I had imagined, but I was settling for less. It was good to have someone to talk to and get perspective on why I might be feeling the way I did. When I realized that my emotions were overwhelming me, I was angry—angry with myself mostly, angry that I had allowed myself to stay in a repetitive cycle with two men for so long. I was ashamed. Who willingly consents to this type of treatment? It was like I was asking for it. I was broken and rejected, I didn't value my life, and the only reason I wanted to live was that I would feel guilty leaving my family and friends to grieve for me. I didn't even know who I was; I lacked identity and purpose. I had no vision for myself outside of being a wife and a mother.

I discovered I had resentment toward my parents. I was holding onto anger from my teenage years for the times they didn't support my choices or relationship with Mr. D. For all the fights I had with my mom, the terrible arguments we had when I was in my teens and my twenties. Resentment toward my dad for always disciplining me but never letting me express myself when I was upset. Through these sessions, I realized that I hadn't received the emotional support I needed in childhood. I needed more than discipline; my brain required adjusting. So here I was, this broken, angry girl stuck emotionally at age four. I discovered that I was an optimist, raised by two pessimists. I was uncovering this resentment but still felt guilty for feeling this way about two people I loved more than anyone else in the world and who loved me and supported me in the best way possible, and the only way they knew how.

Through it all, Mr. L and I remained in contact, and eventually, we got back together. He moved back in, and he met my family. My parents were over their interracial issues by now; they just wanted me to be happy and be with someone who would treat me right. I think they knew that I felt a tremendous pressure to choose a mate that they would approve of, and they didn't want me to carry that burden anymore. Mr. L and I discussed marriage, and we also tried to conceive a child. Things were going well, but I couldn't outlive our past. I was always waiting for the other shoe to drop and for some emotional eruption to blow up everything. I remember my mom asking me if I thought he was "the one." I couldn't confidently answer her, but I remember telling her that he had to show and prove himself, that words and promises weren't going to cut it.

Then it happened: the other shoe dropped, and what an emotional eruption it caused! I call it the "fried potatoes incident." I had plans to make us dinner that evening. I texted him and asked him not to eat the leftovers in the fridge that I would cook. When I got home that evening, I opened the fridge to find—you guessed it— that the potatoes were gone. I was livid. It wasn't the first time he just did whatever he wanted. I felt so disrespected. Looking back, it was such a small thing, but it was the one thing that changed everything. I got so upset with him that I told him I didn't want to be with him anymore, and I wanted to break up—so he said, "Okay!" Typical me! Every time something would happen, big or small, it would feel like the end of the world. As soon as I said it, I wanted to take it back; I felt immediate regret. He said he would not take me back, that I should never have said something I didn't mean, and what's done is done. He locked himself in one of the bedrooms and refused to talk to me. It felt like punishment, but I was no stranger to this routine. Over the years, he would use the silent treatment to manipulate me. He knew it would drive me crazy. That's when I threw the biggest adult tantrum of my life. I was banging on the door, screaming in the hallway, and crying to the point of hyperventilation. He just let me sit there alone. I threatened to kill myself, tried to seduce him—anything to get him to talk to me that night. Eventually, I was so exhausted that I went to bed and cried myself to sleep.

He was a truck driver, so he left the next day to go to work. I couldn't believe how out of control I had gotten. I knew that I needed to deal with the anger and the deep hurt that was always just beneath the surface, ready to pounce. I never wanted to feel that out of control again. I looked into anger management classes and signed up. It helped me tremendously; most of the people who were there were ordered by the court. I heard many stories while I was there; one man got frustrated and threw a sippy cup at a wall and hit his girlfriend in the head. He got arrested and put in jail. This story stuck with me. I thought back to the night I was fighting Mr. L to open the door. That could have been me going to jail. It was eye-opening and what I needed at the time. I learned many helpful tips to control my impulsivity, anger, and rage.

I started looking for a church home; it had been seven years since I had been in church and connected with God. I was far from God and felt guilty for cursing Him in my times of darkness and depression, but something in my spirit after that horrible fight with my boyfriend led me to start looking at the local churches in the area. Growing up, I was Catholic. I didn't attend regularly, but in high school, I began to attend church with my friend Mr. D.; his dad was the pastor. I stuck out like a sore thumb, but I was comfortable there. I loved the gospel choir, and soon I was singing in it. I was there for several years until he and his family moved away to Chicago. I was out of church for a couple of years, but when Mr. D moved back to California, I attended church with him and sang in the choir there as well. It was there where I chose to get baptized again. I was there for a couple of years before I moved.

There were some great churches in my area, but I was looking for something specific. I knew that the church I needed would have to have a choir so I could worship again, and it would have to be racially diverse. I thought it would be hard to find, but soon I found my church. A coworker told me about it, and I knew I had to check it out. The first day I walked in, I felt God's presence. The choir, the praise dancers, and the pastor's humility all touched me, and the message he preached spoke to me. The diversity I desired was present, and it was all confirmation for me. I loved it. It was so different from my usual church experience.

God had given me all that was on my heart in one place. I filled out a guest card, requested prayer, and within a week, a wonderful lady had the card I had completed and called me. I told her I was broken-hearted and had just broken up with my boyfriend. She comforted me, encouraged me, and prayed for me. She was God's first step into my new walk with him. For someone to take the time to spend so much time with a hurting stranger touched my heart. We talked for an hour, and I immediately felt comfortable and safe with her.

Mr. L was still living with me then, so I would invite him to church when he was home, but he wasn't really into it and would never come with me, so I continued to go alone. Anger management and church were keeping me calm, but things continued to be rocky with Mr. L. While he was away, we got into a fight over the phone about money. He again gave me the silent treatment and would not respond to texts, emails, or phone calls. He completely shut me out and left me high and dry financially, leaving me to figure out how I would pay the bills he had promised to help pay. One day while I was at work, he came home, grabbed all his things, and texted me that he was leaving. He was done with me.

At that moment, I felt a peace in my spirit and a calmness that I can't quite describe. It felt like a release of a burden I had been carrying for so long. Nothing in me wanted to convince him to stay or come back. I just didn't want the responsibility anymore of having to take care of him. He was okay with leaving me to pick up all the pieces, and I knew then that this was not my future. That peace I felt was God telling me I was okay and that he would take care of me.

I continued to go to church, created a community, joined the choir, and started serving within the church. I attended women's conferences, Bible studies, and special events. I went from isolating myself to cultivating new relationships with friends both in and out of the church. God was strengthening me and giving me a reason to keep going. I would still have rough days, but I wouldn't wallow in them like before. God was doing these subtle things in me, and over time I began to thrive in my single season and *live* for the first time in many years.

God started making me more self-aware and taught me self-care. He showed me that although I had gone to anger management, was currently attending church, and was growing, I still had some deep healing to do. In this season, I started to see God begin to do a "good work" in me, just as it says in the Bible.

Being confident of this, that he who began a good work in you will carry it on to completion until the day of Christ Jesus. (Philippians 1:6 NIV)

One day while scrolling social media, I came across an online challenge for singles. The objective was to break cycles in your life. I felt an urge to join. I didn't know then that God was about to take me to a new level in my relationship with him. During the challenge, we would pray in the morning and listen to a speaker in the evening. One of the speakers that week spoke on breaking emotional and sexual soul ties. My ears perked up because, for the first time, I felt like I had an explanation for my past struggles. I had never heard that term before. Soul ties? Was this why I couldn't let go? Was this what was keeping me stuck? After the challenge, the group invited me to join an online singles ministry with coursework on becoming "the one." It was a how-to on preparing for a godly marriage. The coursework in this ministry began to completely transform my life. It gave me a whole new perspective on why I was the way I was, why I did the things that I did, and why I reacted to some things the way I reacted all those years.

It felt like God had given me the key to unlock everything I needed for my healing. I had an explanation for the "why," which made it easier to move through everything and get to the place of overcoming.

In my fascinating research mission on breaking soul ties, I came across a YouTube video from a respected pastor. In the video, he talked about the Jezebel spirit. See, Jezebel was a woman in the Old Testament in 1 and 2 Kings. And just as we name a drug after its founder, we also name characteristics after those who loudly portray them. Hence, Jezebel is known in Scripture by her ugly character of dominating and controlling others to the highest degree. It is not gender-specific; it can be a man or woman who displays such a character. I knew I saw this spirit in Mr. L and myself. At the end of the video, there was a prayer to break soul ties and the Jezebel spirit. I prayed and called out to God fervently in all my faith to sever all ungodly soul ties between my exes and me and to break any stronghold of the Jezebel spirit attached to me and my home. I immediately noticed a shift in myself and the atmosphere. Imagine: one prayer caused a significant change in my relationship with the men in my past, for the better.

As I was going through my coursework, God revealed that I felt a deep sense of rejection and desperately needed love like Leah in the Bible. Leah wanted children to get her husband Jacob's love and attention, but it did not work. Even God noticed that she was unloved.

When the LORD saw that Leah was not loved, he enabled her to conceive, but Rachel remained childless. Leah became pregnant and gave birth to a son. She named him Reuben for she said, "It is because the LORD has seen my misery. Surely my husband will love me now." (Genesis 29:31–32 NIV)

And just like Leah, I was a woman on a mission to prove I was worthy of love, that I would do whatever it took to get special, individual attention and to know I was valued and appreciated. But that is not the way God designed love. I guess the old song "I Can't Get No Satisfaction" was the perfect song for me—a song of incompleteness and rejection. I knew that to break the toxic soul ties, cycles, and patterns I had dealt with for so long, I would have to untangle all the lies, labels, and mixed messages placed upon and within me. I took a trip down memory lane and thought about every lie I had told myself and the lies, labels, and manipulations of man and satan strategically placed on my life. It was disgusting. The enemy is evil and knows how to twist us like a pretzel. He had me believing that I had to fight to be seen, heard, and loved, and had to create chaos to get attention. That as a woman, I had to be married and have children to be happy and feel accomplished. That is his nature, and I wholeheartedly believed the lie that I had to earn the love of man and God. I was trying to fix something in nature that could only be fixed spiritually. The lies of the enemy had misled me. I wasn't walking in the fruit of the Spirit—love, joy, peace, patience, kindness, goodness, faithfulness, gentleness, and self-control. I was walking in anger, disappointment, anxiousness, overwhelm, resentment, sin, fear, aggression, and self-destruction. It is the contrast between two passages in the Galatians. The first, Galatians 5:19–21 (NIV), clearly states:

> _Now the works of the flesh are evident_, which are: adultery, fornication, uncleanness, lewdness, idolatry, sorcery, hatred, contentions, jealousies, outbursts of wrath, selfish ambitions, dissensions, heresies, envy, murders, drunkenness, revelries, and the like; of which I tell you beforehand, just

*as I also told you in time past, that those who practice such
things will not inherit the kingdom of God.*

And the second, Galatians 5:22–25 (NIV), shows the contrast:

*But the fruit of the Spirit is love, joy, peace, longsuffering,
kindness, goodness, faithfulness, gentleness, self-control.
Against such, there is no law. And those who are Christ's
have crucified the flesh with its passions and desires. If we
live in the Spirit, let us also walk in the Spirit.*

But then, just like Leah, I suddenly had a revelation. After giving
birth to four children, and during her pregnancy with her fifth child,
she realized she still had not received the love of her husband, Jacob.

Genesis 29:34–35 (NIV) describes how she conceived again,
and when she gave birth to a son, she said, "This time I will praise
the Lord." So she named her son Judah. Then she stopped having
children.

God gave her a revelation of who she was to Him, which birthed
a new attitude, a new way of seeing herself and her God, and she
became a worshiper. She no longer needed a crutch to be loved or
children to give her self-worth. She began to praise the Lord! God was
doing for me just as he did for Leah.

I had to replace the lies, labels, and mixed messages with the
truth! What did the word of God say about me? I had to turn my focus
to Him and recognize that through all my brokenness and self-pity,
He loved me and saw me, and that was all that should matter. I hadn't
been my true and authentic self, the person God created me to be,
which led me to develop ungodly soul ties.

One night as I was leaving the church, it was as though I heard God speak to me audibly. For the first time, my inner ear was in tune, and I could hear Him clearly. He said, "I need you to do what I told you to do, and I need you to do it now." He said, "I want to do something in you, and I want to do it quickly." My spirit said "Yes, God," without question or hesitation. Something about that moment stopped me in my tracks, and I was in awe. There was something breathtaking about hearing my heavenly Father's voice, and I felt an excitement within me about my future that I had never felt before. It was as if God was telling me, "Girl, get ready. All those things you have thirsted for, every struggle, every tear, every heartbreak, that's over!" It felt like I was getting a new life. God needed my obedience, and he needed it right away. That thing he told me to do was to release my exes. Yes, I had prayed the prayers and asked God to sever the soul ties, but really, I wanted God to cut the tie for me, change my feelings, and let me keep the relationship. I tried to manipulate God, and I didn't even realize it, but He knew, and He wasn't having it, so He did what he needed to do to get my attention. When God said He wanted to do something and do it quickly, my first thought was: Yes; finally, God is about to introduce me to my future husband. He will make me a wife, He will deliver on His promises to me, and it's going to happen fast! I mean, what else could it be? This is all I have ever wanted, and now God will reward me for my obedience. I had better get ready.

There was a shift in my relationship with God at that moment. I felt like, for the first time, He was standing right next to me. Although he had always been there, it was as if now I could feel his presence tangibly. I could now feel and believe that He was walking this life out with me together, hand and hand. There was calmness and peace that God had everything under control. He was orchestrating His will for my life.

That husband I was planning on—well, I am still waiting on him. But isn't that just like God? Just when you think you have it all figured out, he surprises you. He had another plan: Kingdom business. He started to bring forth opportunities, and he amazed me every time.

Through anger management, counseling, spiritual insight, and the coursework, there were endless revelations. I came to see that I was comfortable with chaos and inconsistency. If there were no chaos, I would create it. I thrived on drama. I would love as hard as I could and then sabotage it all. Watch it all explode and then fight to make things right again. It all played out in my first relationship with Mr. D. No matter how hard I tried, I was never good enough. It created a striving spirit within me. I started to believe everything was my fault. If he kept me around but I was not good enough, surely I was doing something wrong. I felt needed but inadequate, so I became Ms. Fixer Upper. It was up to me to fix it. And once everything was fixed, I would find a way to break it again because I needed to be needed. As Jonathan McReynolds would sing, "That's how he keeps you in cycles."

The cycles and craziness had me primed and ready for Mr. L. Remember, I was Ms. Fixer Upper, and I needed to connect to people who needed "fixing." Even though he was highly critical of me and fed my rejection, he needed me, and I was ready to be there for him no matter what. Although I didn't know it at the time, this was codependency and narcissistic abuse at its finest.

Both romantic partnerships taught me to keep my expectations low and not to want anything so I wouldn't be disappointed. The cycles that developed from these soul ties and the spirits attached to them created bondage that wore me down and made me angry, sometimes for no reason. I was tired, and eventually, I became resentful, detached, depressed, and suicidal. I didn't know how to make decisions without total confusion; everything felt awkward. I didn't know how to speak up about what I needed or wanted. If I asked for something I needed and got it, the feeling would be so unfamiliar to me that I wouldn't know how to handle it. That strange, unusual feeling reinforced my belief that I was unworthy of anything good happening to or for me. Like the women I watched in my television stories every day, I wanted to be loved, admired, and chosen—the heroine. I wanted someone to fight for me, but I was doing all the fighting. It created a spirit of control, a messiah complex. I needed to take care of everything, because if I didn't do it, then who would? If I didn't do it, it wouldn't get done correctly. I always had something to prove.

But God! God changed my song from "can't get no satisfaction" to "He bought the sunshine in my life." God was transforming my life. He took His time with me and still does. All those years, I was going to church, serving, and worshipping. During the years I had seen as monotonous, where nothing seemed to change, God was doing His thing, ordering my steps, and changing me from the inside out. The storm on the inside had calmed. I could see in yonder skies; the sun was breaking through the clouds.

I began to pursue God like never before. I was dealing with my past in a new way and started the process of deliverance. I had dealt with rejection. I learned to forgive those who had hurt me throughout my life. I discovered that the idolatry of marriage and motherhood in my life was getting in the way of all God wanted to do in me. He had a greater purpose. I repented, asked God to forgive me, and then had to forgive myself. Forgiving myself took time; it was hard. I had to let go of the guilt and shame and stop punishing myself for my destructive behavior. I began to discover that greater purpose after laying down my idols. (That was Jezebel's problem; she worshipped idol gods.) For most of my life, I had felt directionless, but He started to show me all that He had in store for me to do.

I never thought I would safely land in a place where I could be healthy and whole, and I would be okay in my singleness and without children. But I am here in this place now, the perfect landing strip. I still get triggered, I still have moments of wonder, and I still get anxious for the desires of my heart that have not yet manifested. But God is *still* writing my story, and He has turned pain into purpose. He has redeemed my time and the things that I thought I would never get a chance to have. He has given to me according to His will and timing. He has shown me who I am—that my identity is in Him. I feel innately loved by Him, and that brings me so much peace. I would not change a thing because it got me to where I am today, blessed beyond measure, loved, contented, and fulfilled in Him and Him alone. God took his time with me, and here I am, getting to tell my story about how God gave me a new life. His will is always what is best for us, even if we do not understand it.

The Bible says that we ought not to worry:

> *"Therefore I tell you, do not worry about your life, what you will eat or drink; or about your body, what you will wear. Is not life more than food, and the body more than clothes? Look at the birds of the air; they do not sow or reap or store away in barns, and yet your heavenly Father feeds them. Are you not much more valuable than they? Can any one of you by worrying add a single hour to your life?*

> *"And why do you worry about clothes? See how the flowers of the field grow. They do not labor or spin. Yet I tell you that not even Solomon in all his splendor was dressed like one of these. If that is how God clothes the grass of the field, which is here today and tomorrow is thrown into the fire,*

will he not much more clothe you—you of little faith? <u>So do</u>
<u>not worry</u>, saying, 'What shall we eat?' or 'What shall we
drink?' or 'What shall we wear?' For the pagans run after
all these things, and your heavenly Father knows that you
need them. <u>But seek first his kingdom and his righteousness,</u>
<u>and all these things will be given to you as well.</u> Therefore do
not worry about tomorrow, for tomorrow will worry about
itself. Each day has enough trouble of its own." (Matthew
6:25–34 NIV)

Maybe we should all join in and sing that familiar song: "Don't
Worry; Be Happy!"

Pursued

by Tish Rivera

Dear Reader,

As we begin this journey, I must assure you that it was not my strength or power that has brought me to this place of peace and contentment, but the grace and unrelenting pursuing love of Jesus. The backdrop to my story is a woman in the Bible who may have been overlooked, and if she had it her way, being overlooked was a blessing in disguise. You may or may not have heard about her story—the Samaritan woman coming to a well to get water. That sounds so simple, but it is not. This story is in the Gospel of John, chapter four.

So He came to a city of Samaria which is called Sychar,
near the plot of ground that Jacob gave to his son Joseph.

Now Jacob's well was there. Jesus therefore, being wearied from His journey, sat thus by the well. It was about the sixth hour. A woman of Samaria came to draw water. Jesus said to her, "Give Me a drink." For His disciples had gone away into the city to buy food. Then the woman of Samaria said to Him, "How is it that You, being a Jew, ask a drink from me, a Samaritan woman?" For Jews have no dealings with Samaritans. (John 4:5–9 NKJV)

Jesus meets a woman who comes to the well alone. It was a tradition for women to be the fetchers of water. It was not tradition for a man to speak to a woman in public who was not his wife. And stranger still, the Jewish law forbade Jews from talking to Samaritans. But Jesus, the Jew, seemed to have a way of breaking barriers. He asks her for a drink of water because He is tired and thirsty, and there is a well, and she has an instrument to draw the water. But they are not supposed to be talking to each other. The untraditional conversation continues until He finally touches on her brokenness when He asks her, "Where is your husband?" She tells Him a partial truth: that she does not have a husband. He then tells her the rest of her story, saving her the embarrassment. He tells her how she has been married five times, and the man she is with—shacking up with or cohabiting, you might say—is not her husband. We gasp even when we hear a woman in Hollywood being married that many times. But Jesus doesn't gasp; He attends to her need. She is thirsty for a new life, one of hope and happiness. And when their conversation ends, she has received her answer. Jesus has introduced Himself to her for who He was and is, the Messiah, whom they had been expecting. She leaves, running to tell others, "Come see a man who told me everything, could He be the Messiah?" The message He gave her was powerful: *the world—men, in particular—would never quench her thirst.* As you read the details of my story closely, I pray that it will speak to you of the amazing love and redemptive nature of God that He revealed to me, a broken soul!

My dad had custody of me and my sister, and his mother also lived with us. She played a big part in raising us girls. We would visit our mother occasionally. On one of our visits, she decided not to return us. My mother had kidnapped us, and she took us from one drug house to another. I believe I was four or five years old. My sister reminded me how she would hide us in closets because the drug houses were scary.

My grandmother hired a private investigator, and we eventually were found and returned home in deplorable condition. My grandmother kept the photographs as evidence because she was afraid that she would be held legally responsible for our condition. During this time, my grandmother became my mother, and I had little memory of my mother. I remember, as a child, being alone. My dad was always worried about my sister, and I was seemly left to raise myself. I frequently asked about my mother, but no one spoke about her, no one acknowledged her existence, and I began to feel rejected and abandoned. "Why did my mother leave me?"

This question grew into a monster within my mind and soul. We were poor, but we made it. My dad and grandma worked every day, and my sister took care of me. I became incredibly close with my great-grandfather because he spent time with me. I felt loved by my great-grandpa. Indeed, I did. He and my great-grandmother's home was not far from us.

My dad met a woman and looked happy. A part of me was elated that I would have the mother my little heart desired. This fantasy soon came crashing down. Shortly after they were married, her mask came off. She had a son, and he could do nothing wrong, and we girls could do nothing right. We went to church and played the role of the churchgoing family. At home, we were being beaten and abused. One night I could not finish my dinner or maybe didn't want it, and she made me sit there. I told her several times that I had to use the bathroom, but she wouldn't allow me to use it until I finished. My bladder could no longer hold the pressure, and the chair got soaked. She gave me a horrific beating and forced me to clean up my mess. This woman had such anger issues that she would throw glass coffee pots or whatever she could find at my dad. She also had a way of stirring up my dad's anger against us girls. I remember one beating from my dad because she complained about us once again. He beat me severely with a wooden paddle that was at least an inch thick. As I attempted to protect myself, he hit my knuckles, ripping off the skin. When I returned to school the next day, the teachers looked petrified when they saw the bruising, but to me, it was just another day, just another beating.

She would cut our hair very short, intentionally making us look like little boys because she never wanted girls. During this tumultuous time in my life, my dad told me that my mother had found us and that we would meet her at a courthouse in Los Angeles County. I was in elementary school, and we were living in Fresno County at the time. I remember thinking, "Wow! My mom found me, she did want me," and yet, at the same time, I had this monster question in my mind: "Why did she leave me?" The answer to my many questions came very slowly; it would take many years for me to find out the painful truth. As a family, my dad started spearheading for us to become more involved in the church; we would attend what seemed to be every night of the week, and when we weren't in church, we would have Bible studies at home. During these studies, I experienced my first taste of Jesus's power, and the Holy Spirit was introduced to our family.

The time came for us to travel to meet my mother; this journey would change my life. We piled in our station wagon and headed to Los Angeles. Being a bunch of nerves, I did not know who I could share my feelings with, my sister or my dad. I decided to keep everything inside. Finally, we arrived, and we sat in the courthouse, waiting. I was moving from bench to bench in anticipation of this woman's entrance. Then, there she was, the woman who had walked out on us years ago. As soon as I had a chance, I asked her, "Why did you abandon me?" She never answered the question; she would always look away or change the subject. She and my dad agreed she could take us to lunch in the courthouse. Our lunchtime visit was interrupted by our stepfather's presence. My mom appeared to look to him for answers every time I would ask her a question. It would have been nicer if we could have had our mother alone after her long absence from our lives. But it was clear that either she needed him there or he demanded to be there.

We soon left Los Angeles, heading home to Fresno, but our journey would quickly encounter an unexpected turn of events. My dad fell asleep at the wheel and crashed the car under a tracker trailer on the Grapevine, a stretch of highway near Los Angeles. Unfortunately, in the 1990s, and there were no call boxes along the freeway. Thankfully, the truck driver found help with the wreckage and contacted emergency medical services. When the wreckage help arrived, they removed our car from underneath the tractor trailer. My sister later told me that they saw me shivering due to the shock of the accident and asked our stepmother if there were any blankets in the car; she said: "Yes, in the trunk." They, in turn, said, "There is no trunk; just hang on; help is on the way." Eventually, medical help arrived and took us to the hospital. I was frightened. As I was lying on the hospital bed, I heard the doctor say he was astonished we were alive. He kept saying over and over how we should have died in the accident. Moments before this accident, I remember my sister and I falling asleep, and maybe this was a factor that saved our lives. The hospital discharged three of us after a few days, but it would be weeks before my dad would be home. When he returned home, things began to change drastically. My dad and stepmom constantly argued, never letting up.

During this time, my great-grandfather passed away, and I was alone again. I began to fear for my great-grandmother because I was afraid she would say she had no reason to live. She did pass shortly after him. I later found out that she had committed suicide. She was a furious woman, and all us kids knew to stay away from her. No one knew why she disliked us. But we all knew she was outraged. I remember seeing her push my grandmother.

During the funerals and the family's breakdown, my stepmother left my dad, and we moved in with my grandmother, who had inherited her mom's home. We were poor people, and I had to wear clothes purchased from thrift stores or given to me. They called this type of clothing "hand me downs." Kids would tease me because of the clothes I wore and because I didn't have a mother. I remember the anger growing inside, and I started to rebel, but somehow, I could never be cruel or mean. The home beatings continued. I remember my dad would grab a belt and start swinging, leaving bruises all over my body, and he would tell me that I had brought it upon myself. A cycle of abuse started with my dad, so I began to look to my grandmother for acceptance and comfort; I was desperate. She did her best, but she had issues I never fully came to understand. But I am grateful for my grandmother. As a little girl in elementary school, I remember the hurts I suffered at home and the academic struggle at school, along with unrelenting bullying. There was no rest for the weary.

I could not find acceptance, love, or comfort with people, so I began to play board games. The first board game I played was the Ouija board. I thought I would put a little magic in my life. However, shortly after this, I began to see a full-body apparition or manifestation of a demon resembling my great-grandfather. I would have night terrors constant so intense that I could not sleep alone, and although my dad's cycle of abuse scared me, I was more afraid of the night terror. I would beg to sleep with my dad. I began to withdraw even more and lashed out in anger for no apparent reason. It was the beginning of my battle with good and evil—all while I was in elementary school. I remember going to church camp, and now, over twenty years later, I remember having an incredible and unbelievable experience. I believe I saw a vision, and I ascended to heaven during a church camp revival. I remember heaven being like a gorgeous garden and feeling entirely peaceful. Upon my return to consciousness, I began to speak in tongues and lay hands on people. We were of the Pentecostal faith and believed sincerely in the manifestation of the Holy Spirit.

When I prayed for a person's healing, I believed it would happen. I remember one such person was healed from an ailment that doctors said she would suffer for the rest of her life. But God healed her! Even as I grew and entered middle school, I also received miraculous healings. I began to have grand mal seizures, a type of attack that involves a loss of consciousness and violent muscle contractions. The medication prescribed for me at that time wasn't controlling them. I remember feeling like this was ravishing my body. As sick as it sounds, I finally got some attention from my dad due to this illness. He never gave me any good attention; only my oldest sister seemed to earn his attention. Someone prayed for me, and the seizures stopped, never to return. And the affection from my dad also stopped. To this day, there is no evidence of damage done to my brain from the seizures. But I had a bruised heart from the lack of love from my dad.

Shortly after this, I made wrong decisions for my life. I began to rebel against God and my dad. One day as punishment, he wanted me to read the Bible and write a Bible verse. Go figure; my dad used God to punish me. Feeling as though no matter how perfect I was, my dad would always choose my sister, instead of writing the verse, I decided to run away. The police found me and escorted me home, and upon speaking with my dad, they gave him two options: either they were taking me to foster care, or I could live with my mother. My dad called my mother, and I heard him say, "I am done with her, come and get her because I can no longer control her!"

The next morning I packed my bags and went to live with my mother. I realized rather quickly that I had made a horrible mistake. I had a stepsister, and she did not like the idea of me moving in. She felt there was only room enough for her, and the drama began. She hid a birthday card for her father and said I stole it. No matter how many times I denied it to my mom, she insisted I had taken the card. When I confessed to the lie that I had taken the card, my stepsister found the card magically in the closet.

I desperately wanted to be accepted, but I realized that was not going to happen with my mother or my stepsister. The beatings escalated. I remember my mother grabbing me by my hair and dragging me through the house. Although I was so miserable and wanted to leave, there was nothing I could do but bear the pain. My mother would try to convince me that my dad was a horrible man and that the court had not given him custody, but that he had kidnapped us. When my dad, sister, and grandmother would call to speak with me, my mother would eavesdrop. There was no privacy, and the abuse and caged-in treatment intensified.

My mom allowed me to visit my dad for the summer and said she would have a private investigator follow me. If I behaved, she said, I would be allowed back home. I knew my dad would not want to keep me, so I had to make sure I could return to have a place to live. Sad, but true! There was part of me that did not believe her. I agreed to conduct myself properly. I was so happy to be back with my family and felt free, but that was short-lived. My dad and grandmother had to work, and I would wander away, checking out the neighborhood. There was a man in the apartment complex near my dad's house who was much older than me, and I began to visit with him. My freedom to run around without supervision was the nail in my coffin.

It appeared my mom was telling the truth about hiring a private investigator. She said the private investigator told her I had not been listening to my dad and was hanging out late at night seeing this older person. She had no intention of not allowing me back home; she hired the private investigator to find proof that my dad could not and should not have physical custody of me. When I returned home, I knew that my bad behavior had given my mother just what she wanted: grounds to file for full custody. When I was only eleven, the court asked me to choose where I wanted to live. I was desperate to have my mother in my life after all those years of being without her. I chose her along with all the abuse, just to be with her. I told myself it would get better; I told myself a lie. When I told the judge I wanted to remain with my mom, I felt I had betrayed my dad and broken my grandmother's heart. I visited them as often as I was allowed, but my mother began to control the visits. If I did something wrong, she would revoke my visits. I longed for those visits.

My mom now had physical and legal custody of me, and my dad had visitation only. My mother would usually drop me off to visit with my dad. We had a near-death experience on the way to visit my dad.

My mother had a small, two-door sports car. Somehow a speeding truck managed to hit our car in the rear. Thankfully, we did not get pushed into oncoming traffic. I received the full impact, which shifted my spine and left me with debilitating back issues. I received minimal medical care, which did not address my need. My doctor has discussed the possibility of surgery within the next few years if my hands and feet continue to become numb.

Knowing she had total control, a sinister dark side of my mother reared its ugly head. We would go to church on Sundays, but horrendous beatings awaited me for the rest of the week. I remember that when I started high school, she heard I was talking to someone she disapproved of and beat me badly. I had so many bruises on my legs and the rest of my body that she kept me home from school to prevent someone from seeing the marks. My bruises had bruises!

My mother was always kind to other people and other children; I wished I had this mother at home. We maintained the façade of the churchgoing suburban family that had everything together. When we got home, my torment would continue. My mother would tell me how horrible I was and how I disappointed her. I struggled in math, and she perceived that as me seeking attention when, in reality, I needed help. Because of physical and emotional abuse, it became tough to concentrate. While going to church, I tried having faith in God that He would see me through, but years later, the abuse continued, from church to home. But I had to have hope in something or curl up and die.

I was approaching my thirteenth birthday, and I had a terrible dream of my stepdad and me in the car, and he asked me, "Do you find me attractive?" To this day, I believe the Holy Spirit was trying to warn me of what was coming. When I thought my life couldn't get any worse, it did. The dream came true, and my stepdad asked me that same question a few weeks later. I answered, "No, I see you as my dad." Unfortunately, that answer would not stop him. Shortly after this conversation, he began molesting me. He came into my room one day while my mom was at work, and he lay down behind me and placed his hands in my pants; paralyzed with fear, I just stared at him. He then pulled me to the edge of the bed, and he raped me. Thus began the game of cat and mouse. He would petition my mom to pick me up from school so that he could rape me. If I said no to him, he would go to my mom and tell her I was rude and disrespectful, and she would beat me. We went to church every Sunday, faking as if we were a godly family.

I was not allowed to date in high school or hang out with the few friends I thought I had. If I told them anything, they would go back and tell my mom what I said, or they would lie. She must have made some type of arrangement with them or their parents. My mother would believe them and punish me, which could include beatings or canceling birthdays. I could trust no one. I tried journaling, but she would grab my journal from me and read it. I would be in trouble for having my thoughts. I plugged away in school, with math always being my struggle, but I excelled in English and history. Kids picked on me because I was not like them; I never did what typical high school kids do and hang out. My mother and stepfather would come to school and watch me with my friends. Sometimes they would be in places where I could not see them, and sometimes they would suddenly walk up and startled me.

My mother later told me I had a liver condition that I had inherited from her. I didn't believe it was true because it could mean my life might be cut short. I thought it was another one of her tricks to torment me. But it was true, and I had biopsies done of my liver. They were so painful that I felt like I was dying. My mother was so cruel; after these biopsies, she would still expect me to clean the house and do everything as if nothing had happened. With the abuse coming from all fronts, I developed an eating disorder. If I could not control my environment, I could control what I put in my body. When my mother found out, she began to say, "What do you want me to do, put you in the hospital with a tube down your throat? That's what you want, don't you?"

I slowly began eating again, feeling defeated. Although we went to church, I found no reprieve there. Our church adhered to a strict dress code. You must wear nylons; you must wear a slip; your skirt length must pass your knees, and most of all, as a girl, you must never make eye contact with boys or men. Internally I began to spiral out of control. I wanted God to save me somehow, someway, but it never happened. I reached a point of desperation in high school where I could no longer take the abuse and started cutting my wrists. My mother found out and said, "If you want to kill yourself, I can show you how."

My mother didn't want me; I was a pawn for her against my dad and a sexual fantasy toy for her husband. During high school, I hit puberty, and many changes took place in my body. My body, not my mind and soul, began to react differently to the sexual abuse. I experienced my first orgasm with my stepfather, and I was so angry at myself because I felt as though I was telling him I enjoyed it. He then began to pay me to do extra favors for him. He would pay me to allow him to have an orgasm in my mouth, and the payment was not at my request but to add weight to my silence. He also began grooming me, so I was never confident in myself. He would say that my body's imperfections would turn off some guys, causing me to hate my body. Because of his abuse, I didn't love my body. He would tell me that my sex drive was like my mother's. He knew that if I ever told my mother, she would not believe me, so when I told him I would tell, he would laugh in my face. He had her well trained.

High school was a challenging time. I grew up in the suburb of Los Angeles, and race played a huge part in everything. Many people did not accept me because most of them thought I was stuck up, but the truth was, I knew my mother would never allow me to have friends or hang out. It was fear that they saw in me, but they wrongly defined it as a big ego. The students accused me of trying to be African American because my stepdad was Black. They said I belonged with the white people because I was too pale to be Mexican. Boys wanted to talk to me because they thought I was attractive, and girls hated me because they thought I wanted their "man." A girl punched me in the eye during physical education and said I was talking to her boyfriend. Yes, somehow it got to my mother, who said she would have punched me too if I had talked to her boyfriend. With that statement, can you imagine what she would have done to me if she discovered the triangle going on in her house, under her nose? Like the students, she would have wrongly defined me as the aggressive one attempting to take her man. What sickness!

My mother always blamed me and took her wrath out on me. Strangely, one minute she told me that I was better than she was, and the next, I was the worst person she had ever known. One night, as I was sitting at the table, my mother said my stepdad had told her about a conversation we'd had. I immediately knew I was in trouble, and I knew why. The night before, he had told me to keep the bathroom door unlocked so he could rape me while I was taking what would be a perceived shower. We had a game room attached to the laundry room. Separating the laundry room and bathroom was a door that could be locked. I locked that door in an act of defiance and thought he would believe me when I told him I did not intend to lock the door. Being naïve, I thought he bought the story until the next day at the dinner table. I just looked down at my dinner plate, hoping that if I didn't engage her, she would stop, but she kicked my shins and knocked me out of my chair. He then tried to step in, pretending to calm her down. I remember him smirking, and then he told her that she needed to calm down and let me eat. After a full-blown episode of yelling and cursing, she finally did. I quickly went into my room and cried.

As I said before, my mother would find any reason to cancel my birthday party. She canceled one party I was especially looking forward to, for my sixteen birthday. She claimed she canceled my party because I had done something that I hadn't done. I never had a birthday party, and it was made clear that I was not worthy of celebrating. She went from one extreme to another, and so did I. I began having a secret relationship with a female. She showed me acceptance, and I felt truly loved. That relationship didn't last long. I told one of my friends whom I thought I could trust; you would think I would have learned by now. She told my mom, which led to one of the worst beatings I had ever endured. I felt so betrayed, but I soon realized I could not trust anyone and that I was alone. This same so-called friend began to bully me and attempted to have her group of friends attack me. Strangely, my enemies were my mother's friends.

However, during this same traumatic time frame, my stepdad took me to a park and told me that he was marrying my mother. I was shocked; I'd thought they were married already. Instinctively, I began crying, thanking God that this would be my breakthrough—that the abuse was going to stop, and I would be free. Why I thought this would happen, I do not know. Unfortunately, that did not happen. He misconstrued my tears as sadness that the relationship was ending and said, "You always told me to go back to my wife." The plot against me thickens.

Wedding bells were in the air, and my mother was so excited about marrying that pedophile, her daughter's rapist. During the planning of my mother's wedding, she refused to buy me a dress, and she canceled my hair appointment; it was as if she was jealous of me. She would keep me away from her siblings, so I never bonded with any of my aunts or uncles. Now I realize they weren't married; he enjoyed being my sexual molester and my mom's boyfriend.

At age seventeen, almost the end of high school, I could see myself graduating very shortly. Then, maybe I could sing the song Martin Luther King Jr. spoke of, "Free at Last!" Things were beginning to look up for me. A veterinarian chose me to take part in an internship, and I started a regional occupation program. My goal was to become a veterinarian. Soon, the veterinarian asked me to become a full-time employee. Instead of my mother being happy, it caused more issues with us. She would be beyond angry if I had to work later than scheduled because she provided me transportation. Working in the veterinarian field required me to work late if there was an emergency. My stepdad was not pleased either because he did not have as much access to me as he wanted. A perfect storm was forming in my life.

The church organized a retreat, and I was looking forward to attending. I befriended many of the girls, and we became close. I would preach sermons in the Sunday school class, sing in the choir, and perform solos upon request. I was excited to spend time away from my prison. My foundation in Jesus was deepening, even though chaos was surrounding me. I felt like I had climbed Mount Everest; soon, I would be away in college. During this trip, I had a spiritual revelation that I was willing to go wherever God would call me, and I would be His hands and feet. But my mountaintop experience came crashing down!

When we returned from the church camp, I started making my lunch for school on the following day, and my mother began to approach me. In my gut, I knew something was wrong. She began to yell at me for talking to a boy at the retreat and allowing some man to play with my hair. Eyes everywhere! She showed me the videotape. But the truth was, we were put in the same course together, and I merely said hello to the boy and did not speak further. She said she saw us walking together. There was only one path from the cabin, and the boys and girls were on the same route.

As far as some man playing with my hair, I never felt it, but then my hair length was to my waist. She punched me in my jaw like a heavyweight boxer, and I lost it, throwing the sandwich bags and box at her. She then grabbed me by my throat, slammed me on the kitchen floor, sat on top of me, and began punching me like a punching bag. I believed she was going to choke me to death. I couldn't feel my right arm, and I remember begging her to take me to the hospital she refused. Later that night, somehow, I popped my shoulder into place. She asked me did I wanted to stay or go. I said, "GO!" She gave me trash bags, which became symbolic to me that she never valued me; I was her mistake, and now she was throwing out the trash.

I moved back to Fresno with my dad, full of rage and hurt. My sister struggled with me in the house because she enjoyed having the house to herself. It did not take much for me to go into a full rage. I remember her boyfriend was trying to stop us from fighting, and I pushed him so hard it scared him. I was ready to bring wrath upon everyone. I had a soul broken in thousands of pieces. I began my last year of high school with kids of affluence. They drove Hummers and Mercedes. They were also fierce. I gave up hope in myself, my dreams, and what I could accomplish. I tried to keep going to church, but I was done with God, and I believed God was done with me.

I began to have sex with any man I could get my hands on, and they did not have to be attractive; they just needed to act as though they found me attractive and desired me. I began spiraling out of control, drinking to numb the pain. Nothing could stop me. I would disappear for days, get drunk, and have sex. My sister reported me missing after I was late returning home by a few hours. When I came home, the police were there and knew I had been drinking. They attempted to give me words of encouragement, but I didn't care; I was going to use my body on my terms now. Being eighteen and in my senior year had opened particular doors for me that most twelfth graders did not have. I was legally an adult, so I had no technical curfew, which I exploited to the fullest. There were a few boyfriends who were special to me, but they had their own demons. One I liked, but he was an alcoholic, and when I told him I had a liver condition, it scared him. We broke up shortly after because he could not control his drinking, but I believe the liver condition was also a factor.

I finally dared to speak to my dad about the sexual abuse of my stepdad, and when I did, my dad just looked at me with a blank stare—it was like, "OK!" He showed no reaction, absolutely nothing. I later told my mother. Everything my stepdad told me she would do, she did. That is why he had so much control; he had trained her well. And she did not want to lose her husband. First, she said that nothing happened. Then she said that if anything had happened, I wanted it to happen, that I had seduced him, and that if I tried to bring him to court, she would make me look like the biggest slut and would destroy me. Shortly after this incident, my sister began to be rude to me while our mom was on the phone. How dare she dismiss my pain? Rage rose in me, and I went to punch her in the face, but my dad, just released from the hospital, stepped in between us. Before I realized it, he was on the floor, and my sister had called the police. Needless to say, he kicked me out of the house. I later realized that if my dad had not kicked me out of the house at that time, I would have been a felon at eighteen, charged with felonious assault on an incapacitated adult. Shame on me!

I remembered a man I had met and slept with a few times. He was forty, and I was eighteen. I seduced my way into his home. He was an alcoholic and abusive, but it was an emergency requiring emergency means. We would party and drink ourselves into a stupor. I was his trophy, and he loved showing me off to his friends. But there was still a dream in me, so I kept pulling myself up and fighting to finish high school. On a cold, pouring-down rainy day, I strolled into school in a light jacket when a teacher asked if my parents had allowed me to leave the house without a coat. I responded, "What parents?" and walked away. There was nothing they could do. I was legally an adult, and even though it broke my dad's heart, I was on my own. Students saw my boyfriend, the forty-year-old, drop me off at school, and they started a rumor that he was my pimp and I was a prostitute. The torment intensified. I had one good friend, and we are friends today. I shared my true story with many of my teachers, and they began helping me pass their classes. I graduated high school on my own with no support from my family. My teachers ignited hope within me, but life's experiences soon extinguished the flame.

I want to pause and reiterate that God pursued me when I was at my lowest. He always made a way for me even though I was on a self-destructive path. I leaned on my faith, as shattered and fragmented as it may have been. I was not attending anyone's church. I couldn't bring myself to do so because, until this point, the church had only told me what was wrong with me instead of offering to walk with me.

The heart knows its own bitterness, And a stranger does not share its joy. There is a way that seems right to a man, But its end is the way of death. (Proverbs 14:10, 12 NKJV)

I cheated on my boyfriend multiple times because one man was not enough for me to find self-worth. We stayed together, but he would punch walls close by my face and tell me he would never hit a female, but he would hit a b---h, and I was that b---h. While I was taking a nice hot relaxing shower, he discovered our pet lizard had died. He blamed me and entered the shower screaming at the top of his lungs. I thought the shower stall would become my tomb. When I tried to get out of the shower, he grabbed me by the throat, and I managed to push him into the mirror. I quickly dressed and escaped from the house. My life was spared again—God pursued me!

I drove around town, visited different shops, and had dinner, lost in my thoughts and trapped by my fears. It was late, and I finally arrived home. I parked in the garage but remained in the car. As I sat in the car, I contemplated committing suicide. It wasn't the first time I had thought about it. Strangely, unexpectedly, someone from my old church called to see if I was okay. I can tell you now: God was pursuing me before I considered pursuing Him. My boyfriend and I stayed together for a few months after that near-death shower experience. The abuse never stopped, and it was not until he called the police on me for domestic violence that the relationship had to change. The next day, while he was at work, I broke down crying and begged my aunt to let me move in with her. My aunt had taken my grandmother into her small studio apartment. She said yes, and within an hour, I packed my stuff and left. So, there we were, three women sharing a studio. But eventually, a low-income studio apartment became available for my grandmother. Although they only allowed one occupant, my grandmother was my only support, and they approved me living with her. Thank God I wasn't going to be homeless and wouldn't have to take drastic means to stay alive.

I engaged in online dating and eventually met a guy I assessed as Mr. Perfect. I also entered the modeling arena, believing I fit the profile. I had no respect for my body and did not care if I posed nude or seductively. I enjoyed it when a man sexually desired me but could not have me unless I chose to be his prize. I dated Mr. Perfect, but he soon became obsessive. He drank a lot, and I smoked a lot of cigarettes. He didn't appreciate my habits, and the one that disgusted him most was my modeling nude or seductively, so he demanded I stop. I was infuriated with him for daring to control my life. I lived my life on my terms.

One night at a house party, he had too much to drink and decided he would destroy my pack of cigarettes. I was drunk as well, and we began to argue and fight. I decided to walk away. I had no idea where I was, but I left. As I was walking through the neighborhood, I saw a couple on their balcony and begged to use the phone. I told them I had just left a house party because my boyfriend and I had fought, and I needed to call someone. They said yes. I called the only number I knew, my abusive ex-boyfriend, and insanely volunteered for another round of drama. We spent the night together. I finally went home and got the shock of my life when I saw my new online boyfriend sitting at the table talking to my grandmother. The drama was on. I tried numerous times to break up with him. Every time I would, he would attempt to commit suicide. He loaded a shotgun while I was on the phone with him. I called the police for a wellness check, but he told them that I was exaggerating.

We finally agreed to end the relationship, but he soon began to call and beg me to take him back. One day I was walking home, and as I was about to enter the driveway, he pulled in front of me, blocking me from entering the house and demanding I get into the car. I told him I would not and that he needed to leave. I thought I would have to file a restraining order, but he stopped stalking me after this incident. The partying and sleeping around became a constant as I attempted to numb my pain.

My mother was still in the picture, but I would keep my distance because she was antagonistic. She called me on one occasion to ask me to take a lie detector test, which I agreed to do, anticipating she would tell me where to report to take it, but she never did. Then she called to tell me how stupid I was for not realizing that I could go to any police department for the test. It was her way of tormenting me, and maybe she was a little tormented herself. At this point, I was already struggling because my dad and I were not close. Any little confidence I thought I had slipped away.

I continued the liver treatments into my adulthood. It was wrecking my body the way I've seen chemotherapy do to cancer patients. I was working and attending college, pushing my body beyond its physical and emotional ability. I met a man at school, and it was instant chemistry and sparks. However, he wasn't ready to break it off with his girlfriend. The back and forth was becoming tough for me, and I knew I was going about my life all wrong. We dated for a few months, and suddenly, he texted me a message saying he was breaking up—not with his girlfriend, but with me. He said they had found a new spark in their relationship, and he was happy. At the time, I told him I thought I might be pregnant, and he responded with a proposal to pay half for an abortion. Ouch! That hurt. And to add salt to the wound, he said he wanted to forget I ever existed. But he didn't have to fork out any money because I had a miscarriage instead.

My life was in shambles, and I started digging into the Word of God. I remember taking a drive to a lake and praying to God to take my hurt and despair, and I remember feeling the lifting of the heaviness from my soul. I tried to date a couple more times and vowed that I would do it right and abstain from sex. That didn't always work out as planned. The outcome was the same; the men would soon leave, some without reason and some who had family issues. I resolved to date as little as possible. My problem was that I never saw my value, and I never allowed Jesus to answer my search for love.

I continued living with my grandmother; she was amazing, my anchor for support. I was grateful to be given a place to live, but there was an evil presence in this home that would attack me. I didn't understand what was going on, but I knew my aunt was a Wiccan. Wicca is a pagan practice of witchcraft. And my grandmother and I had lived with her. The things in my grandmother's home were strange, and the demonic realm became much more apparent to me. One incident I remember is looking up and seeing a shadow come out of the bathroom. Lights would turn on and off independently. My grandmother was a doll collector, and she kept her dolls stored on top of the refrigerator. One day we left the house to run errands, and upon returning home, we found the dolls in a perfect circle on the floor. She claimed the cats knocked them off, but the cats didn't place the dolls in a perfect circle. I would see shadows and images that unnerved me, and my grandmother called them visitors.

My grandmother tried her best to love me through her brokenness, but I could feel her disappointment when I would go on drinking sprees and return home a total wreck. I decided to find myself a roommate and move out, saving her this pain and hopefully getting away from the strange poltergeist activity. Even though I was not going to church, the Lord always protected me. He pursued me before I considered pursuing Him.

When I finally moved into my very own apartment, I felt I had accomplished a big feat, and that I would be at peace. But there was a tangible, evil presence in my new apartment. I would have headaches and feel as though something was watching me from the closet. It seems weird, I know, but it was my experience. One night as I was sleeping, I felt a scratch on my leg. It began to burn, and when I examined it, it was in the shape of three claw marks, which frightened me. Had the evil spirits followed me? My roommate and her son expressed experiencing weird gushes of wind that scared them both. The next day I attempted to pray over my apartment to bless it, but I felt a physical attack that interfered with my breathing to the point of gasping for air and a pounding headache. I knew I couldn't live alone peacefully, but I definitely couldn't live with my grandmother. I needed my family. I then begged my sister to let me live with her until I could get on my feet, and I would pay her what I could.

Living with my sister also allowed me to hang out with my dad. My dad wasn't well, and he only got worse. He started having strokes and was losing his independence. I believed my sister saw me as Ms. Irresponsible, and soon she kicked me out for not paying enough rent. However, I was paying what I could. I was a full-time student, a full-time employee, and a bartender at night and on weekends. The classification of my situation was "the working poor." That seemed to be the final straw because I had no reliable friends; my demise was imminent. But God provided once more, and I found a studio apartment and a new job that supplied all my needs. During this time, my previous boyfriend found me via social media. We began talking and soon began dating again. I didn't want to talk about God with him because he didn't like the subject. During our dating period, I forgot about making Christ the center of my focus, and my fleshly desire ruled. I walked away from God, and we eventually got married. On the most important day of my life, I was sad because my dad wasn't there to give me away. This was nothing new; he had missed other special days in my life. My aunt and grandmother came to the rescue; they both walked me down the aisle and presented me to my groom.

After a couple of years of no contact from my dad, I felt the need to contact him. I saw it as my last opportunity to speak with him. He didn't recognize my voice, probably because I spent the entire phone call weeping and telling him how much I loved him. Later, I received some good news: my dad wanted to speak with me. My first thought was *no way*, even though I was jumping up and down with excitement to talk with him. I discussed it with my husband, and he told me I should go because we needed closure. Happy but scared, I went to see my dad. His doctor had admitted him to a long-term care facility because he'd had a stroke and could not walk independently. When I entered his room, I saw a different man, a weaker man, but he was still my dad, and I was grateful to be in his presence and wanted to hear everything he had to say to me. The first thing my dad said was, "I am sorry! Sorry I was not the father you needed me to be, sorry that it took me until now to see how amazing you are." He began filling in the blanks of my life.

He told me that he and my mother, long ago, were both addicted to heroin and searching for something; they found each other. When my mother conceived me, she was heavily into her addiction. She used heroin her entire pregnancy, and minutes after they had used drugs, they had to rush to the hospital because my little body couldn't remain in my mother's drug-infested body any longer. They told my dad I was going to die. At that moment, he said he found God. He said he prayed to God, pleading for Him to save me, and he promised to give up drugs. He said that suddenly, I began to breathe. The change did not happen immediately in my dad's life, he would battle his addiction and suffer many relapses, but he said he never stopped fighting. My life from conception seemed to have been a struggle.

He said my mother was not ready to be clean; she wanted the drugs and started diving deeper into the lifestyle and everything that came with it. Eventually, they got a divorce. The agreement between them was that my mother would have visitations, and my dad would have physical custody of my older sister and me. This conversation with my dad was the best conversation of my life. He apologized over and over again for not being the father I needed. But with that conversation, he had gifted me so much.

A month later, he had a frontal lobe seizure and died. I knew then that it was the Holy Spirit who had encouraged me to make that phone call. I sat by his bedside as he took his last breath. This death experience changed my view of death, especially when he said he saw angels. He even began to speak in a different language and in English, saying, "No more work." God was pursuing me long before I considered pursuing Him. My time with my dad had bought me closure, and I knew that he did love me.

I stopped talking to my mother the day after my dad died because she went too far. She messaged me and told me that he was not my father—that I was the result of an affair. I finally put the brakes on. Shortly after my dad's death, I searched for the truth. I accessed the court documents, and I learned that even though I had chosen to live with my mother when I was a child, the investigation advised against us girls living with our mother full-time given her mental state. The court did not take that advice and allowed me to walk into an emotional, spiritual, and almost physical death trap at the age of eleven. But I was resolved!

My husband and I were trying to become parents. Shortly after my dad died, I suffered a second miscarriage. I began to struggle to find my worth. We decided to try fertility drugs and still struggled to conceive. When I finally broke down and said, "No more. I give this to You, Lord," I became pregnant with my son. While pregnant with my son, I did not have the safest job; I was a hospital security guard. One night I was assaulted by a patient who kicked me in my stomach. I began to panic and fear I would lose my baby. Later, a woman entered the hospital and requested an escort to our secured labor and delivery floor. I wore baggy clothes because I did not want to appear pregnant, and this woman, not knowing me or what had happened to me, spoke these words: "He will be okay; he is protected." I could not find her on my surveillance cameras, nor did I see her leave the next day. He pursued me before I considered pursuing Him.

There have been occasions throughout my pregnancy when I knew God was speaking to me, but it was not enough to bring me back to Him. The hurt and pain had built a wall around my heart. Then, I lost my hero, my grandmother. Her death was hard for me because we were having issues and not speaking. Our family was a family of issues, dysfunctional, and I never knew how anyone was doing. Shortly before she died, I felt again that the Holy Spirit was informing me my hero was soon to pass. I sat on my bathroom floor crying because my heart was breaking. I prayed that I would be able to see her one last time. The call came and blessed me to say goodbye to my grandmother. I continue to process the grief and forgiveness of myself and my family.

However, her passing triggered something in me, and I reverted to the thing that once scared me: witchcraft. Maybe I didn't want to let my dad or grandmother go. I began to practice as a medium psychic who can connect the living with the dead. This practice opened a portal that I did not know about, and I was not ready for what would come and go through that portal. That frightened me, and I began burning sage in my home with the understanding that it would cleanse the atmosphere of any negative energy. From there, I began to channel, which is the ability to speak on behalf of the dead to the living. Again, I was getting into dangerous waters far above my head. Because I didn't see this as malicious, I kept practicing. It opened me to intense mind battles. Something strange was happening to me day and night. Things would move in my home. I wanted to run away, and the oppression became so intense I wanted to kill myself. I was experiencing every dark thing one could imagine.

I would pass a particular church daily en route to work, and immediately, my soul would begin reaching out to God. I was in serious spiritual trouble. But the turning point happened one day when my son said he was seeing an orange man, and an alarm went off in me and reminded me of the torment I'd suffered as a child. *No, I cannot do this to my child*, I thought, and I began to seek deliverance. I should have been more careful opening this door when I didn't know what was behind it. It was pure evil.

I decided to go to church; it was on an Easter Sunday. I sat there in church tormented, but I manage to say to God, "I'm here. If you are real, speak to me," and He did. The message preached was about forgiveness and letting go of the past and how to move forward. I was having a difficult time making that connection to God. I believed it was because I hadn't disconnected from my idol god, witchcraft. I had to confess my sins and trust God to forgive me and help me. My deliverance would come in three cycles to thoroughly purge the evilness from my mind, soul, and body. These deliverance processes are challenging and grueling because I had been a disciple of satan. I needed a physical deliverance, and my mind transformed. Everyone's road to freedom is not the same. The devil has since attacked my marriage, finances, and integrity, but I remember hearing how opposition only comes to those the devil sees as a threat to his work.

There are days where satan tries to make me doubt myself, which is doubting God and the work He has done in my life. I still struggle with my anger, but I am working on letting that go. Currently, I am in the next chapter of my life. I am in the process of getting a divorce. But I am also learning how to lean into God wholly in my darkest hour. I have moved from California to Florida; once again, God provided for me. Writing my story has been challenging because it requires me to visit those places of guilt, shame, sorrow, and pain; nonetheless, it tells of my road to redemption where healing has taken place and continues. However, when I surrendered my life to the Lord, I began to realize that this gift came from God, and although the church had called it a curse, it is a blessing when it is in the hands of God and not satan. I asked God to use me to bring someone else peace and hope just as He had done for me.

He pursued me before I considered pursuing Him.

My story may be a difficult read, but these are words spoken in time to the one that needs to hear this story. God uses the imperfect and messed-up individuals to deliver his grace, forgiveness, and redemption story. Moses was a murderer, and David was an adulterer. When God sent Jesus, He did not send Him to condemn the world but to save the world.

> *For God so loved the world that He gave His only begotten Son, that whoever believes in Him should not perish but have everlasting life. For God did not send His Son into the world to condemn the world, but that the world through Him might be saved. (John 3:16–17 NKJV)*

Jesus did not spend most of his time in temples but out with the people, touching the unclean. He changed the life of Mary Magdalene, who had seven demons, and she was never the same again.

Now when He rose early on the first day of the week, He appeared first to Mary Magdalene, out of whom He had cast seven demons. She went and told those who had been with Him, as they mourned and wept. (Mark 16:9– 10 NKJV)

When I look over my life, I can see how the Lord, even as I was making bad decision after bad decision, was still putting hope in me; He was still fighting for me to fulfill His will for my life. He has begun a good work in me. He shall finish it!

. . . being confident of this very thing, that He who has begun a good work in you will complete it until the day of Jesus Christ. (Philippians 1:6 NKJV)

My sister and I have a strained relationship. We always have, but it became more strained as our mother became more involved. My mother and I had not spoken since the day my dad died. But a few years back, she contacted me through my sister and asked about my son, and as a goodwill gesture, she wanted to do something for him. I agreed, but I wanted her to know that nothing had changed between us. She then began posting on social media about how God says to honor your mother and father and how God doesn't like ugly. It appeared she was up to her old tricks again. Some things I just have to "let go"!

I want to encourage you not to give up on your hope and faith. I have had some moments where I have fallen on my face, but the most important thing is when God helped me to stand up. The creator of the heavens and the earth knitted you, dear reader, in your mother's womb. He knew your life's story before you took your first breath, He knew your failures, successes, and stumbles, but He still died for you. I now have spiritual mothers that challenge me and bless me beyond belief. The hardest thing to do is to ask for help. We are a body of believers, just how God planned it, all different and unique, and enlightened by the Word of God. The devil attacks us at our weakest point; therefore, we must be cleansed by the blood of Jesus and transformed by the Word of God. He can restore us to what He wanted for us long before satan convinced us that we weren't good enough. We are not our past. It doesn't matter if you are a prostitute, drug addict, dealer, suicidal, you name it—God loves each and every one, and He will love us to good health, spiritually and naturally. He pursued me before I considered pursuing Him, and I am so glad He continued pursuing me until I said "yes."

> *Not that I have already attained, or am already perfected; but I press on, that I may lay hold of that for which Christ Jesus has also laid hold of me. Brethren, I do not count myself to have apprehended; but one thing I do, forgetting those things which are behind and reaching forward to those things which are ahead, <u>I press toward the goal</u> for the prize of the upward call of God in Christ Jesus. (Philippians 3:12–14 NKJV)*

Like the woman at the well, I received the same *powerful* message: *the world—men, in particular—can never quench my thirst.*

Jesus answered and said to her, "If you knew the gift of God, and who it is who says to you, 'Give Me a drink,' you would have asked Him, and He would have given you living water." The woman said to Him, "Sir, You have nothing to draw with, and the well is deep. Where then do You get that living water? Are You greater than our father Jacob, who gave us the well, and drank from it himself, as well as his sons and his livestock?"

Jesus answered and said to her, "Whoever drinks of this water will thirst again, but whoever drinks of the water that I shall give him will never thirst. But the water that I shall give him will become in him a fountain of water springing up into everlasting life." <u>The woman said to Him, "Sir, give me this water, that I may not thirst, nor come here to draw</u>." (John 4:10–14 NKJV)

Meet Jesus at the well. I did!

Tish Rivera
Daughter of the King of Kings.
Speaker & prophetic seer
Plexus Ambassador

I have since launched a ministry titled, The Living Bread Ministry. My email address is TheLivingBread.11@gmail.com

The Amazing Endless Grace and Mercy of God

by Esinam

I had a great job working with wonderful colleagues and friends. I had a beautiful, well-furnished, comfortable apartment, but I was emotionally tired and felt a little mundane and monotonous. I guess a better word would be "burnout"! I was separated from my family and yearned for a stronger family-like connection. An old colleague emailed me and informed me she had relocated to the United States, lived in California, and was attending a university, endeavoring to improve her life. She sounded excited about attending the university and requested my assistance with her college courses. I agreed to help since I was at a higher educational level. We spoke often, and then she suggested it would be better if I moved to California. She said it would be more convenient to support each other's effort and progress. Already feeling low in the bleak midwinter in Vermont and alone, I thought this could be the change I was looking for, and it was in sunny California. After many conversations about how progressive California was and that finding a job and additional support would be easy, she persuaded me. I immediately felt rejuvenated and happy. The plan was to share an apartment and support each other like family. As I prepared for my journey to California, I prayed that the Lord would give me strength and courage for this new venture.

I started packing, and it took me two months. I hired a moving truck and shipped my household items, resigned from my job, and gave up my established life to go to a new place in the name of friendship. It was a daunting thing to do, but I did it, putting my faith in my friend.

In *Macbeth*, Shakespeare said, "There is no art to find the mind's construction in the face: He was a gentleman on whom I built an absolute trust."

Little did I know, she had laid a snare for me, and I would need God's faithfulness, power, and deliverance like never before.

On Christmas Day 2014, a cold, dreary morning, I boarded a plane to California. My flight arrived late that evening, but my friend was there to pick me up. We were happy to see each other and talked all the way home about how we would together conquer the world. We would support each other. On my arrival, I noticed the six flights of stairs to climb to get to the apartment. Each flight consisted of ten to fourteen steps. I made it, but that was work, and I could only imagine that it would get worse before it got better. Maybe she intended to discuss relocating to the lower level now that I have shown up? Because she knew I had a severe walking disability. But before I could enjoy that happy thought, she showed me my bedroom. It was the smallest room in the three-bedroom apartment. I felt uncomfortable, especially when I knew my bed would be the only item I could place in this room. She also had two children, and I love children.

Three days after my arrival, she gave me a figure of how much rent I had to pay monthly, but without discussing job prospects or support to find one. There was another slap of surprise when she said I was also to pay half of the utilities. I was beginning to wonder what I had gotten myself into. The truck with my household items was scheduled to arrive within two weeks. I offered to pay some of her friends to unload the truck, and thankfully, they accepted the offer. On the day the truck was scheduled to arrive, my host left the apartment early and said she didn't want to deal with the unloading and didn't return until late in the evening. I felt shocked and abandoned. It was a painful revelation of how things would be. My host soon afterward said to me, and I quote, "I don't care about anybody. I care about myself, and I am fighting for myself." Even if her own partner was in trouble, she would tell them it serves them right.

Immediately, I began paying rent and half of the utilities. I had no problem paying, but I wanted to get a job as soon as possible and not deplete my savings. Without asking me, she deliberately assigned me childcare as an additional duty. Her friends were instructed to pick the children up from school and drop them off at home in my care. In addition, I wasn't assisting her with her schoolwork; *I was doing her schoolwork*. Finally, the time came for her to invite her friends over and parade me amongst them. I noticed a lot of pretentiousness and misrepresentation of me as a helpless new arrival who needed a favor. She told them she provided for me because I had no job or income. I was paying rent, half of everything, and taking care of personal expenses. I had no one to talk to except the people around my host. She monitored my interactions closely. If I asked her friends about job prospects and opportunities in her presence, the conversation would be interrupted and the subject changed. She would distract them with other questions because she had already given me a couple of jobs, childcare, and her schoolwork. I caught her more than once eavesdropping on my phone conversations. The truth of the matter was, I was stuck, unable to extricate myself from this place or the lies. I was isolated, lonely, hemmed in, controlled, and stranded. I went from absolute independence to a mini prison.

I couldn't go anywhere unless it was convenient for my host to take me. For months, I paid rent and utilities. It depleted my savings, and I reluctantly resorted to withdrawing from my 401(k) for personal needs. Yet I did childcare and her schoolwork without pay. When I told my host that I didn't have any more money to pay rent and utilities and could only afford to buy my food, she declared war on me. She did everything possible to make me feel worthless. I was overwhelmed with sorrow for the wrong choice I had made. So much was going on that was so shocking I cannot tell it all. I couldn't believe what I was experiencing. I couldn't stop crying and felt unsafe. The trauma I suffered took away my joy, trust, and faith. I felt like an imported servant who was horribly mistreated.

My mind became a battleground between darkness and light. I lay on the floor for many days crying out to God because I knew my spirit was in a dark place. Evil thoughts assailed my mind.

I prayed a lot. Sometimes all I could say was, "Help me, Lord, and thank you." I started researching on my laptop to find what services were available. I found out about paratransit transportation with the American Disability Association; I called them and registered. I wanted to have independent transportation so I could go places to get help in finding a job without depending on my tormentor, a supposed friend. I have a severe walking disability and cannot drive. She knew this.

I found out about the Vocational Rehab office, made an appointment, and began their process. They told me about various jobs, especially state jobs, which I started researching. With transportation, I gained some independence and could go and come at will. I started receiving mail from various sources of support and job opportunities. I asked my host for a mailbox key. When I went to retrieve my mail, it didn't work. She told me not to worry; she would pick my mail up for me. I missed deadlines to apply for jobs because she gave me my mail late, intentionally. I went to the office to get the key to retrieve my mail. I learned my host had given me a fake key and the incorrect mailbox number. I also found out from the office that she was on a government subsidy and was not supposed to rent or sublet. Her goal was to make me feel worthless, foolish, ridiculed, laughed at, isolated, and subject to derogatory attitudes and remarks.

How had I gotten here? I ignored the warning signposts. I had previously worked with this individual. I noticed how other employees walked on eggshells around her. She would demand her way and continuously complain about unfair treatment. I befriended her, and we would have breakfast or lunch together. I wanted to encourage her. I believed her, but I now know I was naive. The friendship did not extend outside the office. And after we reconnected, she requested help with her assignments, but when I couldn't complete the project due to my job requirements, she became furious. This anger and blaming me went on for days. I ignored the warning signposts. When I hesitated to relocate to California, she pushed, cajoled, and accused me of procrastination and refusing to make changes. Her personality was speaking loudly; I was tone-deaf. I ignored the warning signposts.

And now I was in the belly of the beast with no way out. She hadn't warned me about the six flights of stairs I had to climb to reach the apartment, a huge inconvenience. She was well aware of my severe physical walking disability. Going up and down those stairs created more medical problems for me. I often had to find a neighbor to assist me with bringing my shopping upstairs. Now that I was in the belly of the beast, I could see in plain view the warning signposts.

Her demands became more intense when I could no longer pay. All the evil afoot came to a head when my host secretly tried to set me up and reduce me to nothing. She and her friend decided to convince me to go to the welfare office to apply for food stamps. God, in His infinite grace, allowed me to know what they had planned. I knew I would not go along with their plan, but I went and collected all the documents, came home, and stuffed them away. The next day, her friend called to check if I had filled the forms to go on welfare. I told them I had never been on welfare before and did not plan to do that because God would help me, the Lord is my source, and my eyes are on Him.

I told them this could be considered fraud, and they became outraged. They yelled and talked down to me like I was an ignorant, foolish child. I was shocked at the attitude but not at the reaction since I was aware of the diabolical plans. But I was upset at the disrespect and uncouth behavior, so I sent them a message not to talk to me that way ever again. The next day my host left the house early. She returned with her friend together and attacked me, loudly yelling insults and threats. They blocked my bedroom door and were jumping up and down, gesturing and yelling at the top of their voice. I became concerned that they might physically attack me. I tried to tell them why I would not complete the forms and go on welfare, but they would not listen. They wanted to disgrace me. One of our next-door neighbors who heard all the commotion came out later and said to me, "You should have known who you were dealing with; they are not nice." I said thank you, and she left. Another neighbor, a young man who has helped carry my things upstairs before, came to me and said if I needed anything done for me, I should let him know; I said thank you again, and he also left. I didn't need anything at the moment except for the grace of God to endure.

I was beginning to find the boldness to speak up. I told them to never speak to me again in that manner. Even though I was trying hard to redeem myself, I knew deep within me that it would take the grace of God. I asked Him to redeem me, and I didn't know when or how, but I believed He would. I knew His ways are infinite and mysterious.

In His infinite wisdom, mercy, and redeeming grace, He led me.

I visited a church called Harvest and enjoyed the service. The preaching uplifted my mind and spirit. I filled out the visitors' card, not expecting anything. But I was soon contacted by a member of the church. Her name was Dorothy; unbeknown to me, she was the earthly angel the Lord sent me. She visited me with a Starbucks gift card. We had a long conversation, getting to know each other, and she wanted to know my plans. This Holy Spirit–filled woman became a friend sent from heaven to save me from the dark depths. My spirit was dying, and I knew I was heading for a place of no return. She saw the trauma I was going through—how alone, stranded, and unsafe I felt. She understood the effort to destroy my self-esteem, being jobless, and how this was killing my spirit.

I no longer had to contact paratransit for transportation to church because she and her grandchildren would pick me up for church on Sundays and Wednesdays. We spent many hours sitting in restaurants or just in her car, talking about life, scriptures, and the grace of God. She took me to Bible studies, life group meetings, women's prayer groups, and other events within and outside of the church, in the area, or out of town. She took me to movies and introduced me to people, and she strived to build a network of support for me in addition to her friendship. She gave me inclusiveness with her family, making me feel like I belong. She did all she could to build my waning spirit, distracting me from myself so I could focus on the Lord while planning what to do physically to move forward. Every chance she had, she took me out of the house so I would not be alone. *Just for comic relief here: Dorothy designated herself to be my private Uber in addition to being the Uber for her grandchildren.*

One weekend my spirit was so low, I just lay on the floor in my room at God's feet, sang or played music, and cried. This was a common practice for me. When I lack words because of pain, I lay at God's feet and say, "Please help me and thank you." I was in so much pain from the wasted time, the thousands of dollars spent to move here, and the dejection I was subjected to because I trusted a person. I begged God to forgive and save me. The regret was so deep, I felt like disappearing into the ground or not existing anymore.

In *Macbeth*, Shakespeare said, "There is no art to find the mind's construction in the face: He was a gentleman on whom I built an absolute trust."

In contrast, the Bible teaches us differently. I knew that; however, I disassociated this truth with the journey I embarked upon. There can be no absolute trust in a human being because, as the Bible says,

It is better to trust in the Lord than to put confidence in man. (Psalms 118:8 NKJV)

Trust in Him at all times, you people; Pour out your heart before Him; God is a refuge for us. Selah. Surely men of low degree are a vapor, Men of high degree are a lie; If they are weighed on the scales, They are altogether lighter than vapor. (Psalms 62: 8–9 NKJV)

Unbeknownst to me, Dorothy's heart was burdened for me because she could see what was happening to me. When I said I couldn't go to church because I had been crying all weekend and was too tearful, she didn't push me, and she said okay. But that day after church, she and her family drove to my block at the apartment complex, stretched forth their hands, and prayed for me. Later in the week, she talked to me for a long time and encouraged me. Then she laid down the law and said I had to go to church with her the next Sunday, and I said okay.

That Sunday, she picked me up and said we would be going to Stockton for lunch after church. I thought to myself, *Wow, that is special, driving to another town for lunch.* I had no idea that the special lunch was about to change my life from pain to gain. The restaurant owner knew Dorothy, welcomed us, and placed platter after platter of food on our big table. As I was admiring the food, Dorothy handed me an envelope. I was surprised and said I'd read it when I get home, but she said no, if I could please read it now. So I opened the letter, and it turned out to be a life-saving gift. My jaw dropped because it was a jaw-dropping miracle.

They had done the kindest thing. Dorothy and her family had a meeting and decided to move me into her home, where a beautiful room with a walk-in closet and an adjacent bathroom would be mine. I could not believe it. I stopped eating, my eyes widened, and my facial expression said it all. I covered my mouth and tried to breathe calmly because if I didn't, I would have started bawling, and I didn't want to embarrass the family. God, by His grace, had prepared all of this for me.

After reading the note, talking a bit about it, and giving my consent, Dorothy said she would discuss the details with me the next day or so. The thing is, she doesn't play. When she makes a decision, it gets done. So on Monday, she picked me up for lunch, and we sat in a restaurant for hours, discussing the details. I told her that because I have been spending my savings for a whole year paying rent and utilities and buying food, even though I had some money, I didn't think it would be enough for the move; moreover, I didn't know anyone who would move my things from the third floor. She said that was no problem; she would arrange for a friend of her daughter's to move my items, and whatever money I had to pay, she would pay the balance, and did. She was very serious about getting me out of that place. I did not say anything to my antagonistic host; she had displayed her anger toward me because I had no more money.

The next day, my host left the house at nine that morning, and the movers arrived around ten and finished four hours later. I moved into the room prepared for me, and my heavy burden was lifted. I prayed and thanked God and my friend for rescuing me from the snare. My spirit felt so light, and I could breathe again; I lay down and slept like a baby. When I awoke, I got down to business and tackled my job applications. I got many job contacts and interviews and landed a job with the state—another miracle from the Lord. I trained and worked at this job for six months but realized that California was relatively very expensive and too hot compared to Vermont.

Dorothy was very welcoming and treated me like family; I felt like her younger sister. We continued to go to many places. When I became tired of reading, writing, or watching TV in my room, I would find her in her office or bedroom. And we would flop down and chat our hearts out, mostly about God, the Bible, and life lessons. Sometimes we watched sermons or movies together. While enjoying this great reception, I was very comfortable, but I also knew I had to think about my original plan and move forward.

I fasted and prayed. One day as I was on the floor praying, as usual, asking God what I should do, I heard clearly in my spirit to "call Vermont." I sat up and called my colleague at the job I left when I came to California. We checked in and talked a bit; then I asked what was happening at work and what would be her opinion if I decide to come back to my job because it is pretty expensive and hot in California. She got excited and said, "Quick, send your updated resume to the coordinator." She said they had missed me, and they had been chatting about me the day before. We talked a bit more about the job and other developments. I emailed the resume, got a reply, and an interview was set up with another manager and the human resource office, which turned out great. It was now the middle of March 2017.

She asked when I wanted to start, and I said May. Surprisingly, they said no, come back in April. I saw the hand and favor of God (Psalms 69:13, 90:17, Daniel 1:9). I had told Dorothy that I was discussing things with God, and I would tell her what God said.

But as for me, my prayer is to You, O LORD, in the acceptable time; O God, in the multitude of Your mercy, Hear me in the truth of Your salvation. (Psalms 69:13 NKJV)

And let the beauty of the LORD our God be upon us, And establish the work of our hands for us; Yes, establish the work of our hands. (Psalms 90:17 NKJV)

Now God had brought Daniel into the favor and goodwill of the chief of the eunuchs. (Daniel 1:9 NKJV)

I told Dorothy what happened and why. She was hoping I would stay, but she understood my reasons and supported my decision. She took me to get all the things I needed to pack. Her very quiet, sweet, and smiling brother Edward also helped me immensely to put everything together. He took me to the place where I could rent a truck, helped me get boxes, brought a friend to help with the loading, and saw that everything was loaded and boarded for pickup.

I cannot express enough the excellence of God in putting everything in place for me to move back to Vermont. There was a job waiting for me. Since I had left my previous accommodations, someone readily offered me a place to stay until a place of my own would be available. My bank in Vermont loaned me money for shipping, and the company that shipped my household items to California was ready and willing to ship them back to Vermont. I went online, got my airline ticket, and got ready to travel. On April 22, 2017, I flew back to Vermont after shipping my things ahead of me. A couple of days later, I was sitting at my desk, working my shift as part of the on-call supervisor team. By the way, this was a promotion for me.

In every tribulation, there are lessons to learn, and I have learned a lot. The mighty hand of God never forsakes or leaves us when we know and come to Him humbly, because it is only by His grace that we are here. Even when we are lost and grope in the dark, His eyes are on us, His faithfulness is forever sure, and His love is great.

Through the LORD's mercies we are not consumed, Because His compassions fail not. They are new every morning; Great is Your faithfulness. "The LORD is my portion," says my soul, "Therefore I hope in Him!" The LORD is good to those who wait for Him, To the soul who seeks Him. It is good that one should hope and wait quietly For the salvation of the LORD. (Lamentations 3:22–26 NKJV)

Today, I am snugged away here in Vermont with the cold weather, my job, my friends, and above all, my God!

God has walked with me; He has held my hand and carried me in His arms when my strength has failed me. And, what He has done, He continues to do for me daily. I know He is always present. He extracted me from the deep, dark well when I was drowning in sorrow and heartache, felt alone, and contemplated ungodly thoughts the devil tried to feed me. I placed myself squarely in harm's way, full of trials and temptations that put me at the edge of a cliff, teetering precariously to a devastating fatal fall except for the grace of God. It is a real battle of the mind and the heart. I know it, and I also understand that the battle rages continuously daily between the darkness and the light. But by the grace of God Almighty, I don't fight alone; I have an advocate, Jesus Christ, who overcame, and because of Him, I have the victory long before I reach the battlefield.

In the Bible, there is a story about Joseph, whose brothers were going to kill him but resorted to casting him into a well and finally selling him as a slave to Egyptians. But years later, they had to travel to Egypt seeking food, and Joseph was the man in charge. When he revealed himself to them, they became afraid because they knew what they had done. But Joseph said this:

"But as for you, you meant evil against me; but God meant it for good." (Genesis 50:20 NKJV)

I learned from this experience that Romans 8:28 is true:

And we know that all things work together for good to those who love God, to those who are the called according to His purpose.

What the enemy meant for evil, God worked out for my good!

I Am Validated

by Larissa Love

S adly, but truly, I looked for people and things to validate me for a long time because it was satisfying and made me feel good and normal when they accepted me. However, the truth was that the people I encountered never validated me. They discredited me, hurt me, abused me, mistreated me, disliked me, hated me without cause, and were mean just to be mean.

I ran home from school almost daily, crying, and when I was halfway home, I would stop running long enough to give myself time to stop crying and dry my tears. I didn't want to become the topic of discussion and maybe a few cracked jokes. Home wasn't always a haven, because my oldest sister and I gave sibling rivalry a new definition. I would go to my room and slam the door—a signal that said, "Do not bother me!" For the most part, my rule was "do not bring any tears into the house," but I brought plenty of anger, tucked away and well hidden until those closest to me created a reason to arouse my wrath. I was not a kind person. It is almost impossible to be kind and extremely angry at the same time. I didn't like anyone, including myself. I have abused myself and have allowed other people to use me. I have suffered in silence, and it felt like the normal thing to do. "Coping" is the word. Perhaps the ideology that best describes my coping mechanism, in a small way, is Stockholm syndrome. It is said to occur when hostages develop a psychological alliance with their captors as a survival strategy. My circumstances didn't reach that level; however, I created a coping mechanism that allowed me to deal with myself and my anger. It amazes me how the human mind fights to survive.

The environment trapped me, and those trapped with me became my tormentors within our mutual confinement. We were confined within our homes, schools, churches, and neighborhood until we could drive and experience freedom that was short-lived because we always had to come home, back to the hood. Strangely enough, it didn't matter how far I ran to get away; I invariably seemed to run into some of my captors and tormentors. What's a girl to do but redefine her pain and her abusers to make it tolerable, to maintain some sense of sanity? The rationale I developed must have been birthed within me, enabling me to survive at any cost.

Tears of a Little Girl

I was described by most as a skinny, knock-kneed, short-haired, dark-skinned little girl with a terrible speech impediment, and I had no confidence. My speech was awful; I stuttered and stammered every word that flowed from my lips. Anxiety filled me because I could not express myself with words, not even fighting words. Life would have been sweeter without these gifts. I did not ask for them, but I was powerless to change my stammering tongue or physical appearance. May I indulge myself for a moment and say, "Poor me!"

I learned not to talk; instead, I would keep my words few and far between, and spoke only when necessary. My silence was golden. I was constantly reminded of these things by my peers and, yes, even my siblings. Anger only made the stuttering worst, and the anxiety would grow as a result. I had short hair, and in the day, short hair on a girl was enough to cause people to give you a second look—a not-so-kind second look. I got plenty of those. The texture, length, and style were always paramount. A girl's hair was everything, and I didn't have it. There was never a day I was not bullied, talked about, or made aware of my flaws. The daily reminder of these things became my life. I started to believe what they called me; yes, I became *her*, and the flaws became *me*!

I have since learned of the self-hatred taught within the Black culture because of our identity. There is a saying I heard: "The way you see me is the way you treat me, and the way you treat me is what I become." I have no idea who said this, but it became a self-fulfilling prophecy.

I remember the long, quiet walks to and from school. They were a breeze because, usually, there was no one around. I would leave school late to avoid harassment on my return home. I did okay for a long time, staying out of the way of the bullies' traffic. Without any interruptions, I would enjoy those peaceful walks, singing my heart out. As I approached the school ground, my singing turned into a prayer, "Please, no bullying, name-calling, or fights today." Damn, kids were mean. I can't believe I went through all of that to go to school. I would seek out my nice friends for recess to play with and have fun. I remember being on the playground and running around like a free spirit until the mean girls appeared. I was exceptionally balanced. Playing on the uneven bars or swinging were my favorite playtime activities until the mean girls appeared, pushed me, and made me lose my balance and kiss the ground. They laughed out loud! I couldn't use the restroom in peace. Yes, my restroom experience was horrifying. The mean girls would rush the other girls out, turn off the lights and pull the door shut while I desperately attempted to get out. Oh yes, they weren't just mean; they were evil, and I had to endure their malicious behavior.

One day our physical education teacher announced we would be doing relay races, the girls against the girls and the boys against the boys. When it was my turn, I got into position, and the teacher yelled: "On your mark, get set, GO!" I dashed off and ran as fast as I could, never looking back for one second. I ran with all my strength because winning was something I believed I could achieve—I had to achieve. When I crossed the finish line, I slightly turned my head to see where my opponent was, and she was far behind me. I had left her in the dust. Oh, my goodness, I couldn't believe it. I had won, and for once, that meant I was a winner! No one could take the credit if I won or be responsible for my defeat. Winning or losing was on me. I won! Yes, the short-haired, skinny, dark-skinned, knock-kneed girl with a terrible speech impediment won that day.

Everyone at the school knew I was a winner, but what I knew was, I was not a loser!

I finally had something I could do and was great at it. I had to race again and again, and the girls were no match for me. I left them far behind in the dust. My teacher suggested I run against the boys to keep the race competitive. I was super scared and nervous and thought, *How could I do this? I just beat the girls, but can I beat the boys?* At our next class, we had relay races again. This time my teacher approached me and said, "Larissa, you are racing the boys today." I had a few wins under my belt; I had something that validated me. I knew if I lost, I would never hear the end of it. It was time to race the boys; there was no turning back now. Here I go, sink or swim, win or lose. I was ready and in position. As my teacher yelled the commands, I only heard "GO," and I dashed off with super strength. My adrenaline was high, causing my heart to beat fast. I ran like the wind that day, refusing to look back. Upon crossing the finishing line, I slightly turned my head, and a *boy* was crossing the finish line behind me. I had just beaten a boy!

All the boys wanted to race me. I guess their pride was on the line because everyone viewed them as losers until they ran against me and won. So I did—I ran against the boys. I beat them all, and honestly, it was easy. I hoped the bullying would stop. It never did; it got worse. A new title emerged from my unbelievable wins. I was called "boy/girl." It seemed the guys had a vested interest in keeping me down; they weren't going to let me off that easy.

I paid the price so they could hide their shame.

My teacher couldn't believe it, and from that time forward, I was the track star queen. Once the school had track and field, I joined and became the school champion.

But the walks home from school were still the most challenging part of my day. Boys and girls would tease me about the length of my hair. They called me a baldheaded boy/girl. Not only would they tease me with words, but they would also throw rocks at me. I usually had five kids behind me throwing rocks, yelling vulgarity, calling me ugly, and even kicking me. All this happen on my way home from school. I couldn't win for losing. Trying to leave school after everyone else to avoid these issues was no longer working. I tried getting in trouble on purpose to be given detention so I could walk home alone and unbothered. That didn't help me at all, because some of the same kids were in detention.

I hated school, and I hated the walk home.

I cried daily, and I would run home, and sometimes they would chase me from block to block until they got tired. I never got tired; I was a runner. However, I suffered from mental exhaustion. I must repeat this:

I suffered from mental exhaustion.

I would try to get away, and I could hear them laughing and saying, "Get her." I just wanted it to stop, but it didn't. How do you stop people from hurting you without getting into a fistfight? I didn't, and I had to learn to fight. As I became tired of the bullying and harassment, I realized that they would never leave me alone if I didn't fight back. I had a paradigm shift.

The Teenage Years

My older sister was a fighter and somewhat mischievous. I remember coming home with my eyes full of tears for the first time; I was tired of hurting in silence. When I got home, my big sister asked me what was wrong, and I told her. I told her about a girl who lived on our block who had harassed me, spat on me, pushed me down, and caused me to hurt my hands and knees badly. I was angry, burning inside, and I dropped teardrops every step of the way home. My sister knew the girl's sister, and they were friends. However, my sister didn't care about that; all she cared about was me standing up for myself. She made me clean my face and told me we were going to their house, and I would have to fight this girl, or I would have to fight her. I was afraid to go and fight this girl at her home. My sister walked briskly down the street with me in tow. As we approached the girl's house, my heart was beating out of my chest. I looked up and saw them on the lawn. My sister said to the girl, "Since you want to hit my sister, fight her now." We began to fight and fight and fight. I think we fought for a good ten minutes. Once the fight was over, we both had knots. I wasn't afraid to fight anymore, but I was worried about what would happen next. My sister took that fear away as she made me fight and told me if anyone hurt me again, I had better fight. On that day, I added a new title to my identity: "I'm a good fighter!"

In junior high school, we teens wouldn't go directly home. Weekly, students would stop at the park on the way home to either fight or watch a fight. I think I fought more than I watched. My peers would be so ridiculously mean at school, and after school, they would say they were going to fight me. I knew I was timid, and they could see the fear in my eyes and knew I was trying to avoid a fight.

But what they did not know was the intensity of anger and fear that fueled the rage within and guaranteed me a win.

I never lost a fight in junior high school; I never lost a battle ever! My young teenage years were fighting and surviving the war zone on and off campus. Oh, yeah, I was fighting more than my peers at school. I was fighting siblings and cousins because they were bullying me as well, and at that point, all I knew was to fight back. Suddenly, something was empowering about fighting and winning. This was a confidence builder, for sure.

The Woman

As a woman, I was hardcore, cold, and fierce. I had cut my teeth on fear and anger, and they had paid me well. I took nothing from no one and would fight at the smell of trouble. I was angry. I knew it, and I didn't care. After all, it was the mean people who had planted these seeds. My history wrote my current existence, and it was fight or flight. I remember a cashier who treated me disrespectfully. The last thing I recall was wiping everything off the counter before leaving. I was an angry person with a short fuse and had no idea I was toxic. I was toxic to myself. It was hard to recognize the anger as deadly because I saw it as my defense. I defended myself at all times and never thought twice about my actions. I can remember dragging this young lady out of the store and beating her badly because she pushed passed me and didn't say "excuse me." I brought it to her attention, and her words were "f—you!" Well, for me, the "f" meant "fight," so we fought in and out of the store. Needless to say, I won. But did I?

I later learned that my childhood *trauma* produced adult *drama*. Children are what they see, hear, and experience, and we are all sponges in this learning cycle. When we are born, we know nothing. We are on an adventure through this world, learning along the way by responding to stimuli. That's just what I did; I learned along the way. I believed that I was ugly, bald-headed, confused, and too black. I knew that whatever I did well wasn't enough, and I learned that no matter how much I tried to be cool to fit in and be accepted, I wasn't. I learned from experience that some people are bullies, abusers, and evil. Yes, I was learning, but I didn't want to know this evil.

My parents were divorced, and I didn't share with them what I was going through. I guess I was trying to protect my parents from the pain—mostly my mom, because I lived with her. The weight of caring for our family sat on her shoulders. I didn't want to add to it. And I didn't want to get in trouble for the way I was handling things. That was a big mistake, but it was a lesson learned. At ten years old, I learned to lash out due to the bullying at school. The only tools I had were my two fists and, on occasion, one-word bullets. The antagonizing force was just too much, and I couldn't handle it. It is what made me so angry. As they would dig and dig and dig into me, I endeavored to internalize the anger, but as with the Hulk, it always found its way out. And it was ironic how those who created the problem reacted to the outpouring of anger, as though I started the madness. I was just responding!

No, maybe what confused them was me being a little crazier than them. I was calling their bluff, and the bully in them became afraid. It is called "pent-up anger," and I was taking my last stance to save myself and my sanity. As I grew up, I became more of a runner than a fighter because I, the woman, became a mother. I couldn't imagine being in jail away from my children; oh no, running away was wiser and smarter.

How I Overcame My Anger

Overcoming my anger was a choice. To love my children, I realized I had to put my mask on first. Overcoming this out-of-control feeling was something I wanted and needed to overcome. One day I chose to change, and I took it step by step, day by day, and process by process. I knew I couldn't go cold turkey. I knew I wasn't going to wake up one morning and have no more anger. That thought process would set me up for failure. God knew my speed. What was easy for some was ten times harder for me. I needed to take it slow. I remembered asking God for a change because I wanted peace—the kind of peace that made me feel calm and in control. I had been out of control for so long, it had become my norm. If I wanted to learn something new, I knew reading was the place to start.

After all, the best-kept secrets are hidden in books.

And if I wanted to learn about God and His peace, I needed to read books on the subject. I did. However, I am not one who enjoys turning pages, but I listen well. Thank God for audiobooks, including the Bible. I had a devotional book I read daily before or after my prayer time. I was on a journey, and I believed that I would find more than gold at the end of the rainbow; I would find something gold could not replace nor purchase—God's peace!

One of the books I listen to shared the ideas of "the law of attraction" and stated that if you want something in your life, you must believe. I saw this as having the faith of a mustard seed and knowing life will be okay. I knew, despite everything that had occurred in my life, God had always taken care of me. Once again, He found me. I am sure He knew this day would come when having peace would become paramount to me. He found me, the person, and me, the soul, and gave me my greatest gift—calming peace.

I listened daily for months during my four-hour commute to and from work. It was the sound of life. The hearing and receiving truth were changing me.

"Then you will know the truth, and the truth will set you free." *(John 8:32 NIV)*

My "then" had come, and it was *now*! I was finally gathering tools to build a new life on a solid foundation. I didn't know I could do that. What an answer to my prayers. I began to put the learning to work. I began to pray harder and trust God more. The more I trusted him, the more things began to change. The blessing came in an opportunity to move to Chicago. I remember thinking that if I could get there, I could work harder alone, without my critics and judges.

Moving to Chicago allowed me to be alone with my soul and thoughts; it allowed me the chance to accept myself and breathe. The process was slow; it took a year. However, it was a year like no other. I prayed a lot, asking God specifically for what I wanted. I would pray for calming peace, release all inequities, and allow positivity to fill my being. As I prayed, I would add to my prayer request, finances, better relationships with my family, delivery of my emotions, being receptive to others' opinions and emotions. The more I prayed, the more I realized God was healing my inner person, and I was becoming more understanding and receptive to others. I began to see more changes in my life and my family's life. I had to allow the actions of my prayer to take place. If that meant to disconnect from some people, that's what I did, and I trusted the process.

As I progressed, my ways of continued peace came in the form of meditation. I meditated daily first thing in the morning. Meditation brought me another level of peace that I did not expect but was such a wonderful feeling. I started my day with prayer, then mediation, being thankful, grateful, and focused on how I wanted my day to go.

Blessed is the one . . . whose delight is in the law of the LORD, and who <u>meditates</u> on his law day and night. That person is like a tree planted by streams of water, which yields its fruit in season. (Psalms 1:1–3 NIV)

May these words of my mouth and this <u>meditation</u> of my heart be pleasing in your sight, LORD, my Rock and my Redeemer. (Psalms 19:14 NIV)

I <u>meditate</u> on your precepts and consider your ways. (Psalms 119:15)

May my <u>meditation</u> be pleasing to him, as I rejoice in the LORD. (Psalms 104:34)

I cannot express how much this experience of seeking God changed my faith and outlook on life. I am profoundly grateful to have this life-changing information fall into my lap at a time when I wanted to change. I asked for help in the process, and He answered. God is at the forefront of this. He and I have always had this relationship where I said, "Lord, I need substance; just a little bit more, please." If I asked Him for a sign, He would give it. If I asked for help, He provided it. He always knew I needed a little bit more, and He always honored my request. There is a saying that when the student is ready, the teacher will appear.

I am not exactly sure who said that, but in the Bible, when Mary and Martha had lost their brother Lazarus and were in deep distress, Martha went out of the house and encountered Jesus. Jesus told her not to worry because He was the resurrection. She told Him she believed what He said and that He was the Messiah. Then she ran back into the house to comfort her sister Mary. And the scripture says:

> After she had said this, she went back and called her sister Mary aside. "_The Teacher is here_," she said, "and _is asking for you_." When _Mary heard this, she got up quickly_ and went to him. (John 11:25–29 NIV)

That was my experience. When I was in my deepest and darkest moment, I needed a teacher, and the Teacher appeared. I was ready to rid myself of my grave-clothes and everything that represented death. Today, I know what inner peace is, and I know from whence it comes. Just as important, I know how to hold onto that peace. It comes from God, and through prayer and faith, I can hold on tight and know that He will fight my battles.

Psalms 41:8–10 (NIV) says it best:

> Come and see what the LORD has done, the desolations he has brought on the earth. _He makes wars cease_ to the ends of the earth. _He breaks the bow and shatters the spear;_ he

burns the shields with fire. He says, "Be still, and know that
I am God; I will be exalted among the nations, I will be
exalted in the earth."

God has caused the wars inside of me to cease; He broke the bow and shattered the spears that were fear and anger; and then He profoundly said, "Be still, and know that I am God!" He is exalted among the nations, which means *all people*, even a little girl with short hair, dark skin, knock knees, and a speech impediment. May I pause for a minute to say, "Thank you, God!"

Because today, I have learned to be still and know IT IS God who
validates me!

God made this crystal clear to me in Isaiah 54:17, that no weapons ever made to attack me will ever succeed against me and spoken or written negative words against me will never again penetrate my soul and hurt me.

For this to be true, it requires nothing short of a miracle, because naturally, weapons can kill, and hurtful words have wounded my spirit and soul. Therefore, I became determined to no longer casually quote this scripture because I realize that the *protection* God provided me against weapons and hurtful words is also a miracle—a miracle indeed!

LARISSA LOVE

I own a business that prides itself in non-invasive body sculpting, guaranteed results—Embodeed by Larissa, located at 717 K Street, Ste 417, Sacramento, CA, 95814, 916-877-4673, www.embodeed.com. The Company's Instagram: Embodee'd Body Sculpting, my personal Instagram: Embodee'd by Larissa, email: embodeed@gmail.com – let's connect and meet the new Larissa, the validated Larissa!!

His Blood Restores

by Elisha Jones

Suddenly, I lost my private swimming pool, the water broke, and it was time for me to enter into this big world. But I was not alone; my twin was in this with me. We had come to know each other well. And then, an emergency arose. It looked like me, my twin, and my mom were in some kind of trouble. Our parents told us later there was a high chance of all three of us dying during this birth. But, whew, we made it, all three of us—what a way to enter the world! I was the first to exit the womb. What bright lights! I was two minutes older than my twin, which made me the big sister. My twin was a boy. I had bragging rights!

All was well, and it was time for our parents to give us our names. Our mom said she knew before birth what she wanted to name us: Elisha and Elijah. Our names originated in the Bible, after the prophets

Elisha and Elijah. Elijah is the Seer, and he is the chief prophet. He is the one who told Israel that they would suffer many things, including a three-year drought in the land of Israel in 1 Kings 17. In 1 Kings 19, God told Elijah to anoint two kings and anoint Elisha as a prophet. The rest is history. They traveled together and did the work of God concerning Israel until, one day, God raptured Elijah. But first Elijah left his cloak or mantle on Elisha. They had a relationship of great loyalty and unity. I can't say that my brother and I are that close, but we love each other. Maybe one day, we will grow into the meaning of our names. Both names are Hebrew; Elisha means "My God is Salvation," and Elijah means "Jehovah is God."

We are blessed to be the benefactors of a two-parent home, and not only that but a Christian home, and I owe a shout out to my great parents. I call my dad the kooky/goofy one, always telling jokes or playing a joke on one of us. And our mom does not escape his sense of humor either. My mom is more businesslike, always put together, and serious concerning the things of God. She is the woman who makes praying look natural and inviting because she loves God, and she loves to talk to Him.

Six months after I was born, having made it through the first emergency, spinal meningitis attacked my little body. My mom told me how I had a hot fever, and she didn't hesitate to call 911. Once we were at the hospital and the doctors had done their examinations and started me on some meds, they told her that I would have died if she had waited one more hour. My mom told me how she prayed for me and believed that angels were around me. She said that although I couldn't make sounds, I kept moving my eyes in the direction of the corner of the room as though maybe an angel was hanging out there getting my attention. The doctor's prognosis was that I would be blind or deaf, if not both. However, the only residual effect I suffered from this disease was a slight speech impediment, and speech therapy took care of that. Once again, I had escaped death, and now I had escaped blindness and deafness too.

I grew up to be an adventurous little girl. At seven years old, I was always doing something that required risk taking. I am sure my mom would have preferred a more settled little girl. I stretched it a bit too far once when my mom and big sister were off on a trip to a church conference. They had been looking forward to going, and our dad would be caring for us young children. We would be in capable hands. To be entertaining, leave it to me to get the drama going. I told my twin brother to watch me do a magic trick of putting four quarters in my mouth—not one but four. I told you I was a risk-taker. I managed to trip somehow and fell backward in doing the trick, and the quarters lodged in my throat; I couldn't breathe! Fear gripped my heart, and I knew I was going to die. Coincidentally, my big brother, who was in the military, had decided to come home for the weekend. Or was it a coincidence? He performed the Heimlich maneuver on me and was able to dislodge three of the four quarters. The other quarter remained, and I could only breathe a little because, thankfully, it was sitting sideways, allowing a small amount of air to enter my lungs. At the same time, it was also cutting my throat. My dad grabbed me, put me in the car, and took off for the hospital. He believed that he couldn't wait for the ambulance and could get me to the hospital faster. He was driving extremely fast, as though my life depended on it, and it did. He had to get me to the emergency room and get me there quickly because I began to have a big problem trying to breathe. He was speeding, darting in and out of traffic. A white car pulled in front of him, and he slammed on his brakes. When he slammed on his brakes, my head went backward, forward, and thrust back again. And when my head slammed backward, the quarter dislodged and went down my throat; I swallowed the quarter.

Being a typical seven-year-old who understood I couldn't breathe a short time ago but suddenly could breathe again, I considered the emergency over. I asked my dad to forget about going to the hospital and divert this trip to a fast-food restaurant where I could get a hamburger with fries and a soda. Drama queen indeed! He profoundly disagreed and continued to the hospital. Once there, after the doctor heard the story, he couldn't believe that I had wanted to get fast food and a soda. He told my dad that would have been the worst thing I could have done, because the acid in the soda would have caused the quarter to float upward into my throat. If that had happened, there was a high possibility that I would not have survived. My dad did know what was best for me. For almost a year, I was placed on a stringent diet, allowing the quarter to pass naturally, avoiding surgery. One thing was for sure: I couldn't drink soda. When my mom heard about this emergency, she said they were in the air when the crisis took place and couldn't have turned around if she'd wanted to. She and my sister were beyond thrilled that I was alive, but I am sure there was some unbelief that I would have done something like this. Thank God for my big, brave military brother and my dad's refusal to let me die without a fight, taking me for a ride on the wild side. Together, they are my heroes, and on that day, I had received a miracle: they saved my life!

Well, I outlived what could have been a fatality and thank God for every breath, every day. It was a terrifying experience, and even today, it still makes me feel a little anxious when I think about it. I am so grateful for God's intervention. Suddenly, the family was on to other things, and one of those things was moving into a house with seven bedrooms. It fitted us just fine; after all, we needed a lot of room for eight kids. My twin brother and I are number six and seven in the pecking order—this large house allowed for some space between us all. There is nothing like having a bunch of kids crammed into a small space; they get on each other's nerves. So, I would like to say "good looking out" to our parents.

Now that we were all moved in and had lots of space, it was time to get acquainted with our blessing and enjoy it. My plan was to enjoy my new bedroom all to myself, but almost before we could say "hello," I was ready to say "goodbye!" First, my room had a foul order, and my mom tried to get it out but with no real success. Second, I was beginning to experience some weird things that I had never experienced before. For example, suddenly, after my first night sleeping in my room, I became terrified. Why? I don't know; this had never happened before. I was an eight-year-old adventurous little girl who was not afraid. I had proved how much of a risk-taker I was when I put not one, not two, but four quarters in my mouth. But now I was afraid to sleep in my bed.

I would wake up, often screaming, running to my parents to rescue me. My mom was becoming exhausted with this new trend of mine. I slept with the covers over my head, and I remember peeking out and seeing different things. I saw legs walking by the bed, and the legs looked like my dolls' brass legs; in my closet I saw something looking back at me with a face that resembled a shark, teeth and all. I know, it seems strange, but it was my experience, and nothing can negate that I saw all those things. I remember hearing, early one morning, slow, dragging footsteps walking up the stairwell. My dad had already left for work, and he didn't drag his feet. The rest of the family were fast asleep, so I knew it had to be something else. I saw it, and it was ugly and very scary looking, but I will spare you the gruesome details and me too. But I knew I had to get out of my room before it entered. I ran fast to my baby sister's room and hid her under me just in case it came into her room. My mom was a woman of prayer and fed up with this monster stuff. She gave me a Bible and told me to read it, saying it would help me overcome my fears. I did just that, but I couldn't read it in my room. The first day I decided to read my new Bible, I turned off my light, exited my room, and closed the door. I sat on the stairs and read my Bible there. Imagine this little eight-year-old girl, sitting and reading the Bible. Shortly afterward, my mom came home, and she told me to turn my light off and close my door. I was in shock, but when I turned and looked, the door was wide open, and the light was on. These unnatural occurrences were beyond my comprehension, and why was I the target? I did not know, and I did not understand.

I was sick and tired of all this craziness, and it came to a head for me with one episode when my bedroom door was slammed in my face by something when I turned off the light. It was too much, and I yelled out: *"I am not scared of you—get out of my house!"* I was not sure if it paid me any attention, but I must admit that I felt empowered even as a child. I resorted to sleeping in the loft or with my brother and little sister to give my parents a break. From the loft, I could hear things in my room. I became so accustomed to these unusual occurrences that I would turn over and go back to sleep. Strange things continued happening in the house, but they only manifested to me. Once, upon returning home from our family vacation, we saw that my bird, Trinity, had died for no apparent reason.

And then it happened; I will never forget the sound that echoed throughout the house, bouncing off walls and waking up everyone in the house. It was a scream like none I had ever heard; it was a manly scream but spiced with terror. It was a sound coming from my dad, a strong man and by no means a fearful one. We all jumped out of our beds and ran as fast as we could to get to him. He was standing there in fear. When we asked what had happened, with my mom leading the investigation, he began to tell us. He said that as he was walking past my brother's room heading out for work, he saw something big, very tall, pacing back and forth in my brother's room. He looked at it, and it looked at him, and the look on my dad's face said it all. Finally, I had vindication; I knew I wasn't crazy.

On a side note, you may want to consider what you bring into your home!

After my dad's encounter, it wasn't long before my mom gave the landlord our move-out notice. I am sure my mom had told her why we had to move, because a month before we moved, the landlord came to the house with a Buddhist priest to bless the house. She said she knew something was wrong with the house because her son had practiced witchcraft in his room, and she wanted the priest to cleanse the house. I now remembered seeing an object hanging on the wall on the day my mom and I went on a tour of the house with the landlord, which I later recognized as being used in witchcraft. This room that I called my very own had belonged to her son. No wonder I was terrified after the first night. When I saw him, he had long nails painted black and long, black, straight hair as if he had dyed it. His eyes were strange, and he wore black eyeliner. My mom later told me he was around sixteen or seventeen. As we were preparing to move, other families were coming by to see the house. I felt so bad for them and wanted to tell them that they had no idea what unpleasantries this house held for them. But I knew how far not to go with my parents. And it wasn't long before the day came, and we moved out of that demonic stronghold of a house. As we were driving away, I looked at it for the last time, and with a big smile on my face, I said, "Goodbye, house!"

We moved into our new house, and I slept like a baby, the way I was supposed to sleep. No more drama! I was off to enjoy fourth grade. I hung around mostly boys in elementary because we had more boys in the family—five, to be exact. I knew how they thought and played, and that made me feel comfortable. I knew very little about girls because I had a much older sister, and I called her my second mom, and I had a baby sister. I couldn't learn from them for various reasons, and I couldn't teach myself. And, after all, I loved playing basketball, and everyone knows boys like playing basketball. You might say basketball was my first love. Life was good. Our new neighbors were the best, and our families became remarkably close. We were welcomed into their home and would go over for movie nights. We kids played until we couldn't play anymore. I couldn't have asked for anything better than this, but I couldn't stay in the fourth grade forever. Growing up happens without warning, and it doesn't seek permission. Looking back, I so appreciated that era of fun and innocence.

Before I could realize what was going on, I was in junior high school, in double digits, twelve years old. I wish I could say it was more of the same, but playing basketball was the only constant in my life. My tribe changed significantly. I decided to start hanging around more girls, and suddenly, I could hear myself speaking a different language. Unlike boys, I soon found out that girls are more talkative; some call it "chatty." I also soon realized that while boys compete on the basketball court, girls compete off the court for those on the court. Those who like to compete are always seeking to be prettier than the next. And the one who gets to date the number-one athlete scores the highest. I was not sure I liked this change, but I had my dad's personality, always turning everything into a joke. I noticed I started to become an undercover bully. My friends and I would play-fight up and down the hallway, but sometimes those play fights became real fights. I suffered confusion at school and triple confusion at church.

I always attended church with my family, mom and dad leading the way. But—I say this sadly but without hesitation—I suffered the most at church. Our church had a youth group, and within the group was a particular clique. Unfortunately, I was not on the popularity list, and the leader of the group, who was an adult, did not like me. As you can imagine, most of the youth didn't like me because the leader didn't like me. I experienced rejection at the highest level. If there was a sleepover amongst the girls outside of the youth group, they would never invite me. They were so bold, they even dared the boys to talk to me. They would laugh at me, and that would crush me. When we would go to a Christian camp together, no one seemed to care about me, not even the adults. They were the worst because I expected them to care and set a good example. Instead, they disliked me and mistreated me.

This suffering continued for so long that it became customary for me to be insulted by peers and adults. Unbeknownst to me, my heart and soul were becoming dark. Hope seemed to have evaded me; the word for it is "depression." This condition also had a couple of companions that would come along for the ride, "anxiety" and "suicidal thoughts"! It was at youth camps where I experienced the brunt of it all, I guess because so many of us were together in one location. If I dared to defend myself, I would be separated from the group by the adults. They would say very harsh words and treat me like the villain when I was the victim. No one cared! It became apparent when a senior woman, called a "mother," planned a sleepover at her home. Surprisingly, she invited me. I was, as usual, the goofy one, acting silly and trying to make everyone laugh. I sat with a few others who saw themselves as outsiders as well. I then became the topic of discussion, and one by one, they would say some bad things about me. They were roasting me in front of everyone. The sad part was, I didn't get to laugh. What hurts the most was being betrayed by a person whom I believed to be a dear friend. Her desire to be part of the clique overruled her heart of friendship. To add insult to injury, when it was prayer time, it was unbelievable that she prayed to God, saying such negative things about me. It was as though she had invited God to a gossiping session. And once again, the one who I thought would set the right example said, "Yes, God, and amen." My elder participated in slaughtering me. I guess you might say I was the evening sacrifice.

After all the pounding, I began to believe the stories they had written about me with their voices and plastered them upon my soul. I believed that I was ugly, and no one, not even God, would ever value me, according to this religious group's actions. I began to believe that Christians were hateful and rude people. I believed that maybe I deserved rejection. I started to feel that perhaps I should be the one apologizing because I was the problem. Stacked on top of depression were the suicidal thoughts, but then anger sprouted; I became furious, and I acted out. Only the lonely would understand this! I would rather be at school than at church.

Have you ever paused to ponder why things are happening to you? Well, I began to take a good look back over my life. And I found some interesting things that had happened to me when I was between the ages of six and seven. I remembered spending the night over at a friend's house. She had an older sister who was around the age of twelve or thirteen. She told me she wanted to play a game with me; it was a game of touch. She touched me in my private areas and rubbed all over my body. I was in shock but too scared to tell anyone. Looking back, I realized that she had molested me. I then began to look at girls differently and question my identity, wondering if my attraction was to girls rather than boys; this birthed such confusion in me. Not long after this incident, another trusted soul introduced me to porn. I was attacked in my early formative years, from one attack to another, and many more were to come.

It became noticeable that I was not comfortable with church folks. At one point I attended camp with this group of people who did not like me, and the feeling was mutual. I didn't care anymore, and I would fight them, even knowing that I was embarrassing my parents. The leading group consisted of approximately fifteen people, and they were all sitting around in a circle. However, I was in a corner talking to a friend on the phone. I thought everyone would feel good about not having me bother them because I knew at least nine of the fifteen girls didn't like me. Suddenly, I heard someone say, "Let us address the elephant in the room!" Still, I thought nothing of it until I heard my name falling off someone's lips. Looking up, all I could see were fingers pointing at me. I was thinking about how I wasn't bothering them; why are they bothering me? Then begin the name-calling, Elisha this and Elisha that, and the beating continued. Once again, the adults stood silently by as if they were about to watch a heavyweight boxing match. The anger overcame me when my friend—at least, someone I thought was a friend—stood up and got in my face. I was sitting by an open window on the second or third floor, and the suicidal thoughts came rushing in, inviting me to jump. I wanted to die! She seemed to become emboldened and came even closer to my face. She was so close I could sense the warmth and smell of her breath, and then she did something I would describe as stupid. She clapped her hand loudly in my face, and that is when I blacked out. When I came to my senses, those adults who had stood around doing nothing were now holding me down. But I dealt with her, and needless to say, we were no longer friends after that encounter. But the truth be told, she was never my friend.

After this fight, the internal struggle of depression and suicidal thoughts were beginning to overcome me. It looked like they were going to win the war. No one was willing to hear my side of the story.

I am sure the adult input had something to do with that. The news hit the entire church, and my parents had to deal with the fallout. When I returned to school, I received the same reception. Once again, I had no voice. It was all bad. It was a sealed deal, I was the bad person, and all those I thought were my friends departed.

Rejected in despair, I went home with one thought on my mind: today, I will die. I hurried home. Once I arrived home, I rushed to check out every medicine cabinet to see what medications I could find to do the job. I found one. It was a pain killer, and I took a handful. They did nothing to me, and I didn't suffer any side effects from taking that many pills. I was so mad it didn't work. When I wasn't trying to kill myself, I almost did it; now I wanted to kill myself, and I couldn't. I wasn't trying to do a magic trick as I had with the quarters; no, this was an act to end all acts. This marked my first suicide attempt, and it appeared that the darkness was winning.

I wish I could say there were no more church youth camps for me, but there was one more I had to attend. Why? I do not know. But it was significant because it helped to shape my future. At this particular youth camp, once again, everyone was sitting in a circle sharing their stories. Adults, as usual, were part of the group. This time, I noticed something different. As the girls shared their stories, there was a great deal of compassion and empathy shown by everyone. I saw tears fall freely as each girl shared her story. It was impressive to me—so impressive that I thought maybe I could share my story of pain, and then they would understand my anger. I told them how depressed I was and that I had suicidal thoughts, and I expressed to them with tears and a broken heart how deep the darkness was. I was wrong again; I received nothing that resembled empathy and compassion. Instead, I received stares from everyone, including the adults. Someone even said I did too much and was being overly dramatic. I don't know how anyone could see depression and suicidal thoughts as a small matter. But that was because it was me, the angry girl. Not one adult followed up with me to see how I was doing. Their lack of care told me that I was not worthy of another human being's love.

But life doesn't slow down until it is over; it just keeps happening, and I kept getting older, but it wasn't getting any better for me. Once again, I was going through a transition; it was time for me to change to a brand-new school in a different part of town. I graduated from junior high and said hello to high school. I began to hang around the athletics teams. I played whatever sport in whatever season I could, from soccer to basketball to track and field. I submerged myself in sports because that was the one thing I was good at, and I didn't feel ugly while playing the game. I wouldn't dress up and did little to no self-care. Depression was beating down my door; it was my last defense, and it was determined to become my best friend. Fear and low self-esteem ruled me. I had met a dear friend in the eighth grade, and she transferred schools with me. I was at a new school and saw new people, but I was the same old me. I became goofier, showing up late for class, and I didn't care. The darkness was growing. I became a sports fanatic, and my attitude was off; it was ugly. I took everything personally, and because I was always angry, I was easily offended. I was still feeling unwanted, and my emotions dictated my mood. My teammates saw me as a person with an attitude. My coach and team members recognized me as the best player, but I never received any awards because of my bad attitude. There, I admitted it: I had a bad attitude!

Suddenly, something strange began to happen to me during the summer break. I, without warning or any preparation, developed a hunger to know God. I wanted to know this Jesus for myself, and just as I submerged myself into sports, I begin to immerse myself in spiritual things. I couldn't get enough of reading the Bible, fasting, praying, and watching religious shows. I started having what I would describe as nothing less than supernatural dreams because they were spiritual. One of those dreams occurred when I was in a deep sleep, and in it, I had just come home from school. While watching television, I saw a demon behind me, and I took off running, and it chased me. But my sister was there, and as it chased me, she chased it, and when she encountered it, she stood in front of me, covering me, and she rebuked that evil spirit, and it ran. She had authority over it. From this dream, I realized that the same power that had raised Jesus from the grave dwells within His believers, and I did not have to fear demons.

> But if the Spirit of Him who raised Jesus from the dead
> dwells in you, He who raised Christ from the dead will also
> give life to your mortal bodies through His Spirit who dwells
> in you. (Romans 8:11 NKJV)

You may be wondering if demons are real; I can assure you they are. Read the Bible. You will find them, and you will find Jesus casting them out. Amen! (See Mark 1:21–28; Luke 11:14–28.)

After the dream, I had an eagerness to know about the demonic. I read as many books as I could find on the subject and listened to teachers on the subject. Then another dream came. This time I was on the playground hidden in the forest with all my friends, and they were from every nation imaginable. They were the "all nations crew" in living color, and we played and chased each other throughout the forest. But there was a large island of mountains on the other side, which caught our attention. To get to the other side, we had to cross over a body of water, and a fallen tree was the only bridge to cross over.

As you know, trees are round and not flat, which could make this a rather scary attempt. But curiosity got the best of us, and we started to cross over. The water beneath us looked like jewelry, and the trees looked like pearls. Once we had crossed over, someone was leading the way for us on this exploration trip. I never saw him, but I heard someone say to us hurry because he was leaving us. What we were experiencing was indescribable beauty until one of the people with us summoned a demonic spirit, calling it by a name I had never heard before. And immediately, we were being sent back in a hurry. And the things that were once beautiful were becoming ugly. The greenest green grass that I had ever seen was turning brown. As we were crossing back over on the tree bridge, that beautiful water that once looked like jewelry had turned to black, hot lava. As I watched and listened, there were people in that lava, and they were screaming. I noticed a dark figure was blowing fire upon them, and I knew in my heart of hearts that this had to be hell. My friend got a little too close to the edge of the tree bridge and lost her grip; she started falling and screamed as she fell. I was so sad, and I looked up and backward, desiring to see the enormous, beautiful mountains, but instead—you guessed it—I saw a demon instead. This one looked as though he was once of royalty—you could tell; there was just something about him. I froze, and once again, I did not know my authority, and he was about to strike me, but before he could hit me, a cross appeared from out of nowhere. Once again, I was saved.

The dreams kept coming, and each one was building hope in my heart. Lastly, I had a dream that changed my life. In this dream, my love for art and astronomy was on display. It all began when someone ran into the house, screaming that Jesus had returned to get all the Christians. I thought that couldn't be, because Jesus would have taken me with him. Truthfully, that wouldn't have happened because, in the dream, my behavior was sinful. I remember repenting earnestly, knowing I had been left behind. When I went outdoors, hoping to catch a glimpse of Jesus, there was no regular sunlight, only a giant screen of bright yellow heavy fog like on a winter day.

Suddenly, I was flying high into the heavens, and I noticed a dark cloud moving toward me. I could see demons, and they were flying in rank formation like the military. One of them had a giant clock, and I could see the time; it was about to strike midnight. Suddenly, I was in New York City's Central Park, and it looked like World War III. There was the smell of sulfur. It was cloudy with no sun in sight, and the demons were reloading their weapons. Once again, God teleported me, and up to the stars I flew. It was so beautiful, and I was standing on golden sand flashing like diamonds. Looking back to the earth, I saw what looked like the kingdom of hell. I heard a voice—a familiar voice, the one I had heard when I was very young—and I knew it was God. He told me He wanted me to return to earth and to go and tell everyone about Him. It was the same way He had told His disciples in the Book of Matthew:

> *"Go therefore and make disciples of all the nations, baptizing them in the name of the Father and of the Son and of the Holy Spirit." (Matthew 28:19 NKJV)*

> *"But you shall receive power when the Holy Spirit has come upon you; and you shall be witnesses to Me in Jerusalem, and in all Judea and Samaria, and to the end of the earth." (Acts 1:8 NKJV)*

But I resisted and did not want to go; after all, demons had taken over planet Earth. It was a struggle, but I finally said "yes" to God.

When I did, I suddenly awoke in my bed, looking out my window at the trees, and the trees looked like diamonds, glistening before my eyes—unbelievable. But before I could blink, it was gone. Everything back to normal, and I was back on planet Earth.

This dream changed me because I started to make room for Him, and my spirit began to change. I became what I had heard others call a "Jesus freak," and I would tell everyone who would listen to me that Jesus loved them, and He was coming again. But my personality at home still needed some work. The attacks started to get heavy because I was seeking God, and I knew who I was. I was invited to a church by one of my teachers. I took him up on the offer and persuaded my twin brother to accompany me. Upon entering the doors of this new church, I couldn't believe what I saw and definitely couldn't believe what I felt. From the greeter at the door who made us feel like we belonged there to the youth I saw at the altar, crying and worshipping God, I had never witnessed anything like this. As a matter of fact, I had only experienced the opposite. I continued to attend every time I could, and I began to know and feel the love God had for me. I got more involved; I even started a Christian club on my school's campus that glorified God. By the eleventh grade, I had super friends, on and off the basketball court. They were faithful to God and the church, and they were loyal friends to me. They would always check on me when they didn't see me at church because I still had to go to my old church.

Having to go back to my old church after the summer break began to wear down my spirit, and I could feel the depression pressing upon me. I noticed the pattern. First, I would feel rejection, then depression would fall heavy upon me, and then the suicidal thoughts would come as though someone had open a floodgate. It was a cycle, and at this church, it was a recycle. I still had to attend all the youth events, including sleepovers, and experienced the same results. This whole church environment spelled one thing for me: REJECTION! I began to talk to one of the girls and was very candid. I began to tell her about the church I had visited over the summer. I told her how our church was full of hate; they had no love like the love I had experienced at the other church. She understood and thought I was to be the one to bring love to this church. Oh, no, that was too big a task for little me— little broken me. I was beginning to find the missing pieces when I was again thrust back into the madness. Although this girl and I had built a friendship, it was the wrong kind. When we would get together, we only spoke of pain. She told me what I had said about the church was true—another vindicating moment—but yet the church was stuck.

It was time for another summer break, but something had changed. I felt I could no longer defend my newfound freedom. This faith roller-coaster ride was exhausting. This time I went beyond my normal limits and became connected to the wrong crowd. My new acquaintances were druggies and consumers of alcohol in large quantities, and I joined right in. I would smoke a blunt by myself and not be affected. I did not get high, not even dizzy. A blunt is a cigar with all of the tobacco removed and replaced with marijuana, or in today's terminology, cannabis. I would drink alcohol directly from the bottle as if I was a pro—a better word would be alcoholic. I didn't know I was supposed to mix it with a soda or something, and you guessed it, I didn't get drunk. I couldn't escape my misery.

Once again, while in my lonely room, it was as though a tape recorder was on repeat playing in my head the song "let's get this over with," and I again contemplated suicide. I found a belt, looped it around the pole in my closet, which stood relatively high, and around my neck, and took the jump; once again, I couldn't even kill myself. The pole broke. I gave up that day on trying to die. I realized that the new church I had found did me good, and the youths were kind and didn't make me feel rejected. So I separated myself from the bad influences I had gathered and reached out to my new family. I got involved, stop being an introvert, began socializing with godly groups of people, and, wow! My life changed.

> *Therefore, if anyone is in Christ, he is a new creation; old things have passed away; behold, all things have become new. (2 Corinthians 5:17 NKJV)*

Amazingly, I found love inside a church—the last place I thought I would find it!

Life was sailing smoothly, and I was in a good space, emotionally and spiritually. Because we didn't own our home, we found ourselves moving more than we would have liked. Once again, a move was in the forecast. This time, we moved to a city where there weren't many Blacks, and this move happened in the middle of my senior year. That was not the time I wanted to start over, making new friends and getting acquainted with new teachers. I had noticed and experienced racism in a short time being at this new school. I thought all of these changes spelled only trouble for me. But, with my new attitude, I jumped in with both feet. I got involved with the Christian club at the new school. I visited a significant number of churches, trying to find one similar to the one I left. Did I say there was a lot of racism? There was, no exaggeration! For so long, I was it, the only Black in the classroom, and then one day, as I was walking around the campus, I saw a group of Blacks, and when they saw me, I am sure they read my face and knew I needed a connection. I thought I would be the only Black on this campus, and that would have been the making of a lonely movie. They invited me to join their group.

I finally adjusted to my new surroundings, my new community, and found I had stereotyped this community and placed everyone in the same basket. Some teachers were prejudiced, no doubt about it, but not all of them were. I scored and seemed to have found the ones who weren't. My teachers were all friendly to me, and maybe my contribution of having the right attitude made it a little easier for all of us. As a senior, writing essays is a part of life. I decided to write about not bowing down to stereotypes and how I was enough. I put my heart into this essay, and it paid off. I won an award for the best essay in the entire school, and waiting for me was a substantial scholarship in the amount of twenty-five hundred dollars. But the school district decided that my essay was so excellent that they doubled the scholarship. Imagine me, the girl identified by her anger and bad attitude, the girl whose attitude prevented her from receiving awards for her superb skills in sports, was now receiving a scholarship. To add icing to the cake, the valedictorian mentioned my name in his speech. He spoke of how they had never seen a new student fit in so well. I, the Black girl, was recognized by a majority white school that I had been afraid to attend. To top it off, I got plugged into a wonderful local church.

I graduated and chose to attend a local community college. I decided to start a Bible study at college. With this new attitude that God had blessed me with, it was a new lease on life, and I could not get enough of experiencing all the positive things that had passed me by for years while I suffered in silence. I became very busy, and I am not sure if I wasn't overdoing it, but I was like a kid in a candy store. My new church put together a missionary trip to Mexico, and I just had to go. I was spiritually prepared for this trip, and so was the rest of the group. My new community was unbelievable. We had learned about prophesy at our church and quickly applied it on this trip. We would pray and ask God what He wanted us to do and who He wanted us to encounter.

We asked for the details, and He gave us the details. As I prayed, God showed me an elderly lady wearing a purple scarf and a beautiful smile. And He showed me a man with his left arm in a brace and sling. Everyone else had similar experiences. We loaded on the bus, happy, and set off to where the people were. Once we entered the community, I was shocked to see the places where the people lived. I saw houses that had plastic bags as a roof. I realized I was a spoiled American. But then I saw what I could only describe as a miracle: I saw children creating their fun with the things they made. They built their joy, and their smiles and laughter were real. Did God confirm what He had told me earlier? Yes, He did. I met the elderly lady, and she was wearing the colors He had described to me, and we had a wonderful time together. It was a pleasure to pray for her and to see her smile become more distinct. Because our team was so large, we split up, and they returned to tell me that they had seen the man who had the brace and sling on his left arm, so they got to pray for him. God is faithful. I returned home from this trip with new joy!

I had a full-time job, but I wanted to work with children. I found an additional job as a behavior analyst, working one day a week. College was about to start within two weeks, and then I had the experience of my life, one I could have never imagined. I will always remember that day. It was August 19, 2019, and my world changed. In my room, I listened to a song titled "This Is a Move," one of my favorite songs by one of my favorite artists. I had just attended her concert a week prior, sitting on the front row while she sang that song to me.

I was happy and getting ready for my day. I turned on the shower and then realized I had forgotten something and ran back into the room. As I was running back into the room, everything started to spin, and suddenly I had a severe headache. I'd had a migraine two weeks prior, and it went away, so I thought maybe it was coming back to haunt me. As I told you before, I am goofy, and I started to say funny stuff to myself to keep myself calm. But the room, everything kept spinning as though I was on the worst carnival ride ever. Certainly, it was not normal, and I was doing everything I could to keep from falling. I miraculously saw my door, and it was slightly open—thank God, because had it been completely closed, there was no way I would have had the coordination to find the knob and open it. This was unusual because I always kept my door closed. I also realize that had I not run back into my room for something, this would have happened in the shower, and I don't think I would have made it out. Suddenly, I could see only images. I exited my room and walked down the hallway to my parents' bedroom. I could see the large desk that was sitting outside my parents' bedroom. I felt heavy, as though someone was pulling me downward; it felt demonic. I finally reached my parents' room, and my mom was still home, even though she wasn't supposed to be home on this day.

I pushed open the door that is usually locked, but it was not this time, and when I saw my mom's image, I tried to tell her to please pray for me, but my speech became slurred, and it sounded funny even to me. Then came the shaking and foaming from the mouth while making whirl-like body movements. I couldn't sit up, and the weight was still pulling me downward, and I felt my muscles losing strength. Suddenly, I became super cold, and I knew I was dying. My mom later told me that she tried to call 911 on her charged cell phone, but it froze, and the screen turned black. She couldn't get it to work, and it was the only phone she had. She then turned to her technical gadget that is continually playing her requested music, but this time, she requested it to call 911, and I guess it did because an ambulance showed up. Finally, the phone worked, and she called my grandmother, who lived remarkably close. She came over once she realized it was not a joke. This family plays so many tricks on each other that it can be hard to determine when we are serious. My mom went outside as the EMT worked on me; she was in a panic. The house felt tranquil to me; I felt I was dying, and I was at peace but still couldn't believe that my life was over at age twenty. Remember when I wanted to die? What a difference God had made in my life. And I was still goofy as I talked with God about this situation. Suddenly, I heard the song I was playing earlier, "This Is a Move," playing loudly. Then I knew I had more time on the clock. The EMT was asking me questions, and many I couldn't answer. I guess after observation, he realized something was seriously wrong, and that is when he shouted out to his partner, "Get her to the hospital ASAP," as he placed an oxygen mask on me—having the mask on felt like death. En route to the hospital, I was sweating so much that they could not put an IV in; the needle kept sliding out. Finally, they wrapped my arm in bandages to keep the IV in place.

What shocked me most was when I heard one of the EMTs say that he believed that I was faking it, but I could not respond to his lack of education and insensitivity. I hadn't eaten anything, and I begin to lose all muscle control and bladder control, and then had unstoppable vomiting. I blacked out, and when I regained consciousness, I was in the hospital. Then I blacked out again. When I came to, I heard medical personnel talking about a blood clot, and I blacked out again. The next thing I remember was seeing two doctors in my room, and I was fighting. I remember a hefty man laid on me, and I kept trying to tell him I couldn't breathe, but I couldn't talk. The more I struggle to breathe, the heavier he became. The fighting went on for a while. I have not ideal why I was fighting. But after things calmed down, they told me I had died three times, but they were able to jump-start my heart each time. Maybe, for once in my life, I was fighting to live. I heard one of the nurses comment on how young I was. I even saw one nurse with tears in her eyes when the doctor told my mom to call all the family because I would not make it. I blacked out again!

Unbeknownst to me, my church community was praying for me. Those young people who had gone on the missionary trip were backing me up in prayer. I was undergoing an MRI when I began to hallucinate and started to freak out. Once I was back in the room, the nurses kept saying, "Do not close your eyes." But I saw this one nurse who was standing next to my bed, who had blond hair and the most beautiful blue eyes, and I heard her say, "Elisha, close your eyes." They told me later that is when they lost me for the fourth time. I could hear what sounded like hundreds of birds singing, and I kept looking around, trying to find them, but I couldn't. I could only listen to them. I noticed the panic was gone, and I began to see clearly. There was a huge olive tree standing next to several big mountains. I could hear thunder—rolling thunder.

Then, I saw a massive wooden door covered with gold, and as I was about to open the door, I woke up. I was breathing through a breathing tube, and my family was all around my bed. Two thoughts were going through my head: either they are happy to see me alive, or I am about to die, and they are here to say goodbye. The doctors seemed to be still unsure what had happened to me, and that is when my mom spoke up and said, "It's a stroke!" The MRI had revealed a blood clot in my brain, and the doctor successfully removed it. He told us that he went directly to the blood clot for the first time in all his practice and removed it. He said that most of the time, the stem cells are so tangled that it takes a lot of effort to get to the clot. Not mine: he saw it and went straight to it. Nurses would come into my room and say they had seen many crazy things, but my story they would remember forever. I had no residual effect from the stroke. They kept me for a week for monitoring because they couldn't believe what they were seeing. The doctors, nurses, and others, even other patients, called me "the miracle girl"!

My church family community was very lively, sitting for hours at the hospital, according to the nurses. One of my community members stopped by on a day when I had a terrible headache. She prayed for me, and then she told me to lay hands on myself and pray. I did as she said, and I could feel the headache move from my head to my stomach. I hadn't eaten anything because they had me fasting, but suddenly, I vomited all over the room. It was like something you would see in an exorcist movie. It was on the walls, the doors, the bed, and the floor. My friend asked my parents if they believed in deliverance, and they said they did; she said, "It came out." When the doctor came into my room, he asked my friend and parents if they were Christian because he said he only sees this type of thing when Christians pray. He told us he was an atheist.

A week later, I left the hospital whole inside and out, naturally and spiritually. And there was a rebuilding of relationships within our family. Estranged family members became close—what a pleasant change. I suffered from mood swings because my energy level was still low, and my mom encouraged me one day to go for a walk with my friend. I think I overdid it and didn't have the energy to walk back home. I sat down and fell asleep as my friend watched over me. Because I had a headache, my parents took me to the ER, where they kept me overnight. For that evening, my nurse was the same nurse who had cared for me when I had the stroke. She told me about my being upset and fighting, and how she had tried to get me to calm down. I asked her about the blond nurse with the beautiful blue eyes, and she told me there was no such nurse. She said they didn't want me to close my eyes; they needed me to stay awake. I guess it was just another hallucination—or was it? The hospital discharged me with a clean bill of health. From the girl who wanted to die to the girl to whom God said, "LIVE!"

Because of the stroke and ongoing severe headaches, I had to quit my job and college. I could have chosen to see this as a short break for rehabilitation, but I didn't. I saw this as all negative, and I had no passion for attending church. That is when the depression and suicidal thoughts returned. My friends were all calling me and telling me about their lives and how well school was going for them; I don't think they even considered how I must have been feeling. Then, as always, God entered the picture and started painting an entirely new image on the canvas of my heart. I melt when I think of His love for me. He began to reveal and revert the adverse effects resulting from the negative experiences of my life.

Finally, I put away my pride and stubbornness, and I chose to listen to God. I started going back to church, and oh, did I hear God speak to me. The more I sought Him, the more He spoke to me. He picked apart those wrong, self-righteous thoughts in which I judged other people and things so harshly. I didn't understand they were wrong; I thought those were just evidence of me trying to live holy before Him. They were not. They were the things birthed in me from my religious experiences of people judging me and punishing me. Those experiences thwarted my way of thinking, and I became what I hated. Now, God was purging me, and He told me that this was a season for self-care, both spiritually and naturally. My alone time with Him was amazing because I would do things with just the two of us. Suddenly, He took an imbalanced life and balanced it. Today, I am free, not in words only but in deeds. He took away the depression and suicidal thoughts and replaced them with joy and life more abundantly.

> *Therefore if the Son (Jesus) makes you free, you shall be free indeed. (John 8:36 NKJV)*

> *The thief (the devil) does not come except to steal, and to kill, and to destroy. I (Jesus) have come that they may have life, and that they may have it more abundantly. (John 10:10 NKJV)*

Dear reader, if you haven't given Him a test run, I highly encouraged you to give Him a try by accepting Him into your life. How do you do that? Believe that God sent His Son, Jesus, into the world to die for your sins, confess that you are a sinner and accept Jesus as your savior, and then find you a good, Bible-believing church and attend regularly. If you think He didn't do you right, you are not a hostage!

> *… For God so loved the world that He gave His only begotten Son, that whoever believes in Him should not perish but have everlasting life. For God did not send His Son into the world to condemn the world, but that the world through Him might be saved. (John 3:16–17 NKJV)*

My Story

by Thelma Howard

My life is full! I would love to share more of my earlier days with you, but I am dying to share this burning story. It is the story about the day when I realized that I was no longer a drug addict, and I was no longer an unfit mother. It is about the day I became strangely aware of my value, and I knew I had passed from death to life.

I was blessed to be born into a family where both parents were present and actively involved in our lives. Mom was more vocal and present than dad, but our father was the backbone of our family. He loved us, all nine of us, even though he seldom said the word. My mom had a daughter from a previous relationship who added to the village. She came to live with us from Arkansas. My dad had two children from a prior relationship: a daughter, the oldest of the bunch, and a son. They both lived in a different city, not too far from us. Together, my mom and dad had six children in the home: four girls and two boys. Yes, it was a full house, and sometimes, a house full of chaos. I will not name names to protect the guilty. Sadly, my oldest sister, from my dad's previous relationship, was murdered. That hit us hard, but I think it hit my dad the hardest.

I was the baby of the family until my baby brother came along. I found him a little unusual; after all, I was only fifteen months old at the time of his birth. I also found something interesting about him: he was always chugging down a nice warm bottle of milk. I decided I would do some trading. When he was about six months old, I would trade a chicken drumstick or a piece of bread for his bottle. I knew I had to put something in his mouth to keep him quiet. Off I would run to hide and enjoy that nice warm bottle of milk. Then I would hide the bottle. I had to get rid of the evidence, you know! My mother would look all over the house for that bottle and never find it, so she would send one of the older children to the store to purchase another bottle. He would get to enjoy a few bottles of milk, but soon enough I would come to take the next one.

I had been hiding the bottles in an old mattress on our patio where we would play or lie on, enjoying the sun. There was a hole large enough for me to place a bottle inside. I would intend to return to finish it, but why bother with old milk when I could have a fresh bottle? Then, the day came for us to move, and I am sure I had stopped stealing his bottles by then. When my brother lifted the old mattress to move it, all the bottles fell out one by one, and I was busted. Everyone stood around laughing at the many baby bottles with old milk stains in them. The mystery of the missing bottles was solved. Everyone assumed it was me who had been placing chicken legs and bread in his bed, but they thought I was just sharing my love, not trading for milk bottles! To this day, my baby brother and I have a very close, sharing relationship.

Sailing through elementary and junior high, I found myself in high school before I could blink once and click my heels twice. I was extremely shy, and rather than eat with others in the cafeteria, I would grab my lunch and head out into the hallway to read a book while I ate alone. I wasn't a total loner; I had a very dear girlfriend, and she had recently begun dating. I was too shy to notice if a guy was trying to get my attention. We all hung out together and became close. Her boyfriend had a brother, and the rest is history. Amazingly, I observed that he noticed me, but he was just as shy as I was, if not more. But we finally clicked and connected! My mom, and especially my dad, embraced him and saw him as an upright young man. However, one evening, as he walked me to my sister's house, he pulled out a joint—a marijuana cigarette—and begin to smoke it. My parents would have changed their minds if they knew about that, but they didn't, and I didn't mention it. He and I continued to hang out until, eventually, I became pregnant. At the age of seventeen, I became a mother and gave birth to a beautiful baby girl. *I managed to graduate high school with a 3.5 grade point average.* I begin to smoke marijuana with him, and we were both later introduced to a more potent drug, crack cocaine. Association does bring assimilation, and we walked blindly into the abyss of drug addiction.

The saga began, but I didn't become addicted right away. It was a slow process until one day, I suppose I got the right dose of the chemical, because when I smoked that particular crack pipe, I knew something had drastically changed in my brain. The hunt was on, and I was being carried to and fro like the wind of a tornado, not knowing which direction I was going or where I would end up. The drug addiction was slowly but forcibly tearing me apart.

It is imperative that you, my readers, understand the invisible bars of drug abuse, and if you are that person who is a prisoner, know that there is hope, and there is freedom. I believe if you know the "why" more than the "what," you will be able, if you are held hostage by an addiction, to understand why your fight is so furious. As a family member or close friend, you probably have sat in the bleachers helplessly as you watch your loved one out on the field battling what seemed like an invisible enemy. I will assure you that although it is mostly invisible, the enemy is more real than real, and the effects are evident. It is like any pain: you can't see it, but you can see how one reacts to it, including yourself. You probably remember the commercial of the egg frying in the skillet, and it represented the brain being affected by drugs. That's serious! I noticed those addicted to cigarettes were quick to criticize those of us who were addicted to more potent drugs. I assure you, addiction is addiction, and death is usually the result of them all.

My life addicted to crack cocaine led to a life of imprisonment and took away my ability to commit to the children I bore in my own body. I became a full-blown crack addict, but I was also the mother of two children. I had a beautiful daughter born before my addiction, but I was on a slow crawl. I do not believe that marijuana was the gateway to me using more challenging drugs; I believe the gateway was the company I kept, desiring to fit in. Unfortunately, my son had to endure my drug abuse the entire time he was in the womb. It was by the grace of God that he was not born with extreme side effects. I prayed—or better, I begged God to help my baby because I couldn't help him. I couldn't help myself. My mother was praying, and God answered her prayers. The one issue he had was that his left eye was entirely out of focus, but surgery corrected that. The doctor did not associate it with drug use, and that made me feel better. I was an absent parent, even while in the house with my children. That was their worst side effect from my drug addiction.

Addiction is the name given to any habit that makes one a repeat customer, and I came back for more until my life was entirely out of control. I entered this lifestyle at the age of nineteen, still young and trying to find myself; instead, I lost myself. Imagine all the evil in the world and realizing that addiction takes the limit off, and there wasn't anything evil that I wasn't capable of doing. Stealing, lying, robbing people, and even prostituting myself became my new norm. The degradation is a trail of human misery of emotions, mental anguish, and enduring physical pain to get the next high. Once I got that high, it prepared me to repeat the drama, but it was also an anesthetic that induced insensitivity to my emotional pain. That is the street I lived on, Insensitivity Street, in the land of Nowhere.

Have you ever gone on the amusement ride where you stand against the wall, and it spins you around at a tremendous speed, and then the bottom drops out? That's terrifying! That is how I felt when I could no longer take care of my children; my life had bottomed out. My mom and dad had to become their temporary parents when my son was eight months old and my daughter was four. They were in good hands with them, but that was not the way it was supposed to be. It seems like my generation, and maybe the one before, was getting lost in the drug culture, and the babies born during this time had a fifty-fifty chance of surviving. And even if they survived, what would they become?

My parents took excellent care of my children, and after six months, I was able to get them back because I had found a place to live. A few years later, my mom became very ill and was diagnosed with colon cancer. She was sick, and the family was sick, knowing she was not well. In my flawed state, I would take care of my mom. I would never use crack cocaine when I was going to be with her. I would drink because my anxiety was high, and seeing my mom in pain was far too much for me to bear. But I had to be there; she needed to know that I, her baby girl, loved her. In all honesty, I needed to be there to receive the love she shared with me, and I believe every time she touched me, she whispered a prayer. God heard my mom's prayers because He answered her, and others have shared their stories of having my mom pray for them. She lost her battle with cancer at the young age of fifty-three. My dad and mom were a real couple, a fun couple, and we all knew they loved each other. It was sad that she died knowing I was addicted to drugs. But my mom died in hope. She believed God, and God did wonders in her life. It took our dad at least a year before he could part with her personal belongings. She was the best mom we could ever ask for and the most loving person you could ever meet. She was a Proverb 31 woman, and her children rosed up and called her "BLESSED"!

The children's dad and I called it quits and went our separate ways. It is hard for two drug addicts to make it together. The drug is more important than the other person; after all, I left my children for drugs. After a few years, our dad remarried, and somehow, in my addiction, I met a very nice guy who was stable, and we moved in together. He loved my children, and my children loved him. He took care of them and never once took them to my family when I was missing in action. He just hung in there. I later learned that his story was like the story I was writing for them. I was the pen being put to paper to write their sad tale. But he determined that they would have a better story. Along with my drug addiction came incarcerations—more than I would like to think about—but it seems to become a regular part of the experience. They were minor infractions that often landed me in jail but not prison, thank God!

Story break for just a little bit of education on the differences between crack cocaine and powder cocaine: What we learn from life is usually, in hindsight, 20/20 vision. Not only was I fighting an addiction, but unbeknownst to me, I was also fighting an unequal justice system. I was and am so glad I was never caught with a rock of cocaine on me since I have learned what it would have cost me. Had I been caught with five grams of rock cocaine, the sentence would have been up to five years in prison. Five grams is not large at all. But if my counterpart, a powder cocaine user, were caught, they would have to have 500 grams of powder cocaine to be sentenced to five years in prison. Why the disparity? Congress believed the information they received, and without vetting it, accepted the report that claimed that those who used rock cocaine were significantly more violent than those who used powder cocaine. The chemical differences in the drug are zero; it is the same drug. Powder cocaine becomes a rock when it is boiled in baking soda, made into a paste, and then rolled into tiny balls, whereas powder cocaine remains in its natural state. The user of powder cocaine snorts it, and the user of crack cocaine smokes it. By mixing cocaine with baking soda, it becomes a cheaper drug. You might say you are getting a little coke with your baking soda. Because it is more affordable, it appeals to people like me in the inner city or urban areas, whereas more white Americans and Latinos use powder cocaine.

Congress passed the Anti-Drug Abuse Act of 1986. This unequal punishment law remained the law, despite many attempts to have it changed, until 2010. Sadly, many who voted for the bill would not change their minds when confronted with the truth. Finally, in 2010, Congress finally passed what is called the Fair Sentencing Act 2010.

And then it happened again. While I was visiting a known drug house, I didn't realize it was under surveillance, and my number-one enemy as I saw it, an undercover police officer, approached me. Of course, he questioned me, starting with my name, and the rest is history. Once I gave him my name, the warrant when I did not complete my work project appeared. And that warrant landed me in jail to work off the five days. Why didn't I complete the five days? I was chasing my addiction, and my addiction was chasing me.

They designed jail cells to hold two inmates, but I guess reservations were short, and I had a cell all to myself. That was nice. But I promised myself that whoever came into my cell, I would treat them nicely. I wonder why I had to make that promise? And you are probably wondering that as well. Let's just say the streets have a way of changing your perspective, and to survive those streets, I had to wear a hard look, even if I wasn't hard. Sure enough, with each new cell partner I had, I treated them nicely. We kept our conversations generic and mostly spoke of the survival skills we needed to survive the street. Then it happened: guest number three entered the cell. She was very different in more ways than one. She kept reiterating to the officers that they had made a mistake and how she did not belong in jail. But she didn't have a choice; they believed that she did belong there. According to her, it was a paperwork mix-up that had caused this unfortunate situation for her. I started to believe her, but we all say that. As I said, there was something different about her. I had drawn a nude picture of a man on the wall, and as she was entering, I was erasing it. Strangely, her presence demanded respect.

She and I had transparent conversations, and I soon learned she knew some people who at one time were on the street with me; I hadn't seen them in a long time. She spent that night casually talking to me. But, on the second night, I became aware of her convictions. She was a born-again believer, and on this night, she read the Bible to me, prayed for me, and read the Bible some more. This cycle of reading the Bible and praying for me went on and on throughout the night. The next morning, they released her. I had promised to be nice to my cellmates, but not necessarily from my heart. Still, God had sent me an angel to show me true love. As the officer came to get her for release, I heard the officer say to her that she was right; she didn't belong in jail. She replied, "No, I was supposed to be here!"

The day after, it was my turn to be released. The first thing on my mind would normally be to donate blood to get a few dollars to buy alcohol and drugs. But this time, I told myself that I didn't want to drink alcohol because I knew it would trigger the craving for drugs. Instead, I headed straight to my parents' home. As usual, my dad was either gone fishing, in the garden, or maybe helping someone who needed help. That was my dad. This time, he was in the garden. He loved their garden, which was always full of vegetables. I surprised him, and I knew from the look in his eyes and the smile on his face, he was happy to see me. Dad carried a heavy heart for his girls, especially since someone had murdered his oldest daughter. My dad stood there with that smile in his eyes and on his face, and then he asked me, "Would you like to go to church tonight?" I said yes. It was September 1995, four years after I had said goodbye to my mom.

They were holding nightly services; it was called a revival. I was excited about going to church, and my stepmom had given me a dress and a pair of shoes to wear. On my way home from my parents' house, bringing the dress and shoes with me, I ran into an old friend who was my "get high" buddy. He never expected anything from me; we would get high and laugh together. He always had plenty of drugs. He invited me to get high and shoot the breeze as we always did, but somehow I found the power to say, "No, thank you! I am gonna go to church tonight." I went to church slightly nervous but excited, and I returned home a different person, inspired by God and filled with His presence. My dad knew my journey very well. He knew about addiction because he had been an alcoholic since I was a little girl. One day, my oldest sister on my mom's side had asked him to drop her off at church, and he did. He was always the dad that loved us all. He dropped her off and helped her take the baby and her bag into the church. But before he could escape back to his car, one of my sister's friends asked if they could pray for him, and he said yes. God changed him instantly, and that night, he left his alcohol bottle on the altar, never to drink alcohol again. He knew what I needed to break this addiction off me; he knew well.

I begin to wonder, Why now? What was so different now from any other time I had prayed to be free? Then I remembered the lady who prayed for me in the cell. She didn't pray with me, for I did not know how to pray, nor did I believe my prayers counted, but she prayed for me, doing for me what I could not do for myself. I remember so well her praying and asking God to give me a mind and a will to do His good pleasure. Wow!

For it is God who works in you both to will and to do for His good pleasure. (Philippians 2:13 NKJV)

She never preached to me or condemned me; she talked to me. She shared her testimony with me, and though she was not a prior drug addict, she made it clear that lost is lost and sin is sin. She encouraged me so much when she told me I could have a new life. I never thought I could ever be *free*! When I said my boyfriend and I walked blindly into the abyss, it is true. An abyss is an unfathomable deep or boundless space in the Bible, a Greek word meaning bottomless and boundless. That is where I was, in the land called Nowhere.

For God so loved the world that He gave His only begotten Son, that whoever believes in Him should not perish but have everlasting life. For God did not send His Son into the world to condemn the world, but that the world through Him might be saved. (John 3:16–17 NKJV)

I kept going back to church each night, and I received more and more of God's presence. It was His love that set me free; I never knew that God loved me so much. I kept in touch with that lady who prayed me through. I found out what happened to all those disappearing street friends; many of them had met her, given their lives to God, and attended her church. Even my children attended her church for Vacation Bible School. God did even more miracles in my life: He healed me mentally and emotionally. I was receiving Supplemental Security Income from Social Security because doctors had diagnosed me with mental illness. Drugs will make you mental. But suddenly, I was not the same; I had clarity of thought, and I was not suicidal or depressed. As a matter of fact, I had so much joy that I had trouble believing I could be so happy. I was always a jokester, but having joy is different. I asked my dad to take me to the Social Security Office to hand deliver my letter telling them thanks, but I no longer needed their services. That felt good!

Remember the boyfriend who took great care of my children? Well, he is now my husband and has been for twenty-four years. I am reconciled to my two beautiful children and have a bonus daughter from my husband's prior relationship. Together, we have one grandson who is in heaven and three beautiful, lively granddaughters. We are blessed! And the brother whose nice warm milk bottle I used to steal? I was able to share the Gospel with him, and he also accepted Jesus Christ as his Savior and Lord. He even became a licensed minister of the Gospel. My mother prayed, God listens, and then He answered. He is still answering her prayers. The joy is, I get to add to those prayers. God is good! Today, the old drug addict is a new creation in Christ, and I have maintained exceptional employment and am looking forward to retiring within a few years.

> *Jesus said, "I tell you most solemnly that anyone who chooses a life of sin is trapped in a dead-end life and is, in fact, a slave. A slave is a transient, who can't come and go at will. The Son (Jesus Christ), though, has an established position, the run of the house. So if the Son sets you free, you are free through and through. (John 8:34–36 Message)*

> *Therefore, if anyone is in Christ, he is a new creation; old things have passed away; behold, all things have become new. (2 Corinthians 5:17 NKJV)*

Indulge me again, just one more time, to say, "God is good!"

Trusting God through the Storms of Life

by Cindy Tyler-Costa

It was one of those sweltering California summer days in 1996, and I was sitting by the pool with my dear friend Tammy. We had been friends for a long time, and I genuinely enjoyed our friendship, but she was that religious kind of friend I could only take in small doses. She was preparing for Vacation Bible School, better known as VBS. She kindly asked me if my children could attend, and I respectfully declined. I declined because I was running from God and church folks. I wanted nothing to do with the church or its members; they only seemed to hurt me. Tammy knew how I felt because we had many conversations about this, but she faithfully and persistently pursued me, never giving up on me and showing me a different way to see God.

It was as though Tammy was serving a different God than the one others had displayed to me. She loved God with her whole heart. Her life wasn't perfect, but she always showed a firm trust in God no matter what she faced. I knew I wanted that, but I was afraid to seek it because I had experienced so much pain and hurt from the church with their boatloads of rules and regulations. I heard, I saw, and I experienced the constant condemnation, and I assumed that God was just like them and it would only be a matter of time before He, too, would become tired of me because I could not perform all the do's and don'ts that had been preached and demanded of me. I grew up going to church all my young life, but I found myself falling away from the church and God at fifteen. You know we tend to tie the two together. So, I ran away as fast as I could, desperately trying to escape the madness and determined to do things on my own. That is precisely what I did: I ran away, and I did it my way; after all, it was my thing now, and I can do what I wanna do. That was the absolute worst decision I ever made, but that is hindsight. I decided to leave the church and God because I saw the two as one. The condemnation was more than I could bear, and to keep my sanity, this was the right decision for me. Because of my lack of knowledge and experience, I did not know how to deal with this ocean called "the world," and at fifteen, I was now being flooded with a different kind of pain as I tried to navigate these troubled waters called life's experiences. I have heard it said that the ocean is so big that you can take a bucket of water out of it, and no one notices, and you can put a bucket of water in it, and it makes room. That is how the world is; it will make room for you and consume you, or it will spit you out, and no one will notice your absence. I failed miserably, and I opened doors for heartache after heartache.

After experiencing all the heartaches, when I was sixteen, a friend of mine invited me to his church, and I decided to try God again. But it didn't last very long; people kept blocking Him from my view. Once again, I began to experience rejection from the pastors, leaders, and church members because I appeared free-spirited; they didn't want me near their kids. So, I ran a second time, and this time, I was determined to never go back to church. I always believed that Jesus was God's son and that He was in my heart because I did love Him and desired in the depth of my heart to serve Him, but I always felt I wasn't good enough to be called His child. Because I wasn't a "good" person, how could He ever love me? I continually sinned against Him, so why would He want a relationship with me? I carried guilt and shame in my heart for years. I was a hot mess, as they would say. I needed a savior to rescue me, but I didn't have the faith it took to reach up to Him, and I couldn't bring myself to believe He was reaching down for me. I often pondered why Tammy was in my life; was God trying to tell me something? But I rejected her. Every time she talked about God or Jesus, I could feel my skin crawling, and this feeling of wanting to escape the conversation would intensify. There was even a point when I was willing to lose our relationship because I didn't want to hear what she had to say. But she never gave up on me. She loved me through my craziness, gave me space, and continued to ask me to give God another chance.

When I declined her offer to take my son to VBS that summer day, that soft voice reminded me of how much I had once loved VBS as a child and that I should allow my son to have that same experience. I reluctantly called her and said rather abruptly, "He can go with you; just don't ask me to go." I know she must have been rejoicing that I finally said yes. My son went and loved it. He loved it so much, he asked me if I would come to see his performance at the end of VBS.

Because of my love for my son, I agreed to attend. It was awesome, but I wasn't ready to surrender just yet. Then the pastor went onto the stage and said he felt like the kids needed to do their performance again on Sunday morning. Of course, my son asked me to come on Sunday to watch him. Oh, no, I didn't want to go, but I had to do this just for him, just for my son. What I didn't know was that this was a set up by God, and He was going to capture my heart that Sunday and change my life, and He did just that! Again, hindsight! On that day, at that time, at that altar, at that church, I saw God and not the church members for the very first time in my life. On that day, my view of Him wasn't blocked by others, by my emotions, or by the thoughts that I could not live up to His expectations—no, not on that day. On that day, I saw and experienced Him and knew without any conditions that He loved me! My life changed that day when God introduced mercy and grace to my soul. I have *not* been the same.

That was twenty-two years ago when I fully surrendered my life to God. My life was messy, my attitude was terrible, my marriage was awful, and I just really needed Him. My back was up against the wall—the right place for a divine encounter. The Lord surrounded me with godly women to love me through the messy moments of my life. They prayed for me, encouraged me, and begin to teach me how to love and trust the Lord with my whole heart. I had never received such love and support from church members before except for my dear friend Tammy. On the other side of my trying to navigate my troubled waters, God is now showing me who He is, and He is doing it through people. The ones I never trusted.

These women taught me how to build my life on that sure foundation, the solid rock, Jesus Christ Himself. They encouraged me to read the Word, which is the Bible, and seek to obey the Word. But even better, they taught me to trust God, Jesus, and the Holy Spirit,

21

and they would help me; I would never be alone. This was different from a boatload of rules and regulations; they taught me who I was in Christ and my value to Him. They taught me how to stand through the storms of life that would invade my peaceful shores and seek to steal my peace. They reminded me over and over again that when the storms come, I have an anchor. And that anchor was the promises that God had given me in His Word. These amazing women of God didn't have titles by their names; all they had was life experiences with God and lots of love. They trusted God with their whole hearts, and I saw how God had come through for each one of them. Little did I know that the struggles they had shared with me would become a part of my journey many years later.

They prepared me to handle the battles because these amazing women taught me how to trust God, pray, worship, study the Word, and stand on His promises regardless of how dark the situations became. They showed me that God would fight my battles and that He would never leave me. The Word tells us in the Gospel of Matthew 7:24–28 that the storms of life will come to us, but it also reminds us that there are two foundations: one that will withstand the storm and one that will not. A person with a deep foundation will trust God when life is confusing; they will rely on God's strength when they are weak, and they will run to God rather than away. What lessons I had come to learn; what faith I had received because of His love, and now I was on the right side of history—His story!

Shortly after I had recommitted my life and heart to the Lord, life tested my faith. I was at the epitome of happiness. I was so excited because I had scheduled my daughter Amber's dedication to the Lord, and I had invited my family to celebrate this special day with us. I had been praying that my brother would attend because he didn't come around much. I loved him so much, and it meant the world to me to have him, "Big Uncle," at his niece's very special occasion. I hesitated to ask and planned my words for impact. I told him how important this day was and how it would be etched in his niece's memory bank forever that her big uncle was there. He answered, and it felt as if my heart was going to explode when I heard the words come out of his mouth, "Yes, I will be there."

The Sunday before Amber's dedication, I was on edge with excitement picking out her dress and shoes and making sure everyone knew what to expect during the ceremony because nothing was going to spoil this special occasion. I talked to various family members and friends, made phone call after phone call, and as the day's activities were drawing to a close, the phone rang again. What was one more phone call? Well, this phone call changed my life forever. The person on the phone, without warning, informed me that my brother—yes, Big Uncle—had been shot. He and his friend were going fishing. While they were en route to their destination, they came to a stop sign, and of course, the driver did the right thing and stopped. That is when three young men pulled up alongside them and began randomly firing shots at my brother and his friend. They were sitting targets. My brother was shot and died several hours later. My heart broke into a million pieces. How could this be? Why, God, did You allow this to happen? Who does this kind of stuff? How, Lord, will I go on without my brother? It shook my faith, and I didn't understand.

My pastor came to the hospital to pray over my family and me. He encouraged me by sharing that even though I didn't understand, God had a plan, and I should trust Him through this. I decided that day that instead of running away from God, which was my usual practice, I would run to Him. The lessons those godly women had taught me came flooding into my mind, pulsating like a thousand heartbeats, and I learned that true faith shows up in the darkness. I decided to put my trust in God through this storm, and I would seek God for his direction, strength, comfort, and peace. I had always heard that He would give you peace that surpasses all understanding, so I prayed for that peace, and He gave it to me.

I remember sitting on my mom's back porch the day they brought my brother's truck home, and fear and anxiety gripped everyone, yet I was sitting there in complete peace. I knew that kind of peace only came from God. That dreadful day finally came to bury my brother. Later that evening—news flash—there was another shooting of eight people. A young girl had lost her life, and seven others had their lives changed forever on that day. Our city was rocking with fear, confusion, and panic. No one understood what had happened and how this could have happened in our small country town. One of the victims identified the shooters and their vehicle; it was the same description that my brother had given prior to his passing. Because of a young lady's heroic effort and her determination to get up after being shot, she was able to provide the authorities with the information they needed to find and arrest the boys who had committed these crimes. None of the victims had known each other; these were random acts of gang violence. When the killings occurred, my first thought was that these killings were gang-related, but I didn't even know we had gangs in our city. I grew up in a small town and thought that everyone loved each other.

In this one week of my life, there were storms after storms. I knew that the only way I could get through all this was to rely on God and His strength. As information began to come out, my heart broke again because I heard these boys had grown up in Christian homes and had lost their way. Events had happened to them that caused them to run from God and to seek love from all the wrong places. I remembered what that was like, and I remembered that I once ran far away from God and did things that didn't make me feel proud but ashamed.

But thanks be to God; He carved out a way for me to come back to Him. He forgave me for the sins that I committed, and He taught me to forgive myself and others. I asked God for the strength to forgive these boys—forgive them for taking my brother's life and the memories that I would never get to share with my brother. Once again, God gave me the power to forgive. My brother was amazing; he loved everyone, and I knew that he would want me to forgive, love, and go on with my life. I never struggled with forgiveness, hate, or anger toward the boys who did this. However, I allowed God to use me to bring hope and healing to other kids struggling like these boys.

I served on our church outreach team for several years by bringing food, hope, love, and God to the neighborhoods that were stricken by poverty, drugs, and gangs. I watched God do supernatural things on those streets and in His people. God taught me how to forgive and love again through that storm. He taught me that life would bring storms of disappointments and failures, but no matter what I faced, He was there, and He would get me through. That storm in my life was just the beginning of many more to come, but I had learned to put my faith and trust in Christ, the solid rock, and even though the storms would come, I would stand and not fall.

Many years after this, God reminded me of how He got me through that storm. He had been so faithful, and He carried me through times when I didn't think I would make it.

It wasn't long before there was another storm in my life that shook my faith. We will call this storm "Hurricane Brittany." I had just found out that I was pregnant again. This would be our third pregnancy, and we were having another baby girl! There was excitement in the air, and joy filled our hearts. However, at twenty-two weeks, I began to have some complications and was put on complete bed rest. I was a highly active person who loved to be on the go, but my life had just come to a full, abrupt stop. I was a mother of three, and at that time, my husband was on active military duty, which meant he was gone for long periods and to undisclosed locations, which made it far worse without communication.

This was by no means a great time to be bedridden, not that it is tolerable under any circumstance. I didn't know how we would get through this storm. But I did know that somehow God would help us navigate the rough waters. There were days when I felt the waves of discouragement, anxiety, and fear crashing over me. I worried about losing my baby girl or what would happen to her if she was born too early. I didn't know what to do, but I did know who to turn to. I knew that God would give me the strength to get me through this, and He did just that. My baby girl did make her entrance into this world early. She was born at thirty-four weeks, and she was tiny but fierce. The doctors told us that our premature baby girl's lungs did not fully develop, and this would cause her problems for the rest of her life; however, we knew we served a mighty God. We knew that He was the Great Physician, and although we respected our doctors' and specialists' opinions, we trusted God and His plan for our baby girl. We decided to stand on His Word, and we would never give up praying for healing for our little Brittany.

The first four years of Brittany's life were a struggle. She struggled to breathe every night, and she couldn't do the things that her sisters and friends could do because she was a chronic asthmatic. Even though Brittany had daily asthmatic attacks, we continued to stand and pray that God would heal her. When she reached four, her pulmonologist gave us more bad news. This day was different for me; I couldn't accept, anywhere in my being, what he was telling me. I knew that God had a plan for her life; I knew that I had been standing and believing for a miracle for her life, and I just knew that this wasn't how her story was going to end. I walked out of the doctor's office with a bag of medications, and as I was walking to my car, I was yelling at God, "I can't do this; I thought You were going to heal her, why haven't You done something by now? I trusted You! You said You would never leave me, but I'm feeling like You are nowhere near." I remember driving home that day broken.

That night, I was preparing dinner at our home for my pastor and his family. While all the kids were outside playing, Brittany went into a full asthmatic attack. She couldn't breathe, and we were about to call 911 when suddenly my pastor grabbed her and started praying over her, and immediately she began to breathe again. I noticed that something was different; usually, it took her a while to feel normal, but this time little Brittany got up and ran back outside to play. She played for hours and didn't have any issues. Usually, in the middle of the night, Brittany would have breathing-related issues, but she slept through the night that night. I began to notice that she was sleeping every night with no problems. As she ran around with her sisters and friends, I observed that she didn't have any asthmatic issues. I took her back to the doctor, and the doctor said to me, "I can't explain what has happened. Brittany's lungs are completely normal, and she can do whatever she wants to do." I knew at that moment that God had healed her. God had answered my prayers. He was the Healer, and He did what He said He would do. During those four years of patiently waiting on the Lord to heal my daughter, I would remember the spiritual grandmothers who had taught me to stand on His Word and never to give up. God allowed us to go through that storm to teach me to stand on His Word. He stretched me, and I learned how to rely on Him and put my trust in His promises. God knew that we would go through many more storms with Brittany and her health, and He taught us that we could trust Him.

Amazingly, God used a real storm to teach me how to trust Him. My husband and I had set out with our pastor's friend to pick up a boat he had purchased and bring it back. It was going to be a nice boat ride home. As we were preparing to leave, the mariner informed us that a hurricane was heading our way, although it was still far out. We knew we needed to get this boat home onto the safe ground before the storm hit. We checked the weather forecast; it was supposed to be a clear and beautiful evening. So, we set sail on our journey. It was approximately a two-hour boat ride up the Gulf of Mexico. About an hour into our boat venture, we began to hear the sound of thunder and see flashing lightning, and it started to rain heavily.

All these were terrible signs, especially out in the ocean. The weather had changed, which is typical for Florida. We were approaching the deep-water channel and the storm simultaneously. To say the least, this was about to become a very bumpy ride. We were in a twenty-eight-foot fishing boat and getting tossed about in those waters as though we were weightless. Fear set in, and I thought that we were going to flip over in shark-infested water. I was afraid that I would never see my children again. I had never experienced anything like what we were experiencing. It was the feeling of the possibility of imminent death, maybe even a drawn-out, painful one. I remembered all the promises that God had made to me still to come to pass. I started praying fervently and earnestly, reminding Him of all those promises and how I trusted Him. I spent forty-five minutes crying out to God, praying, and begging Him to stop the storm. Suddenly, the waves stopped, the waters became smooth, and we were at our destination. God taught me how to trust Him in a literal storm, and I knew if He could get me out of that ocean, He could do anything. My experience reminded me of the time in the Bible when Jesus and His disciple experienced a storm.

*On the same day, when evening had come, He said to them,
"Let us cross over to the other side." Now when they had
left the multitude, they took Him along in the boat as He
was. And other little boats were also with Him. And a great
windstorm arose, and the waves beat into the boat, so that
it was already filling. But He was in the stern, asleep on a
pillow. And they awoke Him and said to Him, "Teacher, do
You not care that we are perishing?"*

*Then He arose and rebuked the wind, and said to the sea,
"Peace, be still!" And the wind ceased and there was a great
calm. But He said to them, "Why are you so fearful? How is
it that you have no faith?" And they feared exceedingly, and
said to one another, "Who can this be, that even the wind
and the sea obey Him!" (Mark 4:35-41 NKJV)*

A few years later, the winds begin to blow again with Brittany,
and we could sense that another storm was on its way. Brittany was
now six years old, and she was so excited that her favorite band was
coming to our church. She had patiently waited months for them;
suddenly, a few days before their arrival, Brittany began experiencing
nausea, pain in her stomach, and high fevers. After spending several
days in and out of the emergency room, Brittany was diagnosed with
appendicitis and needed emergency surgery. Yes, literally just moments
before her favorite band was to perform, the medical team was wheel-
ing her off for surgery. But, once again, God showed her how faithful
He is. The band had heard all about Brittany, so they called her and
prayed over her. That was a day she will always remember. Brittany
went off to surgery. After a few hours, the doctors came out and told us
that they had experienced some complications during the operation.

They had to make an incision across Brittany's entire abdomen to remove her appendix. They were hoping for a smooth recovery, and they shared that it would take time to heal, and there could be some complications due to the type of surgery she had undergone. Brittany was doing great, but just a few hours before they were going to release her, she began to have internal hemorrhaging, another emergency. Everything happened so fast; we didn't have time to prepare for the storm. We didn't see it coming because it came so quickly. There was no forecast during my morning prayer or Scripture reading. We didn't have any answers, and they didn't know why she was hemorrhaging or where. It was like a tornado had just come through and left destruction and debris strung out all over our lives.

While we were trying to pick up the pieces of our lives, I was also trying to remind myself that God had a plan. I told myself that God had saved Brittany once before, and He would do it again. I saw and watched my baby girl lying there in pain, and I would try to comfort her, but nothing would soothe her; she was scared, gripped with fear and anxiety. I would pray over her, sing His praise, quote scriptures over her, but nothing seemed to work. I tried walking the hallways to get a break and refocus on God, but when I would walk up and down the halls, I would see other moms who had just gotten bad news, and there was brokenness everywhere. There was no peace, hope, or joy in that hospital. Anger, despair, hopelessness, and confusion filled the air. I knew that the only reason I could get through each day was that I had Christ in my life. I knew that no matter what we were facing, I could still place my trust in Him, and I began to realize that others didn't have that hope. If that wasn't enough, Brittany became upset; it looked like we would be celebrating her seventh birthday in the hospital. The night before her birthday, I sat on the end of her bed, and I cried out to the Lord, "Lord if you will heal my daughter again, I promise you that I will do whatever it takes to bring hope to the hopeless inside these hospitals." I didn't have a plan on how I would do that; I was just desperate for God to heal my daughter, and at the same time, the hopelessness I experienced in the eyes of other mothers had gripped my heart. The next day was Brittany's seventh birthday, and when we woke up that morning, we noticed that the gastrointestinal bleeding had stopped entirely. Once again, doctors were confused, so they did more blood work, only to find that her numbers were completely normal. The doctor asked Brittany to eat, drink, and play, which she hadn't done in five days. She did it all, and there was no sign of a bleed, so they discharged Brittany that day. As we were walking to our car, I remembered the promise that I made to God sitting on the edge of her bed, that I would find a way to bring hope to the hopeless inside the walls of hospitals.

After Brittany and I got home, I began to pray and ask God how I could make an impact and bring *hope* to these amazing moms and families. I was currently the women's pastor at my church, and I had a fantastic team of women who helped me. I was a firm believer that God had a plan for my life and their lives. I recalled that I loved it when my husband would come to the hospital to relieve me every night for dinner; I could go to the cafeteria and sit in quietness. It was a time for me to refocus and get prepared for what was to come next. So, I contacted the Child Life Program at the children's hospital; they had been an essential part of our stay while we were there. They offered daily craft and art activities, games, and visits from the hospital's dog. I spoke to the director to share my passion for bringing *hope* to the moms and families. I didn't know what to do or where to start, so I started with what was most important to me: food and quiet time. I asked if our group of ladies could bring a home-cooked meal to the families twice a month. After many months of hospital approvals and board approvals, they finally approved our group to bring in home-cooked meals. We served the parents and families of the pediatric and Neonatal Intensive Care Unit (NICU) every other week for ten years. Over the years, we grew from just making home-cooked meals to making scented dolls, beanies, and prayer blankets. We would sit and talk to the families and share *hope* with them. We celebrated every victory, and we mourned every loss of a child.

After ten years of serving at the children's hospital, things changed, and we were no longer allowed to bring a home-cooked meal for the families, but I knew God still had a plan. The hospital staff asked me to volunteer as a Child Life Volunteer. This position allowed me to be the one who would do arts and crafts with the children. However, there was one problem: I couldn't draw a straight line, and I knew nothing about art or crafts. I chose to trust God and His plan, and I knew that He would lead and guide me to where He wanted me to go. Shortly after I started doing arts and crafts with the children, I began to see how art brought *hope* and healing. It was a tool for the children to express what they were experiencing from the inside out. I saw how art brought families together; I heard laughter from those who were once sad, and I saw families restored. I asked God again, "How can I make an impact in the lives of your children?" That is when All About Hope, my nonprofit organization, was birthed in 2016. All About Hope gives hospitalized children and their families the tools they need to dream beyond their hospital bed by providing "hope" boxes filled with art supplies.

No matter what I face, the night that we were in the ocean in a twenty-eight-foot boat, tossed around like a ragdoll during a severe storm, reminds me to this day: *I can stand.* It was there I learned that my life's foundation is solid, and that foundation is Jesus Christ. The winds and the rains will come, but I will not tip over nor sink. I have faced many storms that God has allowed in my life. I have suffered the death of my beloved brother, my wonderful father, and both grandparents, my children's health, financial issues, my health, marriage, prodigal children, family issues, relationship issues, and work-related issues. But no matter how heavy the rain and intense the wind, God was there for me, and He did not let me sink. He didn't even allow me to leak. He gave me the strength to get through it; He healed me, delivered me, and restored me.

Yes, storms will come, and they will go, and some will be worse than others. But no matter what, I have this hope that He will always be with me. Philippians 4:6–7 NKJV is the scripture I have held onto over and over again:

> *Be anxious for nothing, but in everything by prayer and supplication, with thanksgiving, let your requests be made known to God; and the peace of God, which surpasses all understanding, will guard your hearts and minds through Christ Jesus.*

Today, God and I, along with the great team He has given me, share this great *hope* with the hopeless; after all, it is All About HOPE!

Feel free to go on my website and see the miracle unfold: https://www.allabouthope.net/.

Untitled

by Doral Valley

For as long as I can remember, I have struggled with my identity. My crisis was my identity. First it was not knowing who I was. Then, once I thought I knew who I was, it became my crisis. One definition of the word "crisis" is a time of intense difficulty, trouble, or danger. But for me, the second definition is more appropriate, which says it is the turning point of a disease when an important change takes place, indicating either recovery or death. I will tell you later why this definition defines me best. There is no person alive, or who has ever lived, who does not or did not ever wonder, "Who am I, and why am I here?" Well, that's me. Identity has always been my hang-up. And it hasn't been only about the "who" but also about the "why." My identity is not bound in those simple things: my name, parents' names, gender, and who my siblings are. No, it is bound up in so much more.

I think the million-dollar question is, Why am I here? Not knowing one's purpose—well, that's a crisis. It was for me, and probably for you as well.

Who, God, am I? And why, God, did you create me?

Growing up, I always related to others. I seemed to understand them and their points of view, but I never had anyone who could honestly understand and relate to me. Maybe I gave others what I needed most, a listening ear and an understanding heart, and felt jaded that I never received the same. Simply put, I didn't feel anyone took the time to understand me—to care and relate to me as I desperately needed. There was no one. Many people, mostly adults, recognized my maturity and my high level of intelligence. Still, I could never find a companion to converse with about my deepest desires and to challenge me to grow them. Growing up, I felt alone and different. I would constantly ponder the big "who and what" questions. I use the word "constantly" not to exaggerate but speak to the state of turmoil wherein I found myself. And I didn't only ponder about my existence, but about humankind as a whole. Why were we all here?

During my formative years, in my mind, I was *always* a victim. Here I go again, using words that appear infinite, with no end. I am the middle child of six, born to teenage parents, and allegedly, there is a middle child syndrome. Teenage parenting has high-risk factors. More often than not, drugs and alcohol are involved, and emotional issues such as depression and poverty hang as backdrops. With that in mind, imagine the risk factors for the unborn. I was my mother's third child at age nineteen. I understood that my father had severe alcohol problems, possibly before I was born, but I witnessed him as a full-blown drug addict, addicted to crack cocaine from my early childhood.

Family members believed that my dad spiraled into a state of madness with alcohol and drug abuse when my younger sister, at the age of three, suddenly died. That was the straw that broke the camel's back—my dad's back. I was four at the time of her death. We lived in the most poverty-stricken city in Northern California, which at the time also had the highest crime rate. We were poor, on welfare, and my mom was always out of the home, working hard doing several odd jobs to take care of us. She would work day and night, and my dad was in and out of the home, smoking crack and drinking. As soon as our mom would come home beyond tired, he would come home just to fight with her and steal from us the money to fund his crack habit. Drug addicts do what drug addicts do.

My mother's mom lived with us. Grandmother was a very stubborn and religious woman. Her faith seemed to be the cause of her being so harsh, judgmental, and overbearing. I learned to be scared of God because of how she would define God's character, as though He had a hammer and was on the search for bad people. She made it seemed as though God found great pleasure in casting them into hell fire. Yes, I was scared of God, and I was scared of her. I often wondered, if He was such a good God, why was this world and my life so messed up? I began to think that maybe all of my problems came from Him. I saw Jesus in a softer light because they taught us that He was a Savior, but God, whom they called "the Father"? I thought God was a scary, harsh, and abusive father.

While my young mind was in a state of confusion, trying to process the dysfunction in my home, along came another crisis. Soon after I turned thirteen, I was "taken advantage of" by someone much older than me and not necessarily a stranger. Some may call it rape, but I don't remember what I called it at the time. All I know is, I had just stepped into my teenage years, and what is common in most adolescent girls' headspace happened to me, and I found myself having a crush on an older guy. He was eighteen, a legal adult. He was a friend of a very close family friend who often visited our home, and he would come along with him. They would visit almost daily, and sometimes he would spend the night. It is the primary MO—modus operandi— the older guy who comes over to hang out with the older kids and, at the same time, eyeballs the younger girls. Well, long story short, one late, late night, I allowed myself to be in a place I was not supposed to be, which resulted in me being in bed with him. So, as they say, one thing led to another. The kiss truly smote my flesh, but I honestly did not want to do what he started doing. Although I said and kept saying "no," the shame and fear of being caught kept me from making a scene. I took pride in being a virgin. People viewed my body as fully developed, but I was a child in age and mind. I had also observed older girls around me who had lost their virginity, and I saw it as shameful. I did not want to lose my virginity until I was married.

After it was over, I had to come to terms with what had happened. I told myself that just because I liked him and his kiss, and I allowed myself to be alone with him in a forbidden place, it doesn't mean what he did was okay. Just because I was not as forceful as I could have been does not mean it was my fault or that I wanted this. I gathered the nerve to tell my best friend. She told me to tell someone because it was wrong. But I was ashamed. I eventually told one of my teachers a week or so later because I started itching terribly in my vaginal area, and I did not know why or what to do. I felt close to her, and I thought she would keep my secret. It turns out he had given me genital warts. Imagine me, a thirteen-year-old girl, with a sexually transmitted disease. But because teachers are mandated reporters, the cat was out of the bag when I told her. And my family and his family and our family friend's family all went to war. Everyone was skeptical of each other and questioned if it had happened.

Once the evidence was in and the proof validated that it did happen, they became judge and jury, standing in judgment and deciding who was to blame. However, legally speaking, he was an adult, and I was a minor who could not give legal consent; therefore, the law would say it was the rape of a minor—statutory rape. The definition of statutory rape is engaging in sexual intercourse with an individual under eighteen years of age at the time of intercourse. Statutory rape is a crime regardless of whether the sex was consensual or allowed by the minor. The rumor was that the jury had found me guilty because of flirtation. If I had not been flirting with this grown man, this would not have happened. Then they judged me and sentenced me to a life of guilt and shame, labeled a flirt and possibly promiscuous, and treated much harsher than the rapist. Imagine that: they decided that the standard of conduct was to be set higher for the thirteen-year-old girl and lower for the adult male. And we wonder why these things happen.

It didn't take long for me to lose my convictions, my sense of right and wrong, and begin to believe that fornication was *not* wrong. I no longer cared about virginity, purity, or saving myself for marriage; all hope had left me. If the mind is to protect itself, sometimes it adjusts to the condition. With my conscience somewhat cleared now that I had redefined fornication, it wasn't long before I was sneaking out, lying, dressing provocatively, and willingly having sex. If this was the beginning of adolescence for me with the hope of becoming an adult, the question banging around in my head was, will I make it there intact?

The adult jurors, judges, and executioners had rendered their decision. I accepted it and began to see myself just as they had treated me. The hope of being a good girl was gone, stolen in the night, except many adults were saying I gave it away. Eventually, just before turning fourteen, I ran away because it was too much to bear. In my heart, I blamed God, and I accused Him of forsaking me. By then, I was promiscuous, thinking I could be in a sexual relationship, and believed that a particular guy would love, support, and take good care of me. I was delusional; he lied, cheated, emotionally and physically abused me, neglected and abandoned me, and last but not least, he transmitted sexual diseases to me numerous times. I was taken advantage of in many ways, more than I can count. He harassed me. His sister and his brother's baby mama harassed me, insisting that I babysit, cook, and keep the house clean. I was a real Cinderella living in a house with my worst enemies. His brothers and so-called friends would try to manipulate me for sexual favors. My freedom was in jeopardy by associating with these individuals, who were involved in gang violence, petty crimes, and drug trafficking. Somehow, I thought I was, or would be, accepted, but eventually, I realized that these people would never recognize my value and love me. It was shame and disappointment that drove me to run away initially, but it was shame and regret that was driving me back home.

At the age of fifteen, I decided to leave the streets, those people, and that life and return home because I knew that life wasn't me, and it wasn't for me. The lies told to me and believed by me tried to bury my understanding of what was right and wrong. It wasn't working for me anymore, and everything about it seemed wrong. Going home meant moving to Texas because my mom had relocated there. It served me well being far away from those I had known. I was able to make new friends, meet new people, and see and do new things. It was a great way to start over. I did graduate from high school. I finished one year early, even though I started a year behind. I pushed myself to erase my past and welcome a new life. I graduated with honors, awards, and scholarships.

However, although my life was somewhat on track, my spirit felt broken in a thousand pieces, and I didn't know how to fix my inside. So yet again, I went looking for love in all the wrong places. Cycles after cycles. Immediately after high school, I got into another relationship, and soon afterward, I got pregnant. I prematurely delivered a baby girl at twenty weeks, about a month shy of my eighteenth birthday. I named her Jasmine Andrea Mari, and she died in my arms after a few hours on this earth. My life became horrible. This pain was a new kind of pain, the kind that reached into the depth of my soul. It was a loss undefinable for such an immature mind as mine. Teenage parenting carries with it lots of risk factors. I didn't see myself recovering from this significant loss. I was numb, and again, I felt like a victim ten times over, so unfortunate.

The father of the baby, my boyfriend, began drinking heavily and snorting cocaine—the street name is coke. I tried snorting with him a couple of times, but it didn't ease my pain. I was never really in love with him. I cared for him, and he was always extremely kind to me. He had expressed that he was deeply in love with me, and after years of knowing him and being pursued by him, I had finally said yes to us dating, and then came the baby. My mom liked him a lot, so maybe it wasn't so bad being with someone who had her stamp of approval. She never cared for any of the guys I had previously dated. She had every right not to like any of them because they were poor choices. This guy adored me and treated me well, and with that, I thought I could learn to love him and be as fond of him as he was of me. We talked about marriage, buying a home and doing things for keeps, but I wanted nothing to do with Texas after losing the baby. I had always planned to move back to California and had only stayed in Texas because of our relationship. I told him he could come with me, but I didn't care either way. I firmly set my mind to leave, and if he chose to stay in Texas, he was telling me that he had decided for us to be friends only. He stayed behind, and to this day, over twenty years later, we have not been in touch.

Not long after moving back to California, I got into another relationship. This relationship lasted maybe six years. However, after being in this new relationship for a year, I was pregnant again. A few months into the pregnancy, the physical abuse started. I was the only one working. I had a car, a bank account, and was paying bills, while he enjoyed the benefits. It seemed that my mental and emotional immaturity from thirteen was becoming my lifelong issue. I continued making bad decisions without a thought; I had zero critical thought process.

In contrast, I had some things in place to create success, and my boyfriend—well, he was a drug dealer, and I later learned he was also a drug user. He was pimping, pandering, lying, and cheating. He would leave and be gone sometimes for days with my car, which prevented me from going to work. Other times, he would return late, causing me to be late for work. Early in our relationship, he totaled two of my vehicles. I would break up with him, then take him back time and time again; you may know that cycle of dysfunction. By the time our oldest child was six and our youngest was five, I knew in my head that I was tired and ready for a change. I needed him out of my life. My head and heart couldn't agree, but I was beginning to think out loud.

The last time I kicked him out and refused to take him back was just after he had introduced me to one of his drugs of choice, meth. I was already a daily weed smoker, and occasionally I would drink. More than a few times, with a few friends, I had taken ecstasy pills when out clubbing and socializing. I later begin using meth with a cousin of mine, and when my ex was finally out of the home and my life, I started using it more often. I was depressed and had too much time on my hands. Before our last breakup, he had caused me to lose my job of almost five years, thrusting me into unemployment and unable to take care of my children. I was in between jobs and severely depressed.

One day he came by to visit our girls, but they weren't home. A friend and I were in the house coming down from a drug-induced high after a long night of using meth. She fell asleep. After he told me he only wanted to talk to me, I foolishly let him in. I went upstairs to do something—I forget what it was, because my brain was still foggy and I felt tired. I sat down for a minute and passed out. Suddenly, I felt a sharp object at my throat that awakened me. To my horror, he was standing over me with a knife to my throat. The look in his eyes told me he was very serious. He told me not to say a word or he would stab me. I saw desperation and death in his eyes. He led me downstairs and out the door to the car, quietly threatening me again while forcing me to get on the floor in the back, and strictly warned me not to look up. I remember being so tired from the meth that I kept falling in and out of sleep. I remember him waking me, telling me to give him my PIN to my bank account. It was apparent now that he had brought my purse along with us and expected me to fund this trip that he was taking us on. As I floated in and out of consciousness, the "D" question was swirling around in my head. Was I going to die and never see my children or family again? The thought of death was beyond scary!

I did not know what time it was or how much time had gone by. I could see it was dark, and from what I could comprehend, we were on a long stretch of highway. I was then allowed to sit up in the seat since it was dark. At one point, I saw a sign that said we were just miles from Los Angeles, California. He pulled up to a motel where he threatened again to hurt me and said that I would never see my girls again if I resisted or tried to run. He checked us into a motel, and there he raped me. In his head, he had convinced himself that we were getting back together. He wanted me to promise him I would never leave him again and to swear to him that I belonged to him and him alone. I am sure I said everything he wanted to hear when I was conscious. But I was in and out of consciousness for days, a deep sleep induced by the meth. Then I was awakened in the motel to him tossing clothes my way, shouting orders at me to get up, shower, shave, and get dressed. He said if I was going to act like a whore with other guys, then I might as well get paid for it. It was clear that he planned to prostitute me. He kept asking me to promise I would never leave him, but this was not about love; he was trying to establish ownership. I was being branded in my mind as an animal to show whose property I was.

He was running out of my money and said it was time to get to work. During this time, he hadn't given me any food; he only ordered food for himself and would give me some of what he had, but very little. He would step out into the hall to buy weed and coke and quickly return to the room. After begging and pleading and trying to convince him that if we could go back to Sacramento, I would let him come back home with the girls and me, I realized he didn't believe me. So I pretended to go along with his plan, but I strategized a different plan. As soon as I got into a car with someone soliciting for sex, I would tell them I had been kidnapped and forced into prostitution, and I would beg for my life and for them to take me home. I was too scared to call the police because of all the meth I had in my system; I was scared they would find out, take me to jail, and take my kids.

Amazingly, the first guy who came soliciting had a family in Sacramento and would often go back and forth. Wow! I followed my plan and told him, and to my amazement, he had a heart, and he drove me back home to Sacramento. He made it very clear that I never mention him, especially under the circumstance we met. That was agreeable with me; I wanted to live and return home to my family. I began to soak in what had transpired as he was driving me home. I had been kidnapped, robbed of my substance, raped, and sex trafficked. I was traumatized.

Upon returning home, I tried to pick up the pieces and move on, but I just made more and more bad choices. I was harassed for a while by my kidnapper and tormentor until the District Attorney's office prosecuted him for kidnapping me, violent threats, and acts of violence against me. In the midst of this, a doctor diagnosed me with post-traumatic stress disorder (PTSD), bipolarism, manic depression, and anxiety. If all that wasn't enough, I found myself in yet another violent relationship. I began using meth more than ever until, eventually, I lost everything and found myself having two more kids by two different men. There were times I would go from one homeless shelter to another with all four of my kids. Because I loved them and couldn't take care of them, I had to give them to my mom. I was completely gone and unable to fight my addiction. From the first time I used meth, coupled with the trauma, I was, in my mind, a victim for almost nine years.

I remember always asking God why, but at the same time, I believed there had to be something more; there was something I wasn't understanding. Enough was enough. Eventually, I was ready to do whatever God wanted me to do, even if I didn't understand why. I had felt this way many times before; I cannot tell you how many times, far too many to count. Each time, I could feel my spirit crying out for change and asking God for mercy and opportunity. It was those times when it felt like I was at my "rock bottom"—the rock bottom that would push me to change. There were many times when I could see a way out. Even when I wasn't pleading with God or asking for an escape, I could still *see* and *recognize* particular doors that were open or shut for me and opportunities that had presented themselves. I could have used them as an exit, but I didn't. But this time, there was something special about this specific day, time, and situation; only God knows because I still don't. I had contacted my mother and asked her to come and get me because I had humbled myself and wanted to enter rehab. I remember my mom picking me up, and she had brought along with her a new friend, Ms. Dorothy. There I sat in the back seat, probably smelling like weed, but I felt hope. The first miracle of this reunion was to see my children again; what a sight for sore eyes and a broken heart.

My mom contacted a rehab center for women, which was different from others because it was Christian-based. There were women there from all walks of life, but we had two things in common: we were addicts, and we wanted to be free. For months, I lived in the house, getting acquainted with rules and schedules and speaking words that I didn't normally use—life-giving words, not words of death. We encouraged each other to hang in there and wholeheartedly believed that all of us would make it, but I only held myself responsible for me. The fog was beginning to clear my mind, and my feet started to feel as though they were flat on the floor and not off balance, either from drug use or mental tiredness. I was still and began to think that I could maybe start to trust this process.

That is when it happened. My significant emotional event slammed into me, crushing years of flawed thinking, wrong concepts of God, and what life was all about. It was an ordinary day, and I would pray daily for God's help and strength. I wanted to make it and to have my life well put together for my children's sake. A lady and her young daughter came to the house to share the Word of God with us. I had been watching a minister who was preaching on television who had also gotten my attention. The lady's lesson and the things her young daughter said about God were what sealed the deal. It was all the things I was learning from them, such as:

"Watch and pray, lest you enter into temptation. The spirit indeed is willing, but the flesh is weak." (Matthew 26:41 NKJV)

She shared wisdom and understanding that when the Bible says that the spirit is willing, but the flesh is weak, it means we can have a strong desire to change, but we cannot make it happen with our fleshy strength. Apostle Paul, who wrote many books in the New Testament, said:

> *I do not understand what I do. For what I want to do I do not do, but what I hate I do. And if I do what I do not want to do, I agree that the law is good. As it is, it is no longer I myself who do it, but <u>it is sin</u> living in me. For I know that <u>good itself does not dwell in me</u>, that is, in <u>my sinful nature</u>. For I have the desire to do what is good, but I cannot carry it out. <u>For I do not do the good I want to do, but the evil I do not want to do—this I keep on doing</u>. Now if I do what I do not want to do, it is no longer I who do it, but it is sin living in me that does it. So I find this law at work: Although <u>I want to do good, evil is right there with me</u>. For in my inner being I delight in God's law; but I see another law at work in me, waging war against the law of my mind and making me a prisoner of the law of sin at work within me. <u>What a wretched man I am! Who will rescue me</u> from this body that is subject to death? <u>Thanks be to God, who delivers me through Jesus Christ our Lord</u>! (Romans 7:15–25 NIV)*

Sounds reasonable, right? If we could do it ourselves, we wouldn't need God, and He wouldn't have needed to sacrifice His Son for our sins. The Bible also says in many scriptures that we should pray and ask God to take away our hardened hearts and give us a heart of flesh and ears to hear His Word and receive His love. It took a divine intervention, colliding with my will, for things to happen inside of me. Simultaneously, my flesh bowed to the will of God, and the Spirit of God stood atop my flesh. He declared Himself to be the victor of and over my soul. God is about action, and He is also about time and place. He knew when I was ready and when my need for Him would be stronger than my flesh; by His Spirit, I could follow through. He knew when I would have ears to hear and eyes to see because He knew that each experience I encountered was calling me to cry out to Him. I was reaching my "rock bottom"! It was God who was softening my heart, using my bad choices. It was also at this point that all things became new, and I began to hear and see certain things, many of which I had heard and seen numerous times before. But this time, I was more receptive to them and understood them in a new capacity as never before.

God didn't tempt me with this evil; I was born with this sinful nature. I had a will, and I made terrible choices, but it was not His will for me, nor is it for you or anyone. The scriptures below make it very clear:

Behold, I was brought forth in iniquity, And in sin my mother conceived me. (Psalms 51:5 NKJV)

Let no one say when he is tempted, "I am tempted by God"; for God cannot be tempted by evil, nor does He Himself tempt anyone. But each one is tempted <u>when he is drawn away by his own desires and enticed</u>. Then, when desire *has conceived, it gives birth to sin; and sin, when it is full-grown, brings forth death. (James 1:13–15 NKJV)*

It is imperative that you know, as I have come to know and believe, that the Bible is true, and God will use all things for the good of those who love Him and whom He has called according to His purpose, and that includes using our past.

And we know that all things work together for good to those who love God, to those who are the called according to His purpose. (Romans 8:28 NKJV)

What then shall we say to these things? If God is for us, who can be against us? He who did not spare His own Son, but delivered Him up for us all, how shall He not with Him also freely give us all things? (Romans 8:31–32 NKJV)

I don't know exactly why I stayed in my addiction and depression as long as I did, even though my soul cried out for years to be free. Maybe what made that day an extraordinary day was this thing called time; in my case, "hard time." What was it about this particular cry out to Him that was so unique? It was a cry from the depth of my soul; it was deep, real deep, a cry of desperation because *I had reached my rock bottom.*

Then you will call upon Me and go and pray to Me, and I will listen to you. <u>And you will seek Me and find Me, when you search for Me with all your heart</u>. (Jeremiah 29:12–13 NKJV)

The scripture begins with the word "then," which denotes time—the time when I sought God with all my heart. He heard me, He listened to me, and I found Him because "hard times" had tenderized my heart. And when He heard me, He abruptly broke me free from my chains. Years of addictions and depression, the death of my first baby girl, neglecting myself and my children, a tarnished soul I was until "*then*"! I trusted Him, and he had my attention. He introduced Himself to me with this scripture given to me by this mother and her young daughter:

"BE STILL AND KNOW THAT I AM GOD" (Psalms 46:10 NKJV).

My testimony is untitled because, before my new birth, I had no idea who I was or why I was on planet Earth. It is where we all begin, with questions, especially when our lives are in a mess. These questions mark the beginning of our journey. This testimony is one of many because God is still writing my story. He weaves my stories together like a beautiful string of pearls, and He drapes them around my neck so I can be kept in remembrance of whose I am. Before my new birth, I was in control, I wasn't doing a good job, and my horrible life was the work of my hands and that of the enemy of my soul. Thank God, there was a "*then*." And there is one for you. God is at work, and He wants to write your testimony; let Him do His perfect work in you. Who God says I am—well, that is the definition I use to define me. Because I am His, I know that I have a purpose, value, and hope, but only in Him, through Him, and because of Him. Because He says:

"For I know the plans I have for you," declares the LORD,
*"plans to prosper you and not to harm you, plans to give
you hope and a future." (Jeremiah 29:11 NIV)*

I am not scared of Him anymore; I can't live without Him. It has
been almost seven years since God delivered me, not only from drugs,
drinking, promiscuity, anxiety, depression, and shame, but God has
gone deeper into that place where I could not reach. He has delivered
me from my sinful thoughts and nature. He has healed my heart and
my spirit—all those other things were just symptoms and tactics of
the enemy. God went for the root cause, and He uprooted them and
left no scars!

Today I am free. I still have challenges, but I am no longer bound!
Jesus said:

*"I have told you these things, so that in me you may have
peace. In this world you will have trouble. But take heart! I
have overcome the world." (John 16:33 NIV)*

But I can't say "the end" yet; I promised you something. Why do
I like the second definition of "crisis": "the turning point of a disease
when an important change takes place, indicating either recovery or
death"? I think this definition says it all. I didn't die from my disease
called sin; I was reborn. *It was my turning point!*

I Do

by Anita Joseph

My story is not a tear-jerker. My story is not jaw-dropping. It's the story of my day-to-day, ordinary, yet extraordinary, walk-by-faith marriage. It's about a marriage nurtured in love, mutual respect, and a genuine commitment to one another. It's the story of me trusting in God to do what only He can do to draw my husband to Him. It is a story of gratitude and hope for an even brighter future.

A little over twenty-six years ago, I said "I do." I was young, fresh out of college, and ready to settle down with the love of my life. We were extremely excited about our new life together. We attended church together, and we had both recently embarked on our careers. Newly married, we were in our first apartment and just beginning our marriage journey. We hadn't ventured too far in the marriage when my husband came to his realization and confided in me that although he had made a sincere effort, he did not share the same religious beliefs as I did. First, there was a little panic in my heart. I wondered if this new ideology was temporary. Had I done something wrong? Would this cause irreparable friction in our marriage? What would the people we knew at church think about us? About me? There were so many questions popping up in my head.

My heart ached to hear that news. I had my vision of the path that my marriage would take, and this wasn't it! I genuinely wanted my husband to share the journey of living for Christ. I didn't know if I could do it alone. I didn't know how to do it alone as a married woman. All my Christian friends were either single or married, and the married couples were both serving God. I questioned God. I prayed to God. I shared my heart with God. I thanked Him for such a loving and thoughtful husband with whom there was no doubt that I was going to spend the rest of my life. Over time, I felt the comfort and reassurance of God, as if He were saying, "I got you. I got this." It's amazing how God gives us just what we need, in the right amount, and at the moment that we need it.

I spoke with my pastor about the situation, and he informed me that it wasn't uncommon for one to go through a period of religious doubt. So I waited. Time progressed, and nothing changed. For the first few years after my husband revealed that he did not share the same beliefs as I, he lovingly placed my feelings above his and continued to accompany me to church. What a relief for me! I had always been in my comfort zone when we were together as a couple at church. He was giving me time to adjust and to process this new change. Over time, I realized my need to release him from feeling any known or perceived "obligation" to attend church with me. I realized I needed to allow him the right to make his own choices about God and church attendance freely without feeling guilty because of me. I will admit, it was scary to walk this unknown and unexpected path, but at the same time, I believed that God was with me on the journey.

However, this didn't stop me, time after time, from taking matters into my hands instead of waiting on God. In my attempt at problem-solving, I thought I had found the solution to my husband's dilemma: maybe a new church is what he needed. So, I found another church and started attending. I liked the preaching, the choir sounded great, and I had begun meeting other believers. The problem was, my husband wasn't going! One of the hardest things for me to do was stay consistent in church attendance when my husband was not attending. I know of others who have suffered from this, and many have failed; I was no exception. I stopped attending the new church. It was hard being the only one getting up and heading out to church. It was much easier for me to stay home, sleep in, and enjoy our time together. I was new enough that I didn't feel accountable to anyone at the church, and I knew the members would hardly notice I wasn't there. Deep in my heart, I knew that God desired a closer relationship with me, but I was too preoccupied to give Him me. This is not to say that I totally abandoned my relationship with God, but I was half-stepping. I do recall experiencing extraordinary prayer and journaling time during this period in my life. I just wasn't "all in."

Then, we moved closer to his parents, and I finally attended their church—the church they had always raved about to us. I had never before experienced such exciting worship, meaningful biblical sermons, and time at the altar with just me and God. I realized how hungry I was for a closer relationship with the Lord and getting to know His Word.

God renewed my spiritual zeal and began to fill the void in my heart—the space that belongs only to Him. I was where I needed to be. Suddenly, I was all in! That sudden change in intensity made my husband a little concerned that he was losing me, but I reassured him that was far from the case. Instead of him losing me, I was finding a new part of me. My husband would attend services at times, but I never pressured him to attend, nor did I worry about what others thought of me attending without him. I was gaining spiritual maturity and developing confidence and inner peace in who God created me to be. I was profoundly trusting in my God and the assurance that He had a unique and beautiful plan for my life. I'm not sure I fully realized all of this at that time, but I see it in reflection, and I see now what God was doing in my life. By this time in my faith, I was spiritually strong enough to "go it alone." This didn't mean that I was happy about the situation, but my faith in God drew me to a more profound desire to know Him. I still shared other quality time with my husband, but God's time was God's time, and he had no problem with that.

Fast-forwarding a few years, we had two small children and relocated to a new area. During this time, God led me to a new church called Harvest. It has been fifteen years now and counting. My husband was always open to raising our children with a stable moral upbringing, so he was in total agreement with me to take them to church. For this, I am most thankful! Not only did I have a husband who didn't attack my faith or mock me, but he extended to me the freedom to actively be involved. And the fact that he was not opposed to me raising our children in the Christian faith has meant everything to me.

At this stage in our marriage, my husband continued to attend church with me on occasion when he desired; it always made me happy. I guess because I started attending Harvest on my own, I didn't face many questions as to why he didn't regularly attend. In fact, quite a few people assumed I was a single mom for several of my early years! To say that I wanted to do it solo would be a considerable understatement, but I resolved that I probably would never understand why everything happened as it did and that God's ways are not my ways. I chose to maintain a positive outlook.

After all, I have the best husband, and definitely the best father for my children. His love is evident in everything he does, from his work ethic to the care he puts into planning and preparing meals. Yes, he is the chef; I don't cook, and honestly speaking, I can't cook, not on the level he does. My husband ensures we have all we need. I never question his love and commitment to our children and me. I love him and never get tired of being around him. Together, we have raised two well-adjusted children and have gone through the usual ups and downs of life. My son is now attending college, and my daughter is a junior in high school. I have concluded that everything rests in God's time.

I still stand in faith that my husband will one day join in a relationship with the One who intricately designed him and longs for a deep, lasting fellowship with him. I desire for him to completely surrender and experience the same feelings of wholeness and the sweet love that I feel with my Father in heaven. When this happens, he will rise to a new and immeasurable level of inner peace, well-being, and satisfaction that he may not fully know he's missing. It's like when you're comfortable sleeping on an old mattress, which you think feels great until you get a new one, and only then do you realize what you've been missing. When he surrenders his will for *His* will, we'll be able to share in that love and the fellowship together. God has been patient with me, and I will be patient with God for him.

Perhaps you are in a similar situation and have a mate who is not *presently* serving the Lord. There may be times when you may feel discouraged because things aren't going the way you imagined. Do not fear; instead, rest in God's assurance that He has a plan for you, your mate, and your marriage and that He is in control. I encourage you to allow God to transform you and your marriage into all that He intended.

There are many things I have learned over the years and from different venues. I have excavated valuable information from the pain of my personal experiences. I have found wisdom, knowledge, and encouragement from listening to those who have blazed the trail. All these gifts came from God speaking to my heart and walking with me on this journey. If I could offer any advice and encouragement, it would include the following insights:

Pray for your spouse and your marriage.

Although it is good to have close associates to confide in, your primary resource should be communicating with the Father through prayer. Your family and friends know you, but God *knows* you. Who is better to open up to than the One who uniquely designed you and knows everything there ever was to know about you before you were born? With Him, you can be totally open and honest about your concerns and feelings; I call this "true transparency." He truly knows and understands what you are going through. I must admit, in the early years, although I wanted my husband to accept Christ as his personal Savior, I didn't spend as much time in prayer about this as I do now. Maybe this was because there wasn't much friction in our relationship since he freely allowed me and the kids to attend church. Perhaps it was because, in the beginning, I thought the situation was only temporary. Or maybe it was because it wasn't until more recently, as we have entered into middle age, that the thought that we've lived over half our lives and the truth that death and the afterlife are much closer resonate in my mind. Whatever the reasons, as the years have gone by, the desire to see my husband develop a relationship with

Christ has grown more heavily on my heart and has become a more frequent topic in my prayers.

My initial prayer requests were for God to "fix" my mate. Though God is concerned about him, I've embraced that He is equally concerned with my growth and maturity and wants to build a deeper relationship with *me*. In my many times with Him, He gently reveals areas within me that could use further refinement to facilitate this process. I have learned to allow God to speak to me about me and trust that God has a plan for my husband, whom He cares just as deeply for as He does for me. You, too, can do yourself an enormous favor by taking the responsibility off yourself to "save" your mate. Allow the Holy Spirit to do His work individually in you and your mate.

For example, I know I have possessed deep within me the ability to hold a grudge. During the beginnings of my marriage, there were opportunities where I wanted to unleash this strong-willed ability. Still, the Holy Spirit convicted me and helped me understand that I might not like the consequences. I decided not to hold grudges or have a bad attitude when things didn't go my way. To God's glory, those who truly know me would never describe me as a person with a bad attitude! The same goes for speaking whatever comes to mind. I thank the Holy Spirit for helping to cage my tongue from saying things I might later regret. I had to be deliberate in some things in my marriage to enable me to foster a healthy marriage relationship. God revealed how I could accomplish this during my intimate time with Him. What is God trying to show you about your relationship with Him? About your relationship with your mate?

And by all means, if your mate is open to it, pray with him or her!

Seek God's Word for guidance.

I cannot stress enough how important it is to read your Bible! I struggled in the early years of marriage because I was not very strong or knowledgeable in the Word. I knew some basic scriptures, but not specific scriptures dealing with marriage. If I had to choose one Scripture passage that gave me the most comfort and direction, this is the one:

> *Likewise, ye wives, be in subjection to your own husbands;*
> *that, if any obey not the Word, they also may without the*
> *Word be won by the conversation of the wives. (1 Peter*
> *3:1 KJV)*

This scripture expresses the power of my conversation with my husband without saying a word. It has given me the hope that one day, *in God's timing*, my husband will come to know and accept the Lord. I understood from this verse that I needed to be the Christian wife that God had called me to be, an example of His faithfulness. Striving to honor God's power has been a true testament to my love and respect for my husband. My commitment to God is visible to my husband, and it doesn't make him jealous but lets him know that I am a woman of dedication. One of the highest compliments I received was when someone recently told me that I was the first actual example of the "1 Peter 3:1 wife" she had ever met. To God be the glory, because it is one of my anchoring scriptures!

> *Wives, in the same way submit yourselves to your own*
> *husbands so that, if any of them do not believe the word,*
> *they may be won over without words by the behavior of*
> *their wives. (1 Peter 3:1 NIV)*

And, God's Word further says:

"For I know the plans I have for you," declares the Lord,
"plans to prosper you and not to harm you, plans to give
you hope and a future." (Jeremiah 29:11 NIV)

This verse gave me confidence that nothing in my marriage is a surprise to God and reassures me that God has an overall purpose for my life. This verse declares that God's ultimate purpose for me has always been for my good and His glory. As you encounter the ups and downs of life, this is a truth in which to ground your faith.

What is God's Word telling you? One way to know is to search the scriptures!

Have the right attitude.

It's imperative to realize that you play a crucial role in modeling Christ-like behavior to your spouse. You are the up-close and personal example of Christianity that your spouse sees daily. You provide the evidence that he can examine. Your attitude, when you're facing disappointments and challenges, is scrutinized the most. Setting a watch over your attitude is a responsibility that you must take seriously. You may not feel equipped, but don't worry—in Christ, you are.

I read about the virtuous wife in Proverbs 31 and wondered how I could live up to that ideal because it didn't feel real; therefore, it didn't feel possible. Here's her description:

A wife of noble character who can find? She is worth far
more than rubies. Her husband has full confidence in
her and lacks nothing of value. She brings him good, not
harm, all the days of her life. She selects wool and flax and

works with eager hands. She is like the merchant ships, bringing her food from afar. She gets up while it is still night; she provides food for her family and portions for her female servants. She considers a field and buys it; out of her earnings, she plants a vineyard. She sets about her work vigorously; her arms are strong for her tasks. She sees that her trading is profitable, and her lamp does not go out at night. In her hand, she holds the distaff and grasps the spindle with her fingers. She opens her arms to the poor and extends her hands to the needy. When it snows, she has no fear for her household; for all of them are clothed in scarlet. She makes coverings for her bed; she is clothed in fine linen and purple. Her husband is respected at the city gate, where he takes his seat among the elders of the land. She makes linen garments and sells them and supplies the merchants with sashes. She is clothed with strength and dignity; she can laugh at the days to come. She speaks with wisdom, and faithful instruction is on her tongue. She watches over the affairs of her household and does not eat the bread of idleness. Her children arise and call her blessed; her husband also, and he praises her: "Many women do noble things, but you surpass them all." Charm is deceptive, and beauty is fleeting, but a woman who fears the Lord is to be praised. Honor her for all that her hands have done, and let her works bring her praise at the city gate. (Proverbs 31:10–31 NIV)

Do you see why I felt unequipped to walk in her shoes? She is amazing! Well, guess what? So am I! And so are you! The requirement expected by God and shared with others is to be the best that we are capable of being. And who gives us the ability to meet His expectations? He does, our Heavenly Father. In essence, the virtuous wife loves her husband and children and does her portion to ensure the household run smoothly. It's that simple, but it takes time to develop the right perspective. Having a steady and mature development of a loving and kind spirit to please God presents my husband with a godly example. Early on, I put pressure on myself to be the perfect wife and mother, but keeping that up was too difficult! Know that no one expects you to be superwoman, but rather to be a super woman—a great wife, mother, and friend.

Understand that there is power in your words. Words can tear down or build up. There will be situations that will arise and test you in this area. We know our mates very well, so we often know just what to say that can hurt them, and they know what to say to destroy us. Remember that you can never take back any hurtful words you speak, and you don't want anything harmful to become a barrier in your marriage.

As this scripture states, I endeavor to obey, and I encourage you to as well:

Let your conversation be always full of grace, seasoned with salt, so that you may know how to answer everyone. (Colossians 4:6 NIV)

However, each one of you also must love his wife as he loves himself, and the wife must respect her husband. (Ephesians 5:33 NIV)

Therefore, as God's chosen people, holy and dearly loved, clothe yourselves with compassion, kindness, humility, gentleness, and patience. (Colossians 3:12 NIV)

And whatever you do, whether in word or deed, do it all in the name of the Lord Jesus, giving thanks to God the Father through him. Wives, submit yourselves to your husbands, as is fitting in the Lord. Husbands love your wives and do not be harsh with them. (Colossians 3:17–19 NIV)

I love these scriptures; they gave me hope and guidance and taught me wisdom. They will do the same for you.

Forgive often.

Although true of practically every type of relationship, every marriage will go through ups and downs, and spouses will inevitably say or do something that will require someone to need forgiveness and someone to forgive. No marriage will escape unscathed! My husband and I get along very well, yet we have said and done things that have upset or disappointed each other. We have utterly failed in some areas. The Word says:

Bear with each other and forgive one another if any of you has a grievance against someone. Forgive as the Lord forgave you. And over all these virtues put on love, which binds them all together in perfect unity. (Colossians 3:13–14 NIV)

When it comes to forgiving my husband, I genuinely try to keep in the forefront the many, many things that God has and continues to forgive me. Over the years, I've struggled with gaining the proper balance between shopping and managing debt. In other words, I spend too much money! I have lacked the appropriate discipline in this area. My husband, on the contrary, handles money very responsibly. Multiple times, my husband has come up with a plan to help me get out of credit card debt, and numerous times, I've repeated the same old cycle and landed back into debt. One would think that since I'm the only Christian in the house, I would have been the example and mastered everything that was a stumbling block before me, but that hasn't always been the case. I've got some more growing to do! My challenges keep me humble. I have sometimes gossiped and said negative things about others. What's great is that my husband has never put me down for my shortcomings. Thankfully, it hasn't been a significant struggle for me to forgive him for his shortcomings because I know that I'm not perfect, and we're all masterpieces in the making. Forgiveness is not always easy, but it is necessary. Forgiveness does not mean that you condone a particular behavior. The Bible states this passage of

the Lord's Prayer as follows:

And forgive us our debts, as we also have forgiven our debtors. [I repent of my sins against God and forgive others of their sins against me – a win – win!]. (Matthew 6:12 NIV)

Do not take revenge, my dear friends, but leave room for God's wrath, for it is written: "It is mine to avenge; I will repay," says the Lord. (Romans 12:19 NIV)

Forgiveness releases our right to be the exactor of punishment and to leave such matters to God. Recognizing the debt that our Lord,

Jesus Christ, has paid for our sins should free us to release others from their debts of sin. Realize your total need and reliance on the perfect Savior. That will help keep you humble. Pray for the power to forgive. And forgive often.

Be faithful.

You may feel like not going to church because your spouse is not attending. I know that it's hard to continually have to get up on Sunday mornings while your spouse is resting, watching television, or doing other "fun" things. It was hard for me, and sometimes still is—especially if I stay up late on Saturday night watching movies with my husband, and I'm tired on Sunday morning. Even so, I know that my spiritual growth is essential, so I press on. I go to church to join in collective worship and praise with other believers. I also see myself as a "gatherer," collectively showing my husband and children the love of God. I was touched when my husband commented on my faithfulness to church and church commitments. I realize how important it is that I do what I believe Christ has called me to do for my spouse and children. And if you do the same, it will be a great testament of your faith to your family without you saying a word; your life has broadcasted it!

A word of caution: the church is always in need of helpers, and there will always be an outreach, a new Bible study, a prayer meeting, or another significant event taking place. Being faithful does not mean you attend everything. It is just as vital that you spend quality time with your family. I believe that the proper order of things is: God, family, and church. I have struggled to keep this in proper perspective over the years. In more recent times, I have intentionally allowed the Holy Spirit to guide me to comfortably say "no" when asked to take on one too many church responsibilities. The last thing you want to do is disengage from your mate and family by spending too much time away at church, as this could cause resentment toward the church and problems in your marriage. Be prayerful to maintain a proper balance in all areas.

And although it should go without saying, we should always remain faithful to our mate. The enemy will provide opportunities that may weaken or even destroy our marriage. Although the grass may look greener on the other side, it's probably artificial turf, deceiving you. It's the responsibility of each of us to work to grow our beautiful green, healthy lawn in our marriage.

Teach our children.

Train up a child in the way he should go: and when he is old, he will not depart from it. (Proverbs 22:6 KJV)

Children are a heritage from the Lord, offspring a reward from him. (Psalms 127:3 NIV)

My husband loves our children. Each Sunday morning, while I was getting the kids dressed for church, he would prepare an excellent breakfast for us. At church, I enjoyed worship service, and the kids enjoyed learning about God, singing Christian songs, and making new friends. I recall special times at home with my children—reading Bible stories and watching Christian movies. Each night, we would pray together before going to bed.

Do not deprive your children of their opportunity to grow in faith. If you must be the one to take your children to church without your mate, to read Bible stories to them, to pray with and to teach about the goodness of the Lord, do it! And do it without complaining or making your mate feel guilty. Recognize that it is a privilege and an honor to teach your children about Christ. Your children are indeed a gift whom God entrusts to us for a season. We have to be sure to do our part to give them a firm, godly foundation.

Don't have a pity party.

I once heard a preacher say that our attitude determines our altitude. It may be easy to feel sorry for yourself because of your situation, but I encourage you not to do so. Make up your mind not to wallow in self-pity because your mate is not serving God with you. Accept your present reality, and don't magnify your problem larger than your God.

It's important to realize that everyone is dealing with problems or struggles. Married couples may seem perfect at church, but it's possible that behind closed doors, some of them could have unhappy marriages filled with disrespect, abuse, adultery, and much more. Some singles, divorcees, and widows whom you encounter may feel lonely and long to be married. The same may also hold true for your friends and family who are not believers and don't attend church. Wallowing in sorrow about your issues might keep you from wholeheartedly praising God and may limit your passion for praying and your desire to encourage others experiencing difficult times. Allow God's strength to give you all that you need as you walk in faith regarding your mate's salvation.

So don't have a pity party. Have a praise party! After all, God is worthy of our praise!

Be aware of the middle zone.

Be aware of your possible position in the "middle zone." This is where you'll find yourself navigating in-between relationships with your single friends and your married friends at church. You might feel, at times, somewhat isolated from each group. Since you have a limited amount of free time to spend away from your spouse, this limits your ability for outside fellowship with singles. And although you are married, people frequently see you alone, and since others may not know your spouse, you will probably not receive an invitation to the couples outings. This can be tough! But I get it—who wants a third wheel hanging with them? Singles face this issue, as well.

I want to think that I've done a great job managing my place in the "middle zone." It's not that I like it, but it's my reality, and I have chosen to accept it and make the best of it. There also are numerous events where everyone comes together, so my position in the "middle zone" is fluid. At times, I decide to bypass certain functions because I don't always care to attend without my husband. I also have a responsibility to balance my time away from him. My husband is remarkable, and if I express how badly I want to attend a particular service, class, or marriage seminar, he will sacrifice and attend. The key I've learned is to embrace my status and foster fellowship with others to the best of my ability. I put no added pressure on myself or anyone else. I allow God to fill any voids that I may be experiencing at any given time.

Be thankful.

Blessed be GOD—he heard me praying. He proved he's on my side; I've thrown my lot in with him. Now I'm jumping for joy, and shouting and singing my thanks to him.

(Psalms 28:6-7 MSG)

There is a lot to be thankful for! Even amid trials and dilemmas, there is still room to praise God. The fact that we still have the breath of life in us is a gift. The fact that God's love is so magnificent that He willingly allowed His Son, Jesus Christ, to suffer an utterly painful death. He agreed with Himself to do this so that we might not have to endure eternal separation from Him. This is the most transparent and dearest evidence of His love. When you are enjoying a mountaintop experience, God is with you. When you feel you are in the valley or wilderness, God is right there with you. It is of the utmost comfort to know that the Creator of the universe loves you, me, and everyone this much. Let's choose to rejoice and be thankful and trust in Him for all things.

Where do I go from here?

Marriage isn't always easy, but it is worth it. To write about the day-to-day challenges of being a wife of faith, purity, reverence, and all the in-between would be voluminous. We honor God when we are fully committed to faithfully loving our spouse. It can be scary not to know what the future holds for your marriage and whether your mate will accept the salvation of the Lord. There are times when I have wrestled between faith and fear in these areas. Fear demonstrates a lack of faith that God is in control and has a sovereign plan. To trust in God is to release fear, doubt, and worry and allow Him to do as He will. Faith, to me, is like keeping my foot on the gas pedal and allowing God to steer me in the right direction as He sees fit. Sometimes, out of fear, I take control of the wheel and go down some dead-end street. But God has been faithful in my cries and my surrender to steer me back in the direction that I should go.

I have come to realize that one of my most essential purposes has been to model a Christ-centered life for my husband and children. I pray I am succeeding at this. My son is now in college, and my daughter is in her late teens; they are on their journeys to discover who God is to them in a profound and meaningful way. My husband is already kind, thoughtful, generous, and dedicated. I respect, love, and honor him. How I treat my husband directly correlates with how I submit to Christ's authority. I stand in faith for a time when my husband and I can pray, worship, and serve God together. Then, we will share in the absolute fullness of marriage as God intended, as husband and wife, in the unity of the Holy Spirit. I am grateful for the opportunities that God provides for me to grow in love, patience, grace, and faith, as this ultimately brings me closer to Him.

Maybe, after all, my story is a tear-jerker and a jaw-dropper! Our marriage is blessed, and we value each other. It brings tears to my eyes and leaves me in awe, knowing that we have found the secret of a happy marriage naturally speaking, and I know that one day, we will know it as we join together spiritually as well.

It all boils down to this:

Do I love my husband? *I do!*

Do I trust God to do what only He can do? *I do!*

As I said at first, I say it again: it's amazing how God gives us just what we need, in the right amount, and at the moment that we need it. That was true then, and it is still true today. Come on, get your portion!

Embraced by Love, Healed by Grace

by Elena Cirstea

To all who mourn in Israel, he will give a crown of beauty for ashes, a joyous blessing instead of mourning, festive praises instead of despair. In their righteousness, they will be like great oaks that the Lord has planted for his own glory. (Isaiah 61:3 NLT)

I was born in Romania in 1983. I am the youngest of six children, but the only child who is a product of both my mom and dad. My mom had three children, and my dad had two children, all from their previous marriages. My parents told me that when I was four years old, they became heavily involved in the church. They would attend different prayer groups and began receiving the same message vicariously through different ones that the Lord was going to take them to a faraway land. It became so embedded in their hearts that they knew when the time came and God said go, they would obey and go. That is precisely what happened. That journey was a display of the miraculous hand of God at work in our lives, but that will be another story because my parents have more details than I do. God led us to Portland, Oregon, and we settled there in 1988. God was so good. He provided for us every step of the way.

I remember when we left Oregon and moved to California in 1992. We began attending a Romanian Pentecostal Church, and I loved it. It was in this church that I grew up. I was so excited about Jesus Christ, and I wanted everyone to know it. I started singing in the children's choir and went to all the services, Sunday morning and evening, Monday night, Thursday night, and choir practice on Friday nights. I loved singing to the Lord. I would walk around in my backyard, hanging out around my mom's garden and singing words I felt deep in my heart. I think it was more of a prayer than a song, but I loved singing my conversations to the Lord.

Sadly, even as a young girl of nine years old, adults in my church targeted me. I remember the pastor's wife openly rejected me in church and said some pretty awful things about me on a night when my parents and I were not there. She attacked me personally and said I was not a good girl but a flirtatious girl and wanted attention. I couldn't understand why she would say that when I was so young and not even thinking of such things. Not to mention, my mother would have never allowed me to behave in that manner. Children repeated what they had heard in church and what their parents were discussing at home.

That experience changed my attitude about the church; it sucked the joy out of my young soul and began to push me from the church.

When I was about ten years old, we had the best landlords ever. They were a wonderful couple who were so nice to us. I was a friend of their grandchildren and would visit their home. They occasionally started taking me with them to an American church. My parents encouraged this because they wanted me to become Americanized and settled in my new homeland. I enjoyed going with my newfound friends. But I became a target yet again by an adult. This time no one was accusing me of being something I wasn't. No—this time, I was physically assaulted by my landlord. He began molesting me, and it happened more than once. I didn't say anything to anyone for a long time because I thought if I told anyone, it would be a waste of time, and I would feel even worse because no one would believe me, especially after what the previous pastor's wife had said about me. Those ugly words she had said about me continued to live in my mind. Unquestionably, everyone would believe that I must have done something to attract that attention. More importantly, if I told them what he had done to me, they would surely kick us out of the house. My parents didn't need any extra trouble; they were struggling to pay rent.

While at our church's youth group, I finally decided to tell my youth pastor about what had happened to me. I didn't tell him the molester's name but described him well enough that he would know who it was. He did nothing, absolutely nothing. And I began to think, "Okay, well, I guess that's just the way things work in the church," and I acted like everything was normal. This was the third time adults had pushed me away from the church. In my short time on planet Earth, the adult Christians had discouraged me so much that I wanted nothing to do with them or the church. I told myself that I would still believe in God, but where else could I go to learn about God except the church? How could I separate from the church and continue to be connected to God and live a godly life? These were some heavy thoughts for my ten-year-old mind, and to try to figure it all out by myself became too much! I began accepting how people were treating me. I believe it became a self-fulfilling prophecy that the way people saw me and treated me is what I was becoming, even if only in their minds.

When my parents told me we were going on vacation to visit our homeland, Romania, it was like taking a deep breath, a sigh of relief. I couldn't wait to see my family, mainly to be introduced to them because I was only four years old when we left Romania. But to go back at this age was a reconnection to my past. My parents spoke of our homeland with such passion, and it made me happy to see the expression of joy on their faces. We made it to Romania, our homeland. I witnessed people, places, and things I had never seen. Romania is a European country and is known for its cabbage stuffed with spiced pork and rice. Eating the food was the most important thing to me. Then there are the Carpathian Mountains, salt mines, dense primeval forests, and the Black Sea. But there is another fable it is known for, and that is as the home of the forested region of Transylvania, where the legend of Dracula lives. I know: why such a dark note on such a beautiful country?

It didn't take long before I would experience some of that darkness of Romania. That fresh breath I was enjoying didn't last long because once again, I was a target, and this time, it was my very own uncle who molested me. To be sickly honest, by this point in my young life, I found it normal to be abused by men. I began to define all men as those who only wanted sex because these two older men had shown me where they placed their value and my worth. I internalized the hurt caused by these people and told myself that I was tough, and I started taking charge of my life and what happened to me.

Many years have gone by now, I am all grown up, but I had been marked. I began asking for attention from men in my life, determined that I would be in charge. I would decide what attention I would give rather than wait for men to take it from me. I was so wrong. Oh, I put on a reasonably good act for a while, but it took a lot of masking the emptiness to keep it up for as many years as I did. My masks were drinking alcohol, smoking cigarettes, and taking other drugs to keep from feeling anything for a long time. And then, my masks turned on me; they stopped working and brought me to an even lower point. I learned to hate myself when I was only a child. I hated myself because of what had happened to me and the bad decisions I made trying to fix myself.

The Beginning of the End

If I just let my mom pray now, she will feel better and leave, then I can go, and if I drive fast enough, I can drive off the marina. That is what I told myself. If you could only have heard the noise that was in my head on that day. It was the worst day of my life.

I had spent a large part of my life finding new ways to hurt anyone and everyone around me, and most of all, myself. Things had gotten worse during the last six years. While I was on this downward spiral, I was slowly reaching the point of no return. I did not want any part of this thing called "life." I wanted the noise in my head and the pain in my heart to stop; I just wanted to die. I was determined to commit suicide.

It had become normal for me to lie and manipulate the people around me. I had them thinking I was okay. But I played the victim card concerning my circumstances well enough that my loving family and boyfriend would fall for it every time and would help me. They didn't know they were only helping me feed my dragon of many addictions. I had been chained down so long with my addictions that I could no longer function without them. My masks turned on me. Lying became so natural to me that I habitually exaggerated and puffed up things for no reason at all. I had reached a point when I did not know if I was lying or telling the truth. I started stealing things and lied to myself about that. I would say to myself, "Everyone does this, so why not?" I would boldly tell myself that I was good at this, and stealing and lying were somehow my talents, special gifts from God. I was so confused. To elude my boyfriend's suspicion on how I had acquired items that we could not afford, I would lie and tell him that my mom had gotten the kids or myself those things. He believed me even knowing that my parents weren't wealthy.

The chains in my life had me so entangled that I couldn't break free, no matter how badly I wanted to, no matter how many tears I cried. Even my pleading with God seemed to go unheard. So I added another link in the chain: I started taking prescription pain medications to numb what I was doing with the stealing and lying. I was so depressed; it was too much. I hear people speak of the eight hundred pound elephant in the room; well, that eight hundred pound elephant wasn't only in the room, he was on my back, and I was suffocating, and my head felt as though it would burst.

I am reminded of Sir Walter Scott's quotation, "Oh, what a tangled web we weave, when first we practice to deceive." From the very beginning of when I started lying, first to myself and then to others, I was wrapping myself in a cocoon of spider webs that I would never be able to untangle. I had lost control, and the lies continued. I told myself that taking the prescribed medications would somehow make everything better. I first started taking them sporadically to have fun and feel good because I felt terrible most of the time. But I soon found myself trying to get more than I believed my doctor was willing to prescribe. Because I was afraid of being caught, I decided to lie to my doctor about having back pain and needing something more potent than ibuprofen. I got my supply, but that didn't last long because I started using too much. My body had become so accustomed to the medication that I needed to take a lot more to get the same effect. I would make up stories to my doctor so believable that I got what I wanted, a newly updated prescription. As I said, I had become exceptionally good at manipulating people around me.

I made it sound so good that people just believed me. I learned that if you are going to tell a lie, you must do it with a straight face; I think it's called a "poker face." But it wasn't long before I needed something stronger, and I knew I couldn't fake an injury to get stronger medications. Suddenly, all my chains were starting to twist together and tighten around me, pulling me down. I had to think of something fast before this dragon of addiction reared its ugly head, and everyone would know that I was not okay.

I started manipulating others to feel sorry for me. I would tell them of the tremendous pain I was in and how my doctor didn't care about me or my pain and would no longer prescribe the medication I needed. How unfair it was! The violinist began playing my song of sympathy for all to hear, and some actually listened. A few felt sorry for me and gave me some of their medications. They trusted me and genuinely believed they were helping me, and of course, I could manipulate them so well that I could make them feel bad for not helping me. But again, this wasn't enough. My body started establishing new norms and demanded more and more. It didn't take me too long to realize that I was trying to feed a dragon on a "hot dog" budget.

During this time, everything started to fuse. The weight became so heavy that every decent thing that I had ever had within me left me; every moral thought or desire to be a decent human being went out of the door. I started doing what I once considered to be off-limits: stealing from my family. But now, it was no holds barred; there weren't any boundaries I wouldn't cross. I continued to ask for their medications, but I also started stealing pain medications from those closest to me. They had real medical reasons for their prescribed medications, and I was stealing from them. It got so bad that I began stealing medication from a person who had suffered severe injuries. This wonderful person began to believe they were losing their mind because they couldn't remember taking that much medication. I just sat back and watched it all happen; I watched this person unravel, not caring about the distress that was on their face or the pain in their voice.

I learned a new trade: picking locks and stealing keys to making copies to gain access to people's property. The chain that sealed my fate had finally become wrapped around my neck. What happened next had to happen to me.

On top of everything sprawling out of control in my life, I took it to the next level: I started gambling. I began with scratchers, but like everything else I did, I needed more. I started taking off for hours at a time to go to the casinos. I ran out of money faster than I could catch my breath, causing this adventure to be short-lived. What do you do when you are a thief and find yourself out of money with no other resources? You do what a thief does: you steal, and stealing is just what I did. The boundaries were lifted, erased, and there was no longer anything or anybody off limits—and that included family. No boundary on stealing their medication, and no boundary on stealing their finances. I began taking small amounts that I thought wouldn't be noticed. The first victim was my boyfriend. Then my brother, whose home I spent lots of time at. He loved me dearly and trusted me whole-heartedly. At that time, my parents lived with him, and I would often visit them, mostly to get something from them by hook or crook. Which means I either manipulated them or just stole from them.

Within one month, my life as I knew it before this crisis would come crashing down on me. I imploded like a building after an implosion expert has placed dynamites strategically on specific support structures. When detonated, the building folds inward and caves in upon itself. Something was trying to destroy me, trying to take out the support beams that had been holding me up, to watch me implode. Each family member was a support beam for me. As I mentioned, my brother trusted me even with his bank card. Because I knew his personal information, I decided, without hesitation, that I would take some money out of his account, little by little. I began to think like other thieves, *I will not get caught!* And with that mindset, I finally lost all control and was gambling daily, repeatedly, and losing everything. I had become a lying, thieving, manipulating, pill-popping gambler, and at the same time, a mother of two boys. I was in my late twenties, near thirty, far beyond the age of claiming ignorance of my behavior. This extremely low place got even lower; everything caught up with me, and everyone caught on to me.

It was a Friday afternoon when I went to my brother's home. On that day, everything was like it had always been, but something had happened. My mom said that my brother and his wife were terribly upset because someone had accessed their bank account and stolen from them. My heart sunk into my chest, and I became so weak in my knees that I couldn't stand. At the same time, I was low on my pills and was trying to rip off another family member without them knowing. I managed to steal a couple of pills to take the edge off. Then, I heard my brother explaining what had happened to them. I even played along with the shock and horror of what they said had happened and asked along with them, "Who could it be?" I sat there all night with them, pretending to be concerned about their issues when I was their issue. With no limits, this twisted mind thought, *Well, maybe I can still get away with what I had done.* I didn't think they would find out it was me, so I could keep doing what I was doing. I was so wrong; I heard my mom say that his wife had filed a police report and they would find out who it was. The false hope disappeared, and fear overwhelmed me, not knowing how my family would react once they knew it was me.

April 13, 2013 was a Saturday. I was taking my oldest son to a birthday party and had promised my niece, my brother's youngest daughter, that I would take her with us. Afterward, we were to go back and have a barbecue at my brother's house for his friend's birthday. I woke up, got my kids ready, picked up my niece, and off we went to the birthday party. I was out of pills, and it was only a matter of time before I would begin to feel the pain of withdrawals. I was sitting on a bench at the park and should have been watching the children, but fear gripped my heart, and it pulled extremely hard. This moment in time was a very defining moment.

I worried about the pending withdrawal pains, but I also felt the full weight of what I had been doing. I couldn't move; I felt heavy inside and out. I couldn't speak. I sat on this lonely bench and listened to the things that were in my head. It was my life's playlist set on repeat. No matter what, even in my twisted mind, I knew I had to tell my brother what I did, and I had to tell him now, on this day. I felt so much sadness—a sadness I had never felt before about my behavior. I was still hoping for a way out. But I knew there wasn't, and I had to come clean with all my dirt.

I was aching for drugs, and I was scared; it was by far the longest day of my life. I managed to make it to the party. I pulled up to their house, and the kids went inside. I walked slowly behind them and headed straight to the bathroom. I couldn't find the strength I needed to tell him. I almost just wanted to walk away, but I couldn't. There was only one thought: the thought of telling him that it was me. *"I stole from you, and I have been stealing from you for a long time, and I'm beyond sorry."* The playlist continued to play. I walked out of the bathroom, and there was my mom sitting on the couch. She took one look at my face and knew what I had done and what I was about to do. It was like she heard my thoughts while I was in the bathroom. When I opened my mouth to speak, she just looked at me and said, "You have to tell him now; he is outside." My mother had a way of handling life and its many problems; she believed strongly in God. Her faith was on display every day. I walked out, and he was sitting on the steps; I squatted myself on the steps, looking down at the ground and then up at him, and somehow, I found the nerves and said: "It was me; I did this to you."

He looked up at me and asked, "Why?"

All I could say was: "I'm so sorry, I don't know."

I will never forget the look on his face. It was the saddest look I had ever seen on anyone's face. It was as though I could hear his heart breaking. My brother loved me. My brother trusted me with his life and the lives of his children. The few words of despair that he managed to squeeze out between his tightly shut teeth were, "Can you just leave now?" I left abruptly. I knew if I continued asking him questions as though he had no cause to hate me, it could have been detrimental to my health. Even if it weren't physical, the verbal response would have been destructive enough. I lifted myself off the steps, and I exited his presence with the heaviest heart I had ever had to carry. I took my boys and our dog quickly and left. As I was leaving, I turned off my cell phone. What I needed now was silence.

I temporarily found silence within the walls of my car; the boys were quiet, and so was the dog, but I couldn't find stillness within the walls of my mind. As I was driving blindly with no destination in mind, a flood gate of voices began to pour in. Some of the words that I heard very loud in my head were, *"You are garbage," "Look what you just did," "You are worthless," "You are a waste of space," "You are a horrible person," "You are a no-good mother."* On and on the voices kept screaming. I had heard these voices before, but they weren't as loud. I just wanted to drown them out with drugs. Overwhelmed and scared, I drove for miles. All I knew was, I was sick and tired of myself. The boys began asking me where we were going, but I didn't have a clue.

Somehow, I ended up at a park downtown on C Street. I let the boys and the dog out to play, and I sat by the car smoking cigarettes nonstop. I finally turned my phone back on, and a double-digit number of voice mails popped up. Before I could check anything, my mom called again. I couldn't answer; I felt frozen with fear. I didn't know what to say to her because I didn't have a single clear thought that belonged to me. She wanted to know where we were so she could come to us, but I wanted to be alone. Finally, I thought I could ask her to come and take the boys and dog because, at this point, I was done with me. I didn't know what to do, but I knew I no longer deserve to live as I had destroyed everything and everyone around me. I had my mom meet me at the park. They knew the park well because we had once lived across the street. My dad came with her, and he was not pleased to see me at all. He took the boys and started walking around the park while my mom tried to talk to me. I remember that the louder she got, the louder and fiercer the voices became. She kept saying, "Let's just go anywhere," because she didn't want to leave me there, and I kept telling her to take the boys and the dog and go.

In my mind, I thought that once they were gone, I would find a way to end my life. I must repeat this: my mom is an amazing woman of God. She began saying, "Let's just pray everything will be fine; it's okay." She said that a few more times before I snapped at her and said, "How is anything okay? It's not okay. Nothing is okay!" But she would not leave. Even my dad, at this point, told her, "So let's just go. We can take the boys, and she can do whatever she wants." You see, they had no idea what my plan was at this point, but my mom instinctively knew she could not leave me alone.

Remember earlier when I said, "If I just let her pray, she would feel better and leave me alone"? Well, that's where I was now. I said, "Okay, mom, fine, let's pray," and she began praying. I don't know what she prayed, but suddenly, I couldn't hear anything. I couldn't hear the cars driving by or the boys and other children playing in the park, and although my mom was right next to me, praying at the top of her voice, I couldn't hear her. She is a very intense prayer warrior. No more voices were telling me I was worthless and should end my life. I heard nothing—absolute silence, the silence I had so desperately sought in bottles and pills, in lying and stealing—absolute silence. I felt an intense heat wash over me from head to toe, and I felt a presence like nothing that I had felt before in my entire life. This presence was embracing me. It was as if someone had walked up behind me and wrapped their arms tightly around me. It was the hug of my lifetime. At that moment, I felt peace—not quietness, but peace for the first time. Then I heard this inner voice say, "I love you; it's okay." Once I listened to that voice, I felt embraced by love. Afterward, the noise around me returned, and I could hear everything again—the cars going by, and the children playing, and my mom still praying—and I began to weep.

Something had changed; something shifted in me because there were no more voices, no more emptiness, no more feeling unworthy of life. I didn't know much then, but I knew somebody loved me, and I knew it was God. Finally, once again, I felt I belonged to Him just as I did when I was a young girl. I later learned that where the spirit of the Lord is, there is freedom (2 Corinthians 3:17). It was the presence of Jesus that changed me. His light made the darkness in my life flee. I praised God for the freedom I felt in me and around me.

My mom stopped praying; I finally said I would go with her. Later she told me that something happened to me during that prayer because I was different afterward. Once I got in the car, my mom started asking me questions about everything. I remember merely telling the truth about everything. There was no more lying, no more trying to hide anything. I started to be very aware of what the reality of my current situation was. It became apparent that I would have a hard time ahead of me, especially since I was out of drugs. I knew I would no longer be taking any medications to satisfy my addiction. I feared the withdrawal symptoms because I knew them all too well. Once, I had to be admitted to the hospital when I tried to quit cold turkey. It didn't work for me then, and I walked out of the hospital the same way I had walked in, addicted. So I was a little afraid, but I now had a firm conviction that I would never touch drugs again. This all happened when my mother prayed for me.

God took me off suicide watch that day and gave me life.

I ended up at my sister's house later that night after driving around for a few hours because my parents didn't know where to take me for the night. My entire family was in chaos, and my parents lived with my brother at that time, so I couldn't go there. I couldn't go home because my boyfriend was angry with me. I didn't feel safe. Finally, my sister said I could stay at her home for a night. It was getting later and later, and I was waiting for this horrible withdrawal I expected to come crashing down on me. But it never came. I only suffered a little physical discomfort. The pain, sweating, headaches, and wanting to crawl out of my skin never came. Praise God! I didn't even know that God could or would do something like that for me.

I was delivered and changed. I didn't understand what exactly happened, but I knew I was different. I no longer had the continuous pull on me to sin. For the next few days and weeks, I didn't know what would happen to me. I knew that my sister-in-law had already filed a police report. All I knew was, I didn't want anything to do with the type of life I had been living. I didn't know how to read my Bible, but the Lord met me where I was. He gave me what I needed: clear sight and thought. God lifted the fog. I spent a lot of time praying and crying out to God, mostly because I knew what a horrid and wretched person I had been. I knew I had sinned against Him and everyone around me. From the moment I experienced His presence, I knew I had done horrible things in my life and was so sorry for them. I mourned over what I had done. Looking back now, I can see how God was watching over me all those years, trying to corral me in so I could listen to His voice, the God I had left behind because of the evil of others. He was showing me that He had never left; I had just been ignoring Him. But now I realize how desperately I needed Him and how willing He was to embrace me. Thank you, God!

Because of my dependency and manipulation of others, I was now in isolation. No one wanted to be around me except my mother. But this self-inflicted isolation was needful, and it had become so extreme that the only person I could turn to was God. Thank God my mother had reintroduced us that day in the park. However, the very next day, an opportunity presented itself for me to blame my boyfriend for the path I had chosen; I could have said how I would never have ended up here if it wasn't for him. But I was not about to make a U-turn to where I had just left; no, this freedom felt too good. My sister and I started to make plans for my recovery, and she decided that I would live with her and make a fresh start. I called my sons' father and told him I was leaving and would come home to get my things. He was already in shock because of everything that had occurred the day before. I wasn't listening to any reasons or anything that he had to say, nothing at all; I just wanted a fresh start. I knew something good had happened to me, and I knew that I was different, but I didn't know what I should do. I had felt new, but I was experiencing attacks and fights for my soul. As I drove home to get my things, I started to have the same thoughts as before, and I started getting comfortable with the idea that I could get better and have this great life.

Then I realized that the only thing that had changed was my desire for drugs. I was still playing the blame game. My mind needed renewing, or I would head right back to where I had come from. I knew beyond a shadow of a doubt that if I made a U-turn, it would have been the end of me; there would be no next time. But God, He had bigger plans. He didn't want only to help me stop using drugs and lying. No, He wanted me, and I opened my heart and my mouth and made a declaration, "God wants me!" Guess what? He wants you also. He wanted to change me from the inside out, to change my nature and make me new, and that He did! No more blame games!

Therefore, if anyone is in Christ, the new creation has come: The old has gone, the new is here! All this is from God, who reconciled us to himself through Christ and gave us the ministry of reconciliation: that God was reconciling the world to himself in Christ, not counting people's sins against them. And he has committed to us the message of reconciliation. (2 Corinthians 5:17–19 NIV)

On my way home, I got a call from my sister saying that she had spoken to her husband, and he was not okay with my boys and I living there. He said we could stay for a couple of days, but we couldn't move in. She apologized, but there was nothing she could do at this point. My heart sank. I was disappointed, to say the least, and now a little worried because I had already made my intentions known to my boyfriend. I was walking into unknown territory. I had to be completely honest with him about not having a place to stay, so I needed to retract my words. I had to tell him not only what I had done but what I was feeling. Another hard pill to swallow. And what about his thoughts and feelings? That night he was upset but calmed down, and as the days passed, I kept praying and crying a lot. He was attending school at the time, so I had a lot of time alone. I started listening to some old Romanian Christian songs I remembered from childhood, and I would put my earplugs in and repeatedly play them to help soothe my soul. My playlist had changed.

I knew God had delivered me from the drugs, but to explain this to the people around me was not easy, so I went to a group for addicts to show my inward change. I started attending these group sessions, and I would listen to these people talk about all their horrible cravings and triggers, as they called them, but I had none of that. I shared how sorry I was for what I had done and for the hurt I had caused to the people in my life. I remember a conversation with my counselor about getting my boyfriend to trust me and believe that I would not do this again. He believed that I was going to relapse at any given moment. He was so convinced that he started testing me by leaving his medications on the counters. I can only imagine how many times he had to count his meds. God had been so gracious to me; I had no "triggers," no cravings, and I knew in my mind and soul that He had done a new thing in me!

About this time, I started looking for a job because I had been on unemployment, and my unemployment benefits period ended. I applied everywhere I could; nothing was coming up. During this time, I had noticed that I was hungry for God and wanted more. I wanted to start going to church. I had a conversation with my boyfriend about going to church, and he asked why I wanted to do that. He said if he went, he would go to a church of a different faith than Pentecostal, and at that time, I didn't argue with him about it. I just said that we needed to start going as a family because I wanted my boys to know the Lord. I started looking for churches, but every time I found a church of his faith, he made some excuse as to why he couldn't go. We never went, and I let it go for a while because I was yet dealing with my boatload of shame and believed that I had no right to disagree about anything; after all, my family viewed me as the screw-up. I didn't dare to stand up for what I now knew to be the right thing to do. Please notice my new language; I wanted to do "the right thing."

I knew the truth: I needed God, and so did my family. After about two and a half months of praying and letting go of broken pieces of myself little by little, I finally had enough courage to ask God to show me the church that my boys and I needed. He showed me Harvest Church. Even though I had passed it hundreds of times before, I had never noticed it was a church. I looked it up online and said to my boys, "Okay, guys, we are going to church this Sunday and see how it goes. If it's not the place for us, then we will try another and another until we find one that we can call home." I asked my boyfriend if he wanted to go. He said no and asked why I was going; I said, "I need to." I asked the Lord to give me a sign if this church was where he wanted me to be. I knew I would be fine as long as the Lord was there, but I needed my boys to want to be there also because I could not go without them. I prayed that the boys would love it and want to go back. Sunday came, we went, and I took my sons to the children's church while I went into service alone. I was alone, but I felt the same presence I had felt in the park, and I knew I was never really alone. That day I officially gave my life to Jesus Christ. Once service was over and I went to get my boys, they were so excited and talked about how great it was and that the church had this Wednesday night event for them, and they wanted to go. Answered prayer, and we have been there since August 18, 2013.

That is another date that I know well because the very next day, I started the process of being hired at my new job. Remember that I said I was looking for a job for a long time, finding nothing? Two weeks after I started going to church, I went from business to business, leaving my resume. On this one particular day, I was done passing out resumes and decided to stop at my favorite gas station near my home, where I always purchased my drinks and cigarettes. The girl at the counter knew me as a regular. She asked me how the job search was going because I had mentioned it to her before in passing. But this time, she asked me what kind of job I wanted. I told her anything that would help me pay the bills. On this day, the manager overheard us and came out to talk to me. She told me she couldn't give me full-time employment, but she could offer me a part-time if I wanted it. I quickly said I would take it, and just like that, I started the process of being hired. Within two weeks, she had me on the schedule to work. I only worked one or two days as a part-time employee and later was changed to full time. I worked there for over three years, and then God gave me an even better opportunity.

I finally realized who it was that was out to destroy me—who had caused the trauma in my life, and in turn, I traumatized others. I now knew.

Jesus said to them, "If God were your Father, you would love me, for I have come here from God. I have not come on my own; God sent me. Why is my language not clear to you? Because you are unable to hear what I say. <u>You belong to your father, the devil, and you want to carry out your father's desires. He was a murderer from the beginning, not holding to the truth, for there is no truth in him. When he lies, he speaks his native language, for he is a liar and the father of lies.</u>" (1 John 8:42–47 NIV)

Therefore Jesus said again, "Very truly I tell you, I am the gate for the sheep. All who have come before me are thieves and robbers, but the sheep have not listened to them. I am the gate; whoever enters through me will be saved. They will come in and go out and find pasture. <u>The thief comes only to steal and kill and destroy</u>; I have come that they may have life, and have it to the full. "I am the good shepherd. The good shepherd lays down his life for the sheep. (John 10: 7–11 NIV)

In this scripture, Jesus identifies the thief, the devil, who was trying to destroy me then and now. I see that it was the devil trying to destroy me with help from a few supporting church folks and perverts. And then I read this scripture and saw it. Jesus, the Son of God, is the One who has destroyed the works of the devil, but we only know this when we give our lives over to Jesus:

Dear children, do not let anyone lead you astray. The one who does what is right is righteous, just as he is righteous. The one who does what is sinful is of the devil, because the

devil has been sinning from the beginning. <u>The reason the</u>
<u>Son of God appeared was to destroy the devil's work</u>. No one
who is born of God will continue to sin, because God's seed
remains in them; they cannot go on sinning, because they
have been born of God. (1 John 3:7–9 NIV)

God did not rescue me because there was something extra special about me, but rather because God said I was special—so special that He sent His Son to die for my sins. Guess what? He feels the same about all of us, and a new life awaits you because you are special in His sight. The "world" He alludes to in this next scripture is not the structure; it is the people, whosoever believe.

For <u>God so loved the world</u> that he gave his one and only
Son, <u>that whoever believes</u> in him shall not perish but have
eternal life. For God did not send his Son into the world
to condemn the world, but <u>to save the world</u> through him.
Whoever believes in him is not condemned, but whoever
does not believe stands condemned already because they
have not believed in the name of God's one and only Son.
(John 3:16–17 NIV)

God did and continues to do so many beautiful things for me. He took all the chains that were tangled and twisted around me, and He gave me freedom and hope. He has given me a beautiful life and holds my hands as He walks with me daily.

This is GOD's Word on the subject......, I'll show up and take
care of you as I promised .... I know what I'm doing. I have

*it all planned out—plans to take care of you, not abandon
you, plans to give you the future you hope for.*

*When you call on me, when you come and pray to me,
I'll listen. When you come looking for me, you'll find me.
Yes, when you get serious about finding me and want it
more than anything else, I'll make sure you won't be disappointed. GOD's Decree. (Jeremiah 29:11–13 MSG)*

Life still happens around me and to me. There is pain, emotionally and physically, and there is plenty of hurt and disappointments
to go around. Old shame and guilt sometimes show their ugly heads
and try to creep in and cripple me, but I am not my past. The more
I commit to walking with Jesus, reading His Word, the Bible, and
spending time talking to him in prayer, the more I am reminded of His
promises to keep me strong. He has told me that when I pray, He hears,
and He listens, and His plans for me are for good. He reminds me that
I have hope and a promising future. I could go on and on about how
amazing it is to be loved by God, but I think the Bible says it best.

*Open your mouth and taste, open your eyes and see—how
good GOD is. Blessed are you who run to him. (Psalms
34:8 MSG)*

I am a child of God, *embraced by His Love, healed by His Grace*,
and no one can take that away, and I have no desire to make any
U-turns.

My Life Is Not My Own

by Suki Kaur

I am writing this story at the age of forty-four and the proud mother of three handsome sons, ages twenty-six, twenty-one, and eighteen. I know it is not normal for a lady to tell her age, but for me to be alive at this age, it's a miracle, and so I proclaim my days on this planet with great joy! I am now a God-fearing Christian woman who has been serving God for over ten years. Needless to say, I was not always a Christian, but God works things out in His own mysterious ways. Life happened to me, and then God took over my life!

I was born and raised in Punjab, India. Punjab is a state bordering Pakistan and is the heart of India's Sikh community. The city of Amritsar, founded in the 1570s by Sikh Guru Ram Das, is the site of Harmandir Sahib, the holiest gurdwara (Sikh place of worship). Known in English as the Golden Temple and surrounded by the Pool of Nectar, it's a major pilgrimage site. Also in Amritsar is Durgiana

Temple, a Hindu shrine famed for its engraved silver doors. My homeland was wonderful. The people had so much love, and that love was authentic. They didn't know any religion outside of our birth faith, and with that, we were satisfied.

In 1986, my family came to the United States, and I was thirteen. I am the oldest of four siblings: one sister and two younger brothers. After being in America for only two months, the worst tragedy we could imagine happened to us: our father was involved in an automobile accident and eventually died from his injuries. He was in his mid-thirties and left behind his beautiful bride and the four of us children. We were devastated when we got the news of this horrific tragedy, not knowing what we were going to do next or where we would go. We had nothing left. The man, the husband, the father who had taken care of us, always providing for us, was now gone. The death of my father left a gaping hole in my heart because we were so close. He wasn't around a lot because of his work, but his love was real and strong. How were we to survive without our father, and our mom without her husband, her strength? After his death, some family members did step up to provide some assistance. There is a cultural belief and practice that another man must step up and fill his shoes by assisting the family when a man dies. Well, in our case, it was our uncle, and without hesitation, our mom prepared us to move in with him and his family.

Our uncle, who was supposed to be a father figure to us kids, soon began to display a wave of anger that was scary. He was not prepared to take on five more people in his home. He was the meanest individual I had ever seen, and he would physically abuse us. He would beat us until we couldn't breathe and would lose consciousness. We were left broken, helpless, and hopeless. To this day, there is a scar. There were days I could not go to school because of the bruising on my body. He didn't want anyone to see the evidence of his abuse. You may ask where my mother was while all of this abuse was taking place.

To be fair, custom had my mother bound. It was customary for the women not to get involved when the man was disciplining the children. The truth be told, my mother was also afraid of him and would do as custom dictated, be quiet and obedient. She suffered in silence, which is true of many women within my culture. Yet, she did all she could to protect us and comfort us. I saw the pain in her eyes and felt her fear when she would embrace me. My mother worked the night shift at a fast-food restaurant, which is how she took care of us kids. There was not a moment we all did not pray for freedom, for peace of mind, and for the pure love that we so missed receiving from our father. We dealt with this abuse for the most extended two years of our lives.

My mother managed to save enough money from her fast-food job to put a down payment on a house. She requested her younger brothers' help to buy a house and get her and us children into a safe place. In 1988, we moved into our own home. We had nothing. We did not have a bed to sleep on, so we slept like babies on the floor. Food was scarce, and we ate bread with ketchup for days. Although we were in survivor mode, surviving on whatever we could get our hands on, we were happy. Although we did not have many material things, we had the peace of mind that we all had desperately sought. Finally, we were away from the situation that had left scars on our souls and our bodies.

By then, I was a teenager, a distraught teen, and they would call me by this new name they had given to me, "the Troubled Teen." I started cutting school to hang out with my friends or hang out with boys. This behavior was not acceptable in our culture. Everything my mother told me not to do, I would want to do even more, and I would dive headfirst into the forbidden behavior. I was so angry at the world and my family because of my father's absence, him dying and leaving me prey to that terrible treatment. I became very rebellious. Being a single mother, my mother was once again under a lot of pressure, and this time it was due to her troubled teenage daughter, me. She had to do something, and she decided that the right thing to do at the time was to take me back to India. She pulled me out of high school during my senior year and told me that we were traveling to India to visit my grandparents. I tried to let her know that this was my last year and that I needed to finish school, but she told me not to worry—that we would visit them for a short time and return in time for me to finish my school year.

When we arrived in India after a twenty-four-hour flight and settled in at our family home, I found the surprise of my life: the real reason we had traveled to our homeland was to marry me off. This was my mother's way to tame her out-of-control teenager. Little did I know that everything was already pre-planned for my wedding. My wedding dress, shoes, jewelry, makeup, and even lingerie was chosen and purchased by someone else. She did give me the option to choose my future husband from the selection they had assembled. They introduced me to a couple of men, one at a time, selected by the family, and a few rejected by the family. By this time, I had an extremely sick feeling in my stomach that I would be returning to the United States saying "I'm married now!" at the ripe young age of eighteen. I had hoped to escape that part of the culture of having my family choose my spouse; it is called a pre-arranged marriage. But I now found myself entrapped in its grip. My mom and grandparents told me that it was my responsibility to honor my father because I was the oldest daughter, and everyone wanted to see me married. I knew there was no getting around this. I was now a hostage, and they were not going to relent.

To make matters worse, to add guilt and shame upon me, they even injected my beloved, deceased father into this mess.

My family introduced me to a man whom I thought was very handsome. We talked one day but were never allowed to date or go anywhere by ourselves. It was our custom that boys and girls are not left alone. Since we both were delighted with each other's outward appearance, we both said "yes" and agreed on the marriage. After all, since they forced me into this marriage, at least he should be pleasant to my eyes. We were now engaged! We had two months to plan the wedding. My family was super happy, and different people were in charge of various tasks to make this wedding event happen. They sent out the invitation cards, and everything was ready to go.

Six days before the wedding, my fiancé began receiving letters from a stranger saying, "If you marry that girl, we are going to kill you!" He started to receive these letters daily, and sometimes even two to three times a day. By now, this was a significant concern, and he backed out of the wedding. Trying to save face with the community, my family told him that someone was playing jokes on him. They were devastated and poured out their souls, begging him to reconsider because this would bring much shame on our family, and they could not face the community if he backed out. Although he reassured me that he wanted to marry me, he was understandably worried about his very life. After all, what if the threats were not a joke? I was afraid for him and me because I didn't know who was sending the threatening letters, almost as if they were trying to protect me. What if it was a crazy man who wanted to do me harm as well? We never found out who or what was behind those threatening letters. He backed out, leaving me hurt. Even though I hadn't known him long, I was very attracted to him.

My family was now asking the million-dollar question: What were we going to do now? My mother was so sad, thinking that her eighteen-year-old daughter would stay single all of her life and that no one would marry her now. It is incredible how firm culture can be, and in our culture, shame weighs heavily. With my family feeling overwhelmed with sadness and guilt, they decided since they had a wedding date and the invitations sent out, the only thing they needed to do was find another man in short order. No one would know what had happened. They set out on their mission to find me a husband quickly, and guess what? They did!

They found a man and took him to a friend's house and told me to go there as well. They told him everything, and he agreed. The day finally came when he would become my husband. On my wedding day, I felt hurt, angry, and alone. Once again, I was experiencing the feelings of helplessness and hopelessness. I looked around the room at everyone with tears in my eyes. My family and everyone there had big smiles on their faces, and there I was, looking sad and with my eyes swollen with tears while they chatted about how everything would be okay and would work out. The biggest guilt trip of the evening was me showing respect for my family—my mother, grandparents, but mostly my deceased father—by going through with this wedding. With so much guilt, hurt, and brokenness, I accepted the offer and said yes to putting a smile on my family's faces. Only God knew that I was shut down and dying inside. I married this man whom I did not know, and I did not have a choice. I only did it to save my family's pride. The price of shame can be costly; it cost me, me!

Caution! You are now entering the twilight zone

My wedding day, the day when a girl should be beside herself bubbling over with joy, was the day I had to kill and bury my emotions.

My family was busy preparing and paying for my wedding, but it was my funeral. In my life, I never had felt so hurt and betrayed as I did on that day, seeing everyone so happy that they had pulled off their grand caper. Smiles lit up the room. I suppose they deemed it proper for me to be their sacrifice and to afford them their day of happiness. A sacrifice is supposed to suffer pain, bleed, and plead for release, but find none. I was their sacrificial offering. Although I felt so sad, betrayed, and abandoned, the greatest was the sacrifice of true love. My mother made it clear that she knew what was best for me, and she hoped that I would start behaving in accordance with our faith. Honoring culture was far more important than me finding my true love.

I was now entering into the twilight zone, where everything is not what it appears to be. I had to pretend that I was a happy bride for this to work, and I began doing exactly that. I began to convince myself that the material things that came with this marriage should be enough to sway me from the sadness. We had a home—not just home, a gorgeous home—and I had money, and we traveled a lot together. I remained in India for five months with my new husband and then returned to America married and very pregnant. After eighteen months, my husband joined me in America. I had what the world would call "wealth." I had it all, but my tank was on empty. I was lost, and being forced into this marriage broke my heart into a million pieces.

I am sure you have heard the saying "Money can't buy you love." That was the truth for me. I was still looking for my soulmate because the most significant sacrifice they forced me to give up was to experience true love. I was the sacrifice that kept getting off the altar, because the thirst for true love never left the palate of my soul. I could never pretend enough to quench that thirst. Before I realized it, I had a complete family, with three fine boys, and all the materials defined as wealth. I did not know what was going to be the next phase of my life. I was delighted with the love of my boys, and caring for them brought me so much joy. But nothing removed the thirst deep within me to experience true romantic love. I began my journey of looking for love, but I found myself in all the wrong places. If you don't know where you are going, you are probably going the wrong way. After all, there was no map for this journey, and in my world, no conversation either.

The Attempts to Fix My Life

If you have a flat tire and need to make it to the repair shop, it helps to have some temporary fix-it. To continue driving on a flat tire can create extensive damages, and what would have been a minimum cost extends beyond the budget's reach.

Well, that is what I begin to do: apply temporary fixes while I continued to drive around with a broken heart.

Fix-it number one: I started to drink a lot to fill up the void. Nothing would make me feel happy. I thought I had everything but what I needed. Why couldn't I be satisfied? I had so much stuff. People tell you what you need to be happy, but I wasn't enjoying my life; I was not happy. I cannot say this enough: I did not want this marriage. I didn't hate my husband, but I did not love him. However, after giving birth to my beautiful children and buying a lovely home and everything else we purchased, I thought my heart would change and I would be able to accept my marriage with joy. No, none of these things changed my heart concerning this marriage. *As time moved on without me*, the darkness flooded my soul and gathered around me, and I was diagnosed with depression and prescribed medication that did not help. Things were getting worse as time passed, and I kept falling deeper and deeper into the twilight zone of depression. There was a recording in my head, and it played this script over and over: "You are the problem; everyone else is good; if you get rid of yourself, problem solved." These thoughts of suicide became stronger and stronger. I was suicidal the entire time I was married, and since alcohol could not drown out the voice of despair, I tried fix-it number two.

Fix-it number two consisted of my most desperate acts. I attempted to take my life on numerous occasions, but as you can see by reading my story, I wasn't successful. I was now at a new low and decided to try something different to fix my life.

Fix-it number three was so far outside my norm that I couldn't understand why I thought about doing this. I started praying to the unknown God. I wasn't sure He existed, but I asked anyway for Him to take my life because I had no desire to live; I did not want this life anymore. I placed this god whom I did not know, and whose existence I only suspected, on trial to stand before me. I was going to be His prosecutor, cross-examine him, and, finally, be his judge. First, He had to prove that He existed, and He would do this by showing me the love and mercy that I have heard others say He has. I wanted Him not just to let me die, but for Him to find a way to take my life—to take back this breath that they say He gave because it no longer served me well. After all, I couldn't seem to kill myself. I would waver between wanting to die and wanting to live. I only wanted to die because I couldn't stop the pain. I had heard some things about this god. Some said He listens to us, so I shouted at Him to rescue me. And because others told me that He had emotions, I thought maybe He could feel my brokenness, and if so, perhaps He would heal my broken heart. So, I begged Him, "Please, let me feel Your presence, and make me feel different—make me happy!" I was hoping that this god would be different because I was desperate; I was tired of the mess, tired of the brokenness, and the feelings of being confused, empty, and beyond lost.

One day I met a guy who worked in the same building as me but in a different department. He struck up a conversation, and we began to talk more often; one thing led to another, and we started spending time together. He told me that I was an incredibly special person, and he felt like he was falling in love with me and wanted to be with me. I told him that it would never happen because I was married. He told me he believed that I was going to end up killing myself. He told me he could sense that I was miserable in my marriage. That was true; I had been the entire fourteen years—pure misery. He asked, "How is it working out for you? There is life after divorce, and you will not be the only woman in the world to have gotten a divorce." Again, he reminded me that he believed that I would eventually kill myself and wanted to help me in any way he could to get through this. He said he could see death written all over me. But why would he want to be with a suicidal person?

I felt it in my heart that this was the open door to my grand escape; I had finally found my final fix-it, my knight in shining armor coming to rescue me. My soul mate had finally arrived. I knew at that time that I had to either accept or reject his offer. How badly I wanted to accept his offer, but deep within, I couldn't find the guts to do it. But being at this emotional junction in life where the pain was more than I could take, he seemed to have awakened courage within me beyond my imagination.

I boldly confronted my husband and told him the whole truth and nothing but the truth. I told him where I had been physically, mentally, and emotionally, and I told him how I was pretending to be happy. The flood gate open and I couldn't shut it. I told him that I never loved him, that I married him for my family, and that the children, money, house, and cars were a cover-up. I think I told him probably a little bit too much when I told him I tried killing myself so often because I had no desire to live. I continued to tell him how I never wanted this life, and I still didn't, and then I went for the jugular and said, "I am filing for a divorce!" His heart broke and mixed with tears; he begged me to stay and give our marriage another chance. But I told him I had been trying to give it a chance from day one when I was forced into the marriage and have been for over fourteen years; I couldn't do it anymore. When I pause to think about it, I know it wasn't his fault, and he was becoming a victim just as I had been all along.

I knew if I had stayed with him, I would have eventually committed suicide. I was working two jobs to help my husband, who was going to school. He told me the rest of the family would think it was ugly and not acceptable and sad. The news spread like wildfire, and once again, I had to decide. But I was no longer just a scared girl at an altar. I now had a husband and three lovely sons, my three siblings—one younger sister and two younger brothers—who would all be affected by my decision. I was blunt, stood my ground, and said, "No! I have already made up my mind, and I am going to stick with it. This time I am doing it for me." Everyone who was important to me and had value in my life was against this decision. I had brought shame to the family, and they separated from me. I was disowned and dead to them. The pain of rejection was like none other. Although broken and confused, I stood firm on my decision. I had pain on top of pain, and I could no longer live daily, experiencing the pain every time I awoke or walked into my home. My home was my prison, my institution, and the only joy were those three little boys.

The Divorce Process

I was discouraged and depressed; I had so much pain and confusion. Our boys were affected because of the separation, but I had to do what was best. I would cry all the time and pray to this new God to help me. Suddenly, I started feeling and thinking maybe this God does exist, because every time I would pray, I would begin to hear a song on the radio or hear the exact words I needed come out of a stranger's mouth. It began to happen so frequently that I felt that this God let me know that he did hear me and was trying to get my attention. It was then my blind eyes began to open, and I began to feel like there was a reason why this God did not take my life. Maybe he had a purpose and a plan for my life. Random thoughts like this would flood my mind.

One day I sat alone while the kids were sleeping, and I began to speak to this god as I had never done before. I don't know how I was so specific, but I said, "God, it's me. My life is a mess, and I am lost and confused, still wanting to die because that will solve everything for me. God, I don't know what to do anymore; I need help. I have never felt you before, and I don't even know how I will know if you are real and if you can hear me. God, I would like to know you, and I am willing to do whatever it takes to get my life right, for me to find peace because I don't even know what it is like to have peace in my heart. God, I thought it was the love of a man missing in my heart, but I have found that, and I still do not have peace. I have someone who I think loves me, and I think I love him. I'm still not happy, and I don't know if what I did was the right thing."

I prayed that night and asked this God for two things: First, I told God that I would search for Him—that I wanted to find Him. I told Him how I would start going to different places of worship, and wherever I went, if He was not there, I asked that He please not leave me there. Second, I asked Him that once I found Him, please let me know that I had indeed found Him and could stop looking. I was beginning to recognize this God, and He began to illuminate my spirit.

I started searching right after that prayer, the very next morning, within my birth religion, Sikhism. The temple opened every day, seven days a week. I got up every morning at five and went to the temple; I prayed and waited on God to say something to me. I did not know what to listen for or how He would speak to me; I just trusted. About the seventh day of praying and being in this place, I heard a voice in my spirit, loud and clear, say, "I AM not here!" I got up and never had the desire to go back, and I never did. After that, I checked out every religion I could find. I was the happiest woman in the world one day when some people showed up at my door; I knew it had to be God; He had made way for me. I asked them to take me to their church and if they would teach me the Bible. Both ladies were so willing to help me. I went to their church and heard the same voice again, "I AM not here," and I never went back to that church. I checked out every religious organization I could think of, and I kept hearing the same voice, "I AM not here!" I was so disappointed and wondered why I still heard the same voice. I began to question if what I was experiencing was real. After going to so many churches and not receiving peace, I thought, *How can this be?* As far as I was concerned, there was nothing left, so where was I supposed to go next? Being confused and disappointed, I just kept asking myself over and over again, *What do I do now?*

My friend asked me to have lunch with him, and I said yes. He asked me what I had done the day before, which was Sunday. I told him I had gone to this particular church. He asked me why I had gone to that particular church. I told him it was because I was looking for God, and these nice ladies from that church had visited me. I said I was desperate to find God, so I decided to go with them. He looked at me and said, "Wow! Really? What else?" I said, "Well, I want to find God, and I have been looking for Him. So far, I have checked out every religion, and I keep hearing the same voice saying, 'I AM not here!'" He told me that I amazed him, and then he said, "I told you that you are special! Have you gone to a Christian church?" After thinking about it, I told him I didn't think so. As a matter of fact, that was the only kind of church that was left for me to attend.

He told me about a Christian church in San Jose, California. I was so excited; I thought there was nothing else left out there. I couldn't wait for Sunday to come. Finally, Sunday came, and I asked him to go with me; he declined but encouraged me to go. I was looking for God, and I didn't mind going alone. I went to the church, and as I entered the sanctuary, I felt a kind of peace and a feeling I had never felt before. I was super excited and was practically running to get in there. I meet a lady at the front door, who hugged me and said to me, "You are the most beautiful daughter of the most high God!" I did not know what that meant, but it sounded good to my spirit. After being disowned, to hear that from a stranger who was old enough to be my mother was the sweetest thing I had ever heard. She escorted me to the front, and I told her it was my first time being in a church. *She said, "Welcome! Your life will change forever after this day!"* I did not know what that meant, but it sure sounded good. She found me a seat, and I was looking around and noticed that everyone was worshipping God. They were singing, and no one was looking around. I looked around, and I heard a voice saying, *"Just close your eyes and lift your hands."* I closed my eyes and lifted my hands, and my whole body started shivering, my knees began trembling, I fell on my knees, and I heard this beautiful voice in my head, my heart, and resounding in my spirit say, *"YOU ARE HOME!"* I cried like a baby, and my life changed forever that day! After that, God showed up in every area of my life!

As my life evolved, me and my children moved to Elk Grove, California, and there I found another Christian church that was a blessing to me and my growth in Christ for six years. I am amazed at how I didn't know if this God existed, and now I listen and know His voice. Eventually He told me my tenure was up at my present church. I prayed about that, and a few days later, I ran into an old friend who invited me to my current church, and for that, I praise God!

My life with God grew and grew until even my mother and other family members admitted that a change had happened in my life. I wasn't the same depressed woman they had known. God had truly touched and transformed my life, and they were able to see God's light and transformation that had taken place in broad daylight. God had completely changed me. My family witnessed God's protection over me when I was going through the divorce and how I dealt with the many false accusations; God fought my battles. God performed many miracles for me, and I would share them with my mother and other family members. They all witnessed that I had come alive with Jesus in my life; there was no denying that.

I cried unto this God that I did not know, and He heard my cry and made me understand that He heard me. Today, I am exceedingly happy and content with my walk with my Lord Jesus Christ. He has given me what no man on this earth could give me. I learned that I am a whole person, not a half looking for my other half, but I am complete in Him. As the Lord and I walk together, the road does come up to meet me. He has gifted me with the gift of healing hands, whereby I lay hands on the sick, and they recover, just as the scripture says.

"And these signs will accompany those who believe: In my name they will drive out demons; they will speak in new tongues;… they will place their hands on sick people, and they will get well." (Mark 16:17–18 NIV)

I am grateful that He chose me, and therefore, I can walk with confidence that although I cannot change the whole world, God can use me to change an individual's world, one person at a time.

Being confident of this, that he who began a good work in you will carry it on to completion until the day of Christ Jesus. (Philippians 1:6 NIV)

Praise be to the LORD my Rock, who trains my hands for war, my fingers for battle. (Psalms 144:1 NIV)

The great depression over my life began when my father, whom I loved so dearly, abruptly died, and in such a tragic manner—a vehicle accident. If that was not enough for a young girl to suffer, my mother rushed me off to my homeland for a family visit that turned out to be a trap to marry me off. All my life, my life did not belong to me; it always belonged to those who had authority over me, and they exercised it to their advantage and my disadvantage.

I went on a journey to find this God whom I knew nothing about; I had only heard rumors of Him. And one day, He found me and introduced Himself to me. It is in Him I now live and breathe, and guess what: now my life belongs to Him, the one who loves me unconditionally.

For in him we live and move and have our being. As some of your own poets have said, We are his offspring. (Acts 17:28 NIV)

You are my witnesses, declares the LORD, and my servant whom I have chosen, so that you may know and believe me and understand that I am he. Before me no god was formed, nor will there be one after me. (Isaiah 43:10 NIV)

So that from the rising of the sun to the place of its setting people may know there is none besides me. I am the Lord, and there is no other. (Isaiah 45:6 NIV)

My Life Is No Longer My Own

In the beginning, I told you how I felt like a sacrifice for my family's pride because they robbed me of the ultimate option of deciding who I would love and marry. Well, this God gave me a choice: to choose His Son, Jesus, and have a life now and eternally, or not, and be forever tormented. Not that he was my tormentor; He was not and didn't want me tortured, but He gave me options. He extended to me a way out and was willing to rescue me from myself and from the world with its deadly ideas and habits, including satan. He didn't place a price for it on my shoulders; He had already made a way because His Son, Jesus, had borne it on His shoulders and had been the sacrifice. I knew only a little of what it felt like to be a sacrifice, and I hated it with everything in my being. Others made me the determining factor for their happiness at the loss of my own; that's a deal-breaker. But the Bible says,

For God so loved the world that he gave his one and only Son, that whoever believes in him shall not perish but have eternal life. (John 3:16 NIV)

A very dear friend of mine said, "You don't have forever to start doing what is right, but start doing what is right, and you will have forever to enjoy it!" I think that sums up John 3:16, believing and accepting what Jesus did for me on the cross, the sacrifice that paid for it all, and I, one of "whosoever," shall not perish. I shall enjoy the fruit of my labor forever in Him. And, please, let's not stop at John 3:16; you must also embrace John 3:17:

For God did not send his Son into the world to condemn the world, but to save the world through him. (John 3:17 NIV)

A famous line in a favorite movie says, "Get busy living or get busy dying!" May I encourage you to read the entire Book of John? You will not be sorry you did; it will show you Jesus and how to get busy living. Today, I live to the advantage of the Kingdom of God, which has given me everything. But I am no longer my own; Jesus's sacrifice purchased me. I belong to His Kingdom, and my joy is full.

I had never known this God, and I never thought that surrendering my life to Jesus Christ, the Son of God, would bring me so much freedom, because after my father died, the life I lived was never my own! And today, this new life I live is not my own either, but this is by my choice.

I have been crucified with Christ and I no longer live, but Christ lives in me. The life I now live in the body, I live by faith in the Son of God, who loved me and gave himself for me. *(Galatians 2:20 NIV)*

… Do you not know that your bodies are temples of the Holy Spirit, who is in you, whom you have received from God? You are not your own; you were bought at a price.

Therefore honor God with your bodies. (1 Corinthians 6:19–20 NIV)

Today, I touch the lives of many through my business, Healing Through Touch, a divine massage service located at 3112 O Street, Sacramento, CA 95816. My email is sukikaur916@yahoo.com, and my business number is 916-821-4507. God has blessed my hands.

The Blood of the Lamb and the Words of My Testimony

by Ashley Austin

Everyone who knows me knows I love to write. I write for fun and worship, but writing my story, my testimony, by sharing a short experience in my life has been challenging. I was close to withdrawing from this opportunity, and I gave many reasons for doing so. I said that my story was still being written. But isn't everyone's story unfinished? Then I said it was too much exposure; it would be hard and scary. But I need to learn how to do the right thing scared. The devil, the enemy of all souls, knows the power of a testimony baptized by the blood of Jesus. I pray that my story—my testimony—will be a beautifully wrapped gift of freedom for others, including you. Maybe my story will reach you in time to prevent you from making harmful mistakes like the ones I made. There's a saying that one person's junk is another person's treasure; likewise, one person's heartbreaking life story can be the road map for another to have a life of endless happiness.

The last year and a half of my life have been complicated in ways I couldn't have imagined. My impulsive decision to fight for independence created a roadmap for my life. It is a roadmap of many twists and sharp turns on the edge of the mountain. A real cliffhanger! I wanted freedom so badly that I was willing to throw away everything and everyone in my path. It all started with my longing for a relationship. My religious faith teaches me to trust and wait on God, but the desire became overwhelming, and I said, "Okay, God, I'm not patient enough to wait on you, so I am taking matters into my own hands."

I reconnected with a guy I knew from the past. He was currently in a relationship, and I knew what I was doing was wrong. The woman he was with made him happy, but I believed I could make him more content, so I persisted and persisted, doubted for a bit, and then persisted some more. I convinced myself that we should be together and that it was God's plan. I had visions of us having a family. We had first met when I was fifteen or sixteen, and he was twenty-one, attempting to talk to me. Such a relationship was illegal, and my parents weren't having it. But now I was twenty-four and he was twenty-nine, so age was no longer an issue. Drifting into this relationship pulled me away from my family because my parents didn't forget and wouldn't ever agree. But I thought I was in love, or at least the thought of love caused me to act abnormally. I was impulsive.

My parents advised me not to pursue this relationship, but I was twenty-four, a college student with a job who thought I knew everything and could do anything. I grew tired of hearing their warnings to reconsider my actions, and I turned a deaf ear. I moved into a house with my boss's daughter, whom I considered as a sister, paying seven hundred fifty dollars a month for a room. I couldn't afford the rent. My budget left me with three hundred dollars after rent. It didn't matter; I wanted freedom. I envisioned us conquering the world. I decided to quit my job because it became extremely stressful. I worked part-time as a behavior therapist with children with autism, and when a child bit me, I decided enough was enough. I quit! I found an on-call child-care job that paid minimum wage. It didn't pay enough for rent, and I despised every minute of it. I lacked a connection with the children and their parents. So what did I do? I quit that job and moved in with my boyfriend.

I needed a job and applied for one doing the same work I didn't enjoy and had recently quit. I got the position. The house we stayed in was eight minutes away from my new job, but my time management was horrible. I started the job in October, and they terminated me in January. I applied for many other behavior therapist jobs and received acceptance letters for each one. But they were all part-time. I still wasn't making enough money to pay my portion of the rent; there were no funds for car insurance, food, or personal items. I had to find an additional job, and working two jobs was beyond stressful.

I had one thing in my life that was mine and mine alone. Although I struggled financially, I continued attending college. At least, I did until one day I had to choose between paying for my books and paying my bills. My boyfriend didn't hesitate one second to tell me to drop out and focus on finding a stable job instead. Sadly, I didn't hesitate to do precisely what he said: I dropped out of college. I had graduated high school seven years prior, and I still didn't have an associate's, bachelor's, or master's degree. My grandmother was and is my inspiration. She pursued her education and got it; why couldn't I? I became depressed and gave up trying to take care of myself or have a relationship with my family, and I stopped going to church. Not that college meant everything to me, but it was the only thing I had going for *only* me; everything else spun around my relationship.

Soon, I knew my relationship was heading for disaster because of the lack of passion and interest; it stressed me out. Then a flicker turned into a flame, and I cheated on my boyfriend. I had vowed to keep my virginity until marriage. But I saw my live-in relationship with my boyfriend as similar to marriage. I confessed to my boyfriend what I had done, and for my punishment, he made it clear that it had to be an eye for an eye. He said it wasn't about forgiveness but vengeance; therefore, he had the right to cheat. I accepted my punishment with an aching heart. My dream of having a job as a behavior therapist disappeared because I needed a position that paid more money. And I was still hoping to have fun in this broken relationship.

I finally landed a job at a casino as a childcare attendant. Because I had childcare experience, I was getting paid one dollar over minimum wage. I lived forty-five minutes away. Night after night went by, and I would eagerly get in my car and head home, but something sparked my interest in the casino, and I asked myself why there were so many cars in the parking lot on holidays. Why did people leave their children in childcare until two o'clock in the morning to gamble? So, I ventured into the casino one night and played the slots; I won a hundred and seventy dollars. That felt good, because I didn't have enough money to make ends meet. Playing slots for only one night became a habit, and I lost more than I won. I was depressed and addicted to playing the slots. My boyfriend didn't seem to notice that I was coming home later and later. He either didn't notice my late arrivals, or he didn't care.

My twenty-fifth birthday arrived, and my friends threw me a party at the house, and we celebrated. They made me a strawberry cake with marijuana in it, and I drank all night, putting myself in a stupor. Around midnight, one of my brothers called to wish me a happy birthday. I was so excited to hear his voice. But I found myself crying at three o'clock in the morning about God only knows what. I was nauseous and began to make promises to myself. One, I would get myself out of this dead-end position. Two, I would start surrounding myself with positive people. Three, I would *maybe* get out of this unhealthy relationship, and, four, I would make an effort to create a better relationship with my family.

I don't remember when I fell asleep, but my memory was fuzzy when I awoke hours later. I vaguely remembered some of my promises, but they were short-lived, and the cycle repeated itself every month. When my rent came due, I only had fifteen cents in my bank account, and I wouldn't get my next check until the end of the month. I asked a few of my family members if they could help me out, and they did. But every month, I felt like I was "robbing Peter to pay Paul." I got a second job near my parents' home, doing childcare for a former friend. She paid me, sad to say, only twenty dollars a day to watch her children from five o'clock in the morning until five o'clock in the evening. I was desperate.

One day while driving to work, I told God that if He would heal me from my emotional pain and physical pain, I would give up everything in my life that wasn't pleasing to Him. Yep, I was bargaining with God. The next week didn't go so well. I felt like God was punishing me for everything I had ever done. I got strep throat, I couldn't go to work, and I found out that my boyfriend had tried to make a pass at my best friend. There went everything! With all of this came even more emotional pain; even my physical pain increased. I felt like God wasn't holding up his part of the deal. I know that sounds spoiled. After all these things began to happen to me, I became suicidal and stopped trusting that God wanted to see me do well and prosper. For the next two months, I sabotaged everything I had going in my life that was good: my job, some good friends, and some good family relationships.

At one point I was driving from work after putting my last two dollars and fifteen cents in the gas tank—definitely not enough to get me home. You may ask why I was driving home if I couldn't make it. I don't know; I had no other option but to hope. And again, I made the same promise to God that if he got me home, I would give up everything. My car stopped on the off-ramp of the freeway, and I was screaming out to God, crying while banging my hands on the steering wheel, when I saw lights behind me; it was two highway patrol officers. They went beyond the call of duty and not only pushed my car off the road, but they also gave me a ride home. Yes, God got me home safely; yet I paid little attention. Shortly afterward, I quit my job. I stayed in the same situation I was in, living with my boyfriend until finally, my back was up against a brick wall. A wall that I had erected all by myself. I broke and called my mom, bawling, and asked her if I could come home. She said yes—only a mother's love.

At the time, I was so glad that she said yes; I didn't take time to think about the loss of independence that comes with living with parents after a burst of freedom. But was that freedom? The adjustment of being back with my parents was a little awkward; I was very irritable, annoyed, anxious, and depressed. I was still angry at God for not answering me on my time and terms. So, as if I could punish God, I didn't go to church for a few months. My parents are lovely, godly people, and the church is their life. I finally took my friend up on her invitation to go to church. I told God, "I'll know you want my life to turn around if something in this service tugs at my heart directly." The pastor ministered a heart-touching message that day, but nothing specific stood out to me.

"This is it!" I thought. "I'll do life my way." While at the altar, a lady spoke with the minister and told him God had placed something on her heart. I may have seen her before, but we had never formally met. He introduced her as Mama Love and gave her the mic. She said, "God gave me a word to share with the church," and she began saying many things, but this is what I heard: "You thought I didn't hear you when you were in your car, but I heard you." I don't know what else she said, but that was all I needed to hear. I was swooned and came undone, and I knew God was calling me out. Okay, God, you've got me; I'll put forth my best effort to follow you. That was it! That was the word I needed to hear. I knew that God had called me to live for Him. My next step was to find a community to assist me in making life changes.

To my surprise, I saw an announcement about a sisters' retreat at the church. I had never gone to one before, but I thought if God could speak to me at church, what beautiful things would he say to me at the retreat? I decided to go, but first, I had to put away my discomfort about being vulnerable and open my ears to what God had to say. I heard many positive words at the retreat. I heard that with God, I was the victor and no longer a victim. One of my friends came over to pray for me while I was at the altar and shared a prophetic word with me. She said that as I was sitting at the altar, she saw a vision of God pouring anointing oil over me, and me resting in his presence. God took the time to remind me repeatedly that I am now the victor and not the victim.

I'd been baptized when I was thirteen, but I realized my experiences had caused me to reach a new level in my relationship with God. I wanted to get baptized again, and they were baptizing at the retreat. After being baptized, I sat and spoke with some ladies from the church; they talked to me and encouraged me to stay firm in my decision to follow the Lord. One of the ladies asked me for my story. I began sharing my testimony and how and why I was at the sisters' retreat, and I said, "Some lady named Mama Love, I think, had shared a word at church that God had seen me in the car in great distress." Unknowingly, she was sitting next to me as I shared my soul, as I shared my testimony. Wow! She had played an active role in my testimony. To me, that was more confirmation that God had called me and took me through the things I went through for a reason. I sought more earnestly to find and become a part of a community to help me live this new and redeemed life purchased by the blood of the Lamb.

A quote says, "A ship is safe in the harbor, but that's not what ships are for." I had only been back with my parents for three months after living with no rules, running away from God's calling, and giving up on everything except for that relationship I didn't need. I moved in with my parents after making compromises in every area of my life. I prayed for a better community. Before I opened my eyes after the prayer, I started receiving invitations left and right from friends to begin attending hangouts and services with a positive community of people. Suddenly, upon being back for a few months, a Christian college community small group start inviting me to be a part of their family. They were active and took trips and went hiking. They would go out to eat and didn't mind paying for anyone who didn't have money and didn't mind picking someone up if they needed a ride. I had never experienced anything like that, and I couldn't imagine such love existed. They scared me.

When I first started getting invites to hang out, I would tell myself that they were lying or were fake. I also said to God, "By the way, I've known you for sixteen years, and you don't answer prayers that fast, so I don't believe you did this." All of this seemed so fake; I couldn't believe these people were the answer to my prayer. I would decline the invites but later decide to go to a few events to snoop and see who they were. I fell in love! This group of people and the experiences I had with them startled me. I had always believed that I had to earn love, sacrifice, and pay for it. I remained skeptical about hanging out. I didn't want to slip up and open my heart to these strangers. I didn't want to share my story with them; maybe they wouldn't like me after learning my ugly past, even though it had pushed me back to seeking God. I thought, "God, do You want me to blow my cover? I'm a mess, God; make them leave! Let them disappear and never invite me out again!"

But I kept going back. This community would meet up in small groups of ten to twenty young women. We would study the Bible, learn a lesson, and strengthen each other with updates and encouragement. This was the right place for me after returning from a rough patch of life and needing some accountability and love. There was also a larger group, and we met in an auditorium at the university. The large group was the one that scared me the most! People of all different colors, gender, and cultures would meet up and share one common theme: Jesus, living with Him, and living like Him.

The community consisted of young people, and they were physically active. The first time I went out with them was for a hike, which was honestly my first hike. I thought it would be fun, an easy walk. Psych! I got lost with the friend who'd invited me to the group and another girl I met there. I thought we would be on the evening news telecasting the military airlifting us out of the woods. Surprisingly, I wasn't scared. I was praying and laughing hysterically, and we eventually found our way out. Honestly, that's one of my favorite memories. The group also had a fall retreat where all of the group would go to Santa Cruz. My friend kept asking me if I was going, and I kept telling her no and kept making excuses, but I had no reason not to go.

When I finally decided I'd go, my mom provided me with a new excuse. She informed me that appraisers were coming to look at our home, and I needed to clean my messy room. I then used that as an excuse: "I can't go; I need to clean my room." To me, it sounded like I couldn't go because I need to clean out my fishbowl—petty—but these people were determined. The girl I was riding with said, "We can pick you up from your house later." Perfect! My excuses were over.

Just as I finished cleaning my room, she texted me and told me she was outside. Great, and now I was on my way to Santa Cruz. I felt vulnerable, and I prayed the entire way there, "God, don't let me get all icky, don't let me scare them away." I liked them a lot. I felt the need to pray in the car on the way there, and I'm so glad I did because we almost hit a deer but avoided it. I shared prophesy with some of the people that I was too nervous about sharing with before. Prophesy is communicating with someone what you believe God is showing or telling you to share with them. That is what Mama Love was doing when she said, "God told me to tell you." I was saying things about people's lives that only God could've told me. It was amazing. As it states in Romans 12:6 (NKJV):

> *Having then gifts differing according to the grace that is given to us, let us use them: if prophecy, let us prophesy in proportion to our faith.*

There was a lighthouse, and I love lighthouses. I was able to visit it. I took lots of pictures and watched the waves crash right in front of it and managed not to get splashed in the process. I even got a new tattoo that weekend, and I opened my heart to some unbreakable bonds. I realized that I wouldn't have been able to experience any of this if I had left my ship docked at the harbor. This group that I was afraid to interact with has been extremely beneficial to my life. Through prayer, my precious time with God, I have been able to break off strongholds and soul ties that I had allowed to take hold of me and that didn't want to let go.

As life went on past the two retreats, I still struggled with depression, anxiety, and self-doubt. I was working in God's gift. But that didn't change the fact that my debt was in collections, my driver's license suspended, my registration late, I needed new tires, and on top of it all, I didn't have a job. I fell into severe depression again, and I became suicidal once again. I would snap at my family because they were the closest to me. I decided enough and started to see a therapist concerning my mental health; I think she was a Christian because she told me to listen to my favorite worship song when I would feel anxious. I've learned breathing techniques, journaling skills, and so much more. God gives us peace of mind and wisdom to know what to do when we feel like we have no options.

Mama Love and I became close, and I went to Thursday morning prayer with her sometimes. When asked what I needed prayer for, I brought up my transportation dilemma, and she told me that she and another lady from the church would like to help me get my car on the road; I was elated. They told me to write a list of the things I needed to pay off, and they would help me to do so; however, due to my lack of research, I miscalculated the expenses and was still left with things to pay off on my car. I immediately fell into guilt; these women were nice enough to spend money on me, and I couldn't even accomplish my tasks. And then it hit me; perhaps God didn't want me to get relieved, delivered, and healed all at the same time because if I received my deliverance all at once, I wouldn't be able to appreciate it fully. At least that was my logic.

Since living with my family again, I had several jobs in behavior therapy and childcare and would use alternative means for transportation to get to work. But I finally realized I was spending most of my check just getting to work, and I decided that the location of these workplaces would be a deal-breaker. If I couldn't take the bus, walk, ride my bike, or get a ride, then I couldn't do the job. I decided on Good Friday to visit the daycare where I used to work. For some reason, those children could make my day five thousand times better. While I was there, my old boss asked how I was doing, and I told her about my difficulty finding a job. She offered me work hours there while I found the job I wanted. The job was two minutes away by car and five minutes by bike. I didn't know this at the time, but God showed me that if I sow good seeds, I will also reap them. Working at my old job has been humbling, convenient, and helpful. After I made this commitment to humble myself, suddenly, I was offered a job with more hours within a reasonable distance of our home. My relationship with my friends and family got better, my health and my family's health improved, and I am doing much better in college. Yes, I went back to college.

I have learned many things, mostly about myself and how to read my environment. I have learned to be careful when people say they believe in God and ask questions, because you can never be too sure about their definition of God. I have learned that I need to guard my heart and my mind. However, I saw myself from time to time doubting my worth. But one day, while worshipping to the song "Reckless Love," I heard the words saying that there was no wall He won't kick down, no lie He won't tear down, coming after me, and at that moment, I knew my worth to God. I am finding the mercy of God right where I am, and it's beautiful, it's blinding, but most of all, it's mine. This scripture reminds me of who I am:

Then I heard a loud voice saying in heaven, "Now salvation, and strength, and the kingdom of our God, and the power of His Christ have come, for the accuser of our brethren, who accused them before our God day and night, has been cast down. And they overcame him by <u>the blood of the Lamb and by the word of their testimony,</u> and they did not love their lives to the death. (Revelations 12:10–11 NKJV)

I invite you to follow my visual diary on Instagram: noshoesnectariness

Things That Crawl from Under Rocks

by Gloria J. Cunningham

I am just a country girl born in the hills of Arkansas. I am child number two of thirteen children, and we lived in a two-bedroom house. My dad and mother slept on the living room floor, and the boys and girls each had a room. My dad later added another bedroom. Yes, he built the house. My dad was good with his hands. But there is one thing I have learned about the country: you never know what will crawl from under the rocks, and we have lots of rocks in Arkansas. I finally reached the boiling point in my life—a point where I knew I needed to unburden myself of the layers of pain, confusion, and pure desperation that were stacked on me and had become my burial place. I could feel my chest getting heavy as I continued to fight to breathe, just trying to live. I began to push and push to get a breakthrough, and to accomplish that, I had to take a look back and deal with my reality. I looked myself in the eyes and stared into the depth of my soul. I searched out the secrets, praying that God would give me the strength and grace to handle the truth about to be uncovered. Life's journey brings its problems, mishaps, those "should have, would have, and could have done," and finally, the truth of what did happen. Yes, life happened for me, and it wasn't very polite; it didn't ask me permission. It hit me in the heart and took my breath away.

As far back as I can remember, I had a deep sense of right and wrong. It was awakened in me when I was eight years old in the third grade. I can remember the day as though it happened yesterday. A lady—my school called her a missionary—came to visit our school. She carefully took her props out, made of flannel material. She conveyed the incredible story of Jesus Christ and what happened at Calvary for each individual, and she said it included me. Her story awakened my spirit, and I wanted to know more about this Jesus. There was a television show called *The Flying Nun*, and I wanted to do good like her throughout the world. Watching this show was a wonderful escape because even though I was young, I recognized the bad things that were going on in my family. Today, "dysfunctional" would be our description—a new name for an old problem.

The South culturally tends to encourage close-knit families. Because the economy is terrible, the family consists of mom, dad, and siblings, along with grandparents, uncles, aunties, and cousins—or any of these at any given time. It is called the survival of the whole. You would like to think it is the safest place for a child, but that is not necessarily so. It is the hiding place for domestic violence, sexual abuse, oppression, and depression in many instances. In the midst of

it all, the South has qualities worthy of being praised, such as teaching respect and hospitality, producing hard-working individuals, and
women who know how to take a small amount of food and feed an
army. If I was in a courtroom presenting my case, I submit that while
my family taught me to respect others, they also taught me not to tell
secrets. Terrible things are hidden in "secrets." And "children should be
seen and not heard" means that given a child's story versus an adult's,
the adult wins. Parents and other adults punish children when telling
the truth if they are naming an adult as the wrongdoer because it is
considered disrespectful. The ambiguous teachings were confusing
and, in reality, told other children and me to "shut our mouths." The
secrecy and silence can create a safety net for pedophiles and abusers.
There are terrible things that crawl from under the rocks!

It wasn't often that my father allowed my mother to do anything
without him. Everything that she did required his permission. On
one occasion, my parents planned to have a night out with my mother's sister and husband. My parents and their friends loved to party,
which meant drinking, smoking "them there" cigarettes, and dancing
the night away. Whenever they went out, because I was the oldest
girl, I was the designated babysitter. For some strange reason, my dad
suddenly didn't feel like going, but he gave my mother permission to
keep the date. That didn't relieve me from being the babysitter, because
men supposedly weren't babysitters; that was a woman's job. You have
probably figured out that the oldest child was a boy, and he didn't do
babysitting either.

I was thirteen, and in the South, a thirteen-year-old girl is very
responsible and knowledgeable on how to run a house. Older women
teach girls how to cook, clean, take care of the children, and even
marry. I had planned on getting some good sleep, but not so: the baby
woke up wanting a bottle. I stumbled half-asleep into the kitchen to

make a bottle, and as I was returning to my room, my father physically stopped me. There he was in his underwear, which shocked me. He called me to him, and I always obeyed. He began to run his hand up my leg and into my underwear. I was terrified. This was the last thing I thought would ever happen to me, and I screamed: "You are my *daddy!*" I temporarily lost consciousness and passed out on the floor from the stress and unbelief that this was happening to me. Thank God he stopped and told me to get up and go back to bed. The icing on the cake was when he said, in that country accent, "I was just checking to see if you were out there messing around with them boys"—as though I was to believe that. However, the stake that pierced my heart happened when he said, "You better not tell your mama, because if you do, I will kill her and you." That was the day I lost all trust in men, because if I couldn't trust my daddy, who could I trust? I remember when the darkness fell upon me and entered my soul; that night, I became suicidal. Things that crawl from under rocks.

The next day, it was as though nothing had happened, but to reinforce his power, he beat me badly because I had burned the beans, and he did his best work in front of his friends. He beat me, and his friend watched and didn't dare say a word. After all, he did the same thing to his family. Their badge of honor was beating the children and the mother and ruling their family with an iron fist. I learned this is how the boys were taught. They were trained and raised to become men who treated their families as property and the receivers of their anger and frustrations in life. I suppose it was the one time they felt they had power as a man.

My dad betrayed all of us and had me thinking that everything should be perfect. He would make me strive for perfection. How can an abuser model perfection? I guess the one saving grace for me was the escape I experienced every time I would go to church with my neighbors. I loved the church and attended as often as I could; I felt refreshed. From time to time, they would have what is called a revival. A revival was when we would have nightly services, and there would be singing and preaching. They would also have a Mourner's Bench. It was a southern thing, an array of benches arranged at the front of the church for those who wanted to repent for their sinful lives. A person would sit on the bench until he or she believed they were ready to confess their sins and serve God. If and when an individual felt they had accepted God, they would get off the bench, step forward to the minister, and confess their newfound faith. I did this. After confessing my faith in God, the preacher shook my hand, told me to turn around to face the audience, and presented me to the church family.

The next step was baptism, and the preacher dunked me in the nearby water hole. But it was learning about Jesus and the different Bible characters that kept me excited about going to church. I joined the choir; I loved to sing, and I must admit, our family had gifted singers.

Strangely, my dad and mother started going to church, and we started singing in the church as a group. But it seemed like we were acting religiously and not genuinely worshipping God from our hearts. It was all crazy and felt contaminated with hidden agendas. A tent revival came to town, and Dad and Mother claimed they had an experience with God and surrendered their lives to Him. I was fourteen at the time, trying to enjoy some part of my life, when suddenly, after their conversion, they wanted to interrupt the one stable thing I had going for me, going to church with my neighbor. My parents insisted I attend a different church with them, but it was no fun for me. I wanted no part of my parents' new identity; going to church with my neighbor had been my escape from the madness. I joined with some of the neighborhood girls to form a backup singing group to retain some independence. I had chosen to live, and this was one step between me and death. I kept forging forward as best as I could and endeavoring to get through junior high school. I noticed a young girl at church my age, and she seemed so happy. The expression of her happiness provoked me to jealousy. I wanted what she had. And although I did have a more in-depth experience with God, it didn't seem to be enough to keep me.

Something broke in me when my dad sexually assaulted me, and considering all the beatings before that experience and the more severe beatings afterward, I was delusional. Maybe if I could have continued attending the church of my choice, escaping the madness, I could have tolerated my dad and mom. I became more suicidal and started sneaking out to nightclubs at the young age of fourteen. I was trying to find love in all the wrong places and smiling in all the wrong faces. I became rebellious and out of control. Why should I have to respect my dad? And my mother could not protect me, the other children, or herself. My life became a blur, and before I knew it, I was eighteen, a declared adult.

My life became free and wild, and I kept feeding the monster of confusion within me. At the same time, I was trying to have a good time. My emotions and behavior were erratic. Trying to be sexy and appealing to the opposite sex, I became promiscuous. But my behavior left me feeling disgusted; I was a real Ms. Jekyll and Ms. Hyde. I gave up my virginity to a married man, someone to whom I knew we could never be together. He told me that lie; you know the one—"My wife and I are separated." Honestly, I didn't feel ashamed or guilty for sleeping with him because I believed the lie. His compliments helped. He told me I was "pretty," and I was hearing those words for the first time, which made me feel special.

I was eighteen, but I hadn't graduated from high school. The months couldn't come fast enough; I could smell freedom. That day finally arrived, and, oh, what a relief it was. I asked my parents' permission to leave home. Although I was an adult, it was customary in the South to honor your parents by requesting their consent, especially being a girl, a recent graduate, and new to adulthood. This honor was for my mother, not my father.

My best friend and I moved in together, and I wish I could say we moved into a lovely apartment and lived happily ever after, having lots of girl fun, but that is not what happened. We moved into a room we rented from an elderly couple, and a sewing factory hired me. We decided to take a trip back home, but we forgot to secure the house and left the door open. The elderly couple was very angry with us because we put their safety at risk. I guess the risk was too high, and they evicted us. To justify our wrongdoing, I said, "They kicked us out." Have you ever heard of the saying "from the skillet to the fire"? Well, that is what happened to me; I found myself in the fire. My friend and I moved to Little Rock, Arkansas, into her boyfriend's cousin's apartment—a guy, I might add. I should have seen the handwriting on the wall, but I was so happy with the reality of moving and staying away from home that I was willing to risk what little peace I had. It wasn't long after we moved in that I supposed the cousin thought that since my friend and his cousin were a couple, he and I should be one as well. That wasn't my plan at all. I had a boyfriend, my high school sweetheart, who was at basic training. It didn't seem to matter to the cousin that I wasn't interested in him, and before long, he forced his way into my room and raped me, more than once, and threaten to beat me up or worse if I refused him or told on him. Terrible things are hidden in secrets. My boyfriend started to visit me often, and I was happy to see him because I thought this would make this rapist leave me alone. I soon learned that rapists are opportunists; they don't mind waiting. My boyfriend kept showing up, making me feel happy and safe. It wasn't long before the visits slowed, and one weekend he was a no-show. I was worried and contacted the military base, his best friend, and as a last resort, his mother; no one seemed to know where he was, but the military did confirm he was on leave. But he wasn't at my address. He later wrote me a letter to apologize, and I didn't buy the excuse and cut him loose. Within months, I resolved the issue with the rapist by moving back home. Things that crawl from under rocks.

A year later, my dad's mother, Grandma Mary, became very ill and passed away. I will never forget her passing because she died in the month I was born, March. We had her funeral, and it was a painful experience for me. The family came from all over. It was nice to see my cousins who had moved away and other family members. That is what funerals do, reconnect families. I decided it was time to attempt a grand escape and get out of the state of Arkansas, away from my immediate family. I discussed with my aunt Bobbie Jean my desire to live with her in Florida, and she agreed. I was nineteen and ready to take on the world. Off I went. Once I settled in living with my aunt, I began visiting nightclubs, and it wasn't long before I was singing with a band, except this time, I was singing secular music. I took on the name Chi-Chi, and my fake identity became a part of me. The more they called me by that name, the more I enjoyed my fictitious life. I wasn't a bad person; I was a loving person looking for love. We played the kind of music and sang the kind of songs that made me think and feel things I probably ought not.

My aunt was a seasonal employee for a farmer working group. They were individuals hired to go from farm to farm, city to city, or state to state, working in fields depending on the season. If it was the peach season, they would travel to whatever city or state harvested peaches and work until that season was over. The travel could almost be endless because every season produced a particular crop for harvesting. My aunt was the cook for the group. The man in charge of the business was called the overseer, an old slave term. Because of my aunt, he hired me. He assigned me as a babysitter and tutor for his little girl because his wife was extremely busy with the business. She was such a pretty little girl, between five and seven years old. She was easy to care for and very smart. I enjoyed taking care of her. I was also the bookkeeper for the business. My life was picking up steam, the married man was history, and I had found a new love. The only problem was that I had to leave him behind because he couldn't travel with me at that time.

We were off to the Carolinas to do farm work. We always traveled by bus or van. Once we arrived, we set up camp. The camp consisted of a large house with many rooms that housed the workers. They looked like old plantation houses. Overall, they treated everyone very nicely. We weren't the only group; there were other groups that had come to work the fields as well. After work, especially on weekends, the camps would join and celebrate. There was plenty of drinking, partying, and gambling.

Along with that came the deviant sexual parasites of prostitution and drug addictions, which fueled each other. They were in one camp and doing damage. I didn't do either, so my life was calm. I did learn how to gamble playing cards and became very good at it. I tried to downplay it, but it was gambling. My life was moving as smoothly as I could imagine. Each city had social workers who visited us in the field and provided us with a low level of health care. They would question us about our health and see if we had any concerns, and they would perform preventive care and minor treatment. If we needed further care, they would refer us to the medical clinic.

I saw this as an excellent opportunity to acquire birth control; after all, I was sexually active. My mom prevented me from requesting a prescription from my doctor in Arkansas, convinced that I didn't know what it was all about. But I did. She thought that if she allowed me to have birth control, she would be encouraging me to have sex. Well, I was an adult and didn't need her permission. I was later taken to the clinic for tests and to get birth control. I was so excited to finally be getting on birth control because I did not want to get pregnant. I underwent the tests and examination and was ready to get my birth control prescription and head back to the farm. There was only one problem—a big one. The nurse walked into the room and made an unbelievable announcement: "You are pregnant!" When she gave me the news, I screamed with terror; they could hear me in the hallway. Even though I was an adult, I kept repeating over and over, "I don't know what to do; they are going to kill me!" "They," of course, were my mom and dad—but really, it was more like my dad would kill me. I still feared him.

The nurse tried to calm me down, reassuring me they would help me. I finally stopped screaming out loud, but I was still screaming inside. I was in a panic of fear because I was not ready to become a parent. I returned to the camp, and my aunt and her friends were acting strangely. When I told my aunt I was pregnant, she told me she already knew. She said she noticed that I hadn't used any of the feminine products she had purchased. Why hadn't I noticed the obvious? I told her how the nurse had said the clinic would help me. I overheard my aunt and her friend whispering out loud, saying the people at the clinic will help me by "getting rid of it." Can you believe this? I had no clue what they meant. I was clueless and very much afraid. The unknown can be the most frightening thing; it lurks in the darkness of ignorance, and I could only see its shadow moving. I knew it was there because my heart pounded with unimaginable fear.

Well, I don't care what they say about those people at the clinic; they kept their word and purchased me a bus ticket as well as paid my taxi fare from the bus station to the clinic. They sent me to another clinic in a different town. I arrived at the clinic, and the receptionist gave me a form to complete. I noticed I was not alone; there was a row of women doing the same thing, filling out forms before seeing the nurse. After the nurse reviewed the information with me, she gave me a cup of water and a pill to take. I had no idea what it was for, but the other ladies did the same. After approximately four minutes, I started to become dizzy. A lady escorted me into another room in the back that looked like an examination room, but there were more medical instruments than in an exam room. She told me to undress and put on a gown. I was dizzy, and I started to feel strange, not knowing what was going on. I began to cry. The lady was nice as she prepared me for the examination. She didn't talk much. None of them did; they just scurried about doing their tasks.

When they told me to lie back on the table, I thought I was getting ready for another examination. I was incoherent. Suddenly, the doctor and other nurses filled the room. As the doctor began the examination, I felt pressure, pain, and abnormal inside. I began to cry out loud and scream in fear and panic. Then the kind nurses became unbelievably nasty, and one of the nurses told me in the worst way, "Hush, you didn't do that getting that baby!" The pain was unbearable, nausea turned to vomit, and fear became a full-blown panic attack. What had happened? What did they do to me? More importantly, what is about to happen to me? They allowed me to stay in the room for a short time, and once they believed that I had my balance, the nice-nasty nurse told me it was time to leave. Except, they didn't provide me with a taxi to back to the bus station. The nice-nasty nurse walked me outside, pointed to a tall building that I could see through the trees, and said, "That is where you have to go to catch the bus. Now get to walking." In pain, dizzy, losing blood, and nauseous, I began to walk slowly, barely putting one foot in front of the other. I didn't know what they had done to me—maybe performed an abortion? I received no counseling, no nothing but the element of surprise. I walked slowly, but I walked, and I kept walking for what seemed to be at least ten miles. I finally made it to the bus station and back to camp. I left there in severe pain, with feminine products, medications, and birth control pills. Yes, they helped me. They had done precisely what I overheard my aunt and friend saying what they would do—get rid of it! Things that crawl from under rocks.

I did not realize what was happening to me long term when each of these significant events took place in my life. I later learned that prison walls were being constructed around me and just for me, and at that time, *I did not know it was going to be a maximum-security prison.*

I had spoken to my boyfriend, the father of the now-aborted baby, and after two months, he was able to visit me. We lived together, and he was a habitual marijuana smoker and found friends at the camp who enjoyed it as much as he did. I was a giddy kind of girl; maybe it was nervous laughter, but I laughed a lot. I was funny enough that I didn't need to indulge in drugs. Finally, the season was over, and it was time to return to the city. Back to Florida we went. My aunt and her boyfriend decided to move three towns away. I continued to work for the overseer doing childcare and tutoring and bookkeeping because the business continued. I also became the cook, replacing my aunt. Unbeknownst to me, my boyfriend was on probation and was not supposed to leave the state, and he had violated his probation when he came to be with me. That move cost him his freedom, and now I was home alone again. There was another camp and then another camp; work was constant.

I went home to Arkansas on a short vacation; wow! I was home again, but my mom took one look at me and told me I needed to come home to stay. I guess there was something about how I looked that concerned her. I dared not tell her that I had been through hell. Maybe I didn't need to; perhaps it was written on my face and locked in my eyes. She didn't like the farm work I was doing, and I promised her I would get a real job, but I was not about to come home to live; I enjoyed my freedom. I visited my family for two weeks, and afterward, I was ready to go back home to Florida. My family's home in Arkansas no longer felt like home. I kept my word; I began looking for a different job and found one as a waitress. My manager happened to be from my home state, and I believed the job would be a good fit.

I was happy with my job. I loved my customers, and they loved me and I knew it. But I still felt sad and lonely even though I was in my very own two-bedroom apartment in the beautiful state of Florida. I guess you might say I wasn't good company. The boredom led to another issue that I had never imagined. A friend introduced me to a drug called "Black Beauty." It was a drug prevalent in the 1960s and 1970s and rumored to have been given to soldiers. It was supposedly overproduced, creating a surplus, and the surplus hit the streets. It wasn't made illegal without a prescription until 1965 by most authorities. What does it do? It speeds you up, and you can find yourself doing a marathon in a few hours. I was already giddy, and now I was speeding around silly. I was still empty, running on fumes; I call them glances of hope. To the rescue, my older brother was out of college and came to live with me. That made me feel a little better, because I enjoyed my big brother. The job was good to me and for me, but my private life was in shambles; I kept falling in and out of love.

I remained connected to my hometown, family, and friends, and one of those old friends was my high school sweetheart. I told you to keep reading; well, the military guy came back. I felt somewhat sorrowful for the things I had done since he had left to join the military. But I never believed that he was faithful to me either. We were always off and on. When I would go home, he would be there, home on furlough. And we would sometime connect for fabulous visits. I enjoyed so much being with him. After one of our visits to our hometown, upon my return home, I received a letter. It was a letter from my mother, but within the letter was a letter from him. It appeared he had left this letter in my mom's mailbox, maybe hoping I would get it before I left, but I didn't. I opened the letter, and to my surprise, it was a marriage proposal. It was kind of cute the way he did it but strange at the same time. I called him and asked what this was about, and he explained that he was no longer dating the other girl and wanted us to connect and get married. Can you see something here that I didn't?

I relinquished my apartment and moved back home so we could get to know each other better. I didn't trust him. I saw this time as dating and building a good foundation, but then he gave me an ultimatum: it was either "yes" or "no." The rest is history. I said yes! He seemed so happy and decided we should live in Texas. He moved there and began to get everything ready for our wedding. He found a job; as a matter of fact, he was working two jobs. After three months, he sent for me and had his friend move me. However, he was renting a room along with some old classmates of ours. I later got a job working with special needs children. In that beautiful month of December 1978, we got married. I was twenty-two. Because I had been on birth control pills for so long, it took me months before I could get pregnant, but finally, I did. It was during the pregnancy that things began to change. The marriage was a struggle from the beginning, and domestic violence reared its ugly head when I was three months pregnant. We may have gotten married because of our high school connection and because we were both on the rebound. When you feel alone, you tend to go to that which is familiar.

I gave birth to a handsome boy. It was the happiest time of my life as a woman, but my husband began to act erratic, and on the second day at the hospital, he didn't come to see the baby and me after work as I expected. I knew something was wrong. In all honesty, I had known for some time that something was wrong, but I wanted to try to make this marriage work. I had been searching for a long time and had gone through a few relationships to get to the altar to say, "I do!" Six weeks later, things got worse when, one night, he didn't come home. I panicked; I called the police department, the hospital, and all our friends looking for him, and I couldn't find him. He showed up the next morning, and my anger was high in the danger zone. We had to have a heart-to-heart talk. Then he started confessing. He informed me of a prior relationship he'd had when we were apart. He said she had gotten married and lived in California. It was hard to realize that he didn't break up with her; she broke up with him and got married. He went on to say that supposedly she had left her husband, and once again, they had become a unit. And then he dropped the bomb: he confessed that he had gotten her pregnant. Things that crawl from under rocks.

I didn't feel married because marriage is more than a piece of paper. We separated. It was a short, painful death, but a death, none-theless. I went back to my last stomping ground, Little Rock, Arkansas, and connected with my best friend. We had been friends for a very long time, and I could always count on her love for me and her help in any way she could give it. What a friend! After I'd been scuffling about trying to get my life together, my husband decided he wanted to save our marriage. Remember, getting to the altar was a big thing for me, and I didn't want to give up on my marriage. He requested that we both move back home to Arkansas and try working on our marriage. I agreed, and back home we went. I didn't think he literally meant going home, but that is where we landed—in my parent's home.

Finally, we moved to a trailer park, and one night we had a disagreement, and domestic violence showed its ugly head one more time. I left because I was not going to raise my son in that type of environment. My son was about one year old at the time, and I knew if I didn't get out, I would become my husband's punching bag and be seriously injured or killed. I didn't want my son to grow up committing violence against women. No, thanks! That would be our last fight. I accepted the death of our marriage and moved back to Florida. Things that crawl from under rocks. I am going to let you in on a secret: I knew what was under his rocks. His untrustworthy behavior wasn't new. He was my high school boyfriend, but I failed to tell you that he was my boyfriend Monday through Friday morning, but the weekends belonged to his other girlfriend. And to be transparent with me first and then you, he was with her on his military leave weekends, leaving me to worry. It was this same girl, now a woman, whom he got pregnant during our marriage. I tolerated his behavior and taught him how to treat me—still trying to learn!

At twenty-five, two years later, I was once again alone, but not completely alone; I now had a son who needed me. Once I was back in the city—well, city life has a life all its own. I was back in the swing of things and once again looking for that one true love. I ran into a young man from my past, and we got together to waste time. I didn't want to date forever; I wanted a forever mate. Sad to say, most mothers in the

South raised their girls with two purposes for our lives, and we were continually being asked, "When are you going to get married and have babies?" And, if you have babies and are not married, "When are you going to get a man to help you with them babies?" I was twenty-five and feeling old, wondering what my future would be, when I would be fulfilled. I decided to give this relationship a try, and when he told me he could not make babies, I thought, what a relief! I surely didn't want any more children; I needed to be the best parent possible for my son. I was too busy trying to be visible to others, having a value in their lives, and forcing myself to believe they loved me.

My brain and heart were always in conflict; it was a war. Did I believe he couldn't make babies? Yes. I threw away the birth control, practicing silliness to its highest degree, trusting someone's word. Was he lying? Yes. Did I get pregnant? News flash—yes! The first time we had sex, I got pregnant. There is no time to be considered a safe time to have unprotected sex. I was in shock and felt stupid. I didn't tell him right away. I guess there was more for this naïve lady to learn. We had been around each other for a while, and we talked a lot. He had told me mostly all his secrets.

But no one tells all their secrets, and I was about to learn that. I later learned it was not a medically proven fact he couldn't make babies. He based his belief on his prior girlfriend's experiences, who kept getting pregnant but having miscarriages. There was no logic, and it was all a lie. A miscarriage meant she had gotten pregnant, and he was the potential father. He said he wanted to be a father, and if he did, his child wouldn't have to worry about anything. He, like me, was on a guilt trip. He shared his outlandish beliefs, but they were his beliefs. He told me he played football in college and played the girls who were attracted to him. He had gotten many of them pregnant and convinced them to have abortions. He felt God was punishing him because now he wanted a child, but his old girlfriend only had miscarriages. It was not the right time to tell him I was pregnant.

Like my childhood sweetheart, he had joined the military and was about to be shipped off to basic training. I finally mustered up the nerve to contact him, but his mother answered and told me he had left for basic training. He had told her to give me his address. I sent him a letter and told him I was pregnant, but he never responded. He returned home from basic training, and I saw him and requested that we meet to talk, but he never connected with me. I called again to speak with him, and again, his mother answered and informed me he wasn't there. I had to unload on someone, so I told her I was pregnant and did not know what to do. She assured me that he would be over that night, and he was there. She was a mother who believed in accountability. Later, he said he wasn't the father and wouldn't believe it until the child was born. He was on active duty and never contacted me until long after the baby was born. His mom was so nice to me and intervened; she encouraged me to seek medical care for the baby and me. He finally accepted my pregnancy when I was four months along, but he did not communicate with me. His mother had convinced him.

Something went seriously wrong with the pregnancy. I was six months pregnant with three more months left but went into full labor. I was afraid that my baby would die. Then the doctors began to fear for both our lives. My sweet little girl was born feet first. She was a micro-preemie, born three months early and weighing one pound and fourteen ounces. It was a serious struggle, and she came into this world fighting for what mattered most, her life. After seeing the baby, his mother convinced him that this baby looked just like him. He accepted the baby on his mother's word. But he was in love with someone else, and they got married. I wasn't hitting any home runs with men; I was striking out. I was twenty-six, a single parent with two children, and now I had a preemie who needed my care. Her care was demanding, and I gladly gave my all. I had to take a leave of absence from work to care for her. She fought for her life, and I did all I could to help her win. But emotionally, I was a wreck. I felt like a Mack Truck had run over me, backed up, and parked on my chest.

I was beyond stressed that breathing was a task; life was taking my breath away. Somehow, I kept moving. Suddenly, her father appeared after getting married and said he wanted to help me with the baby; she was two years old. He said he wanted to help and to give me a six-month break. Our daughter was born with many medical issues, one being multiple sclerosis, or MS. I agreed because I never wanted to keep her from her father, and his wife appeared civilized. I trusted they would take good care of her. But he had a hidden agenda to take her away from me. He would call and taunt me by telling me he was taking my daughter overseas, and I would never see her again. I was afraid of him, and I did not know how to stand up to him. I suffered in silence and later learned this was a form of domestic violence.

The six months turned into two and a half years, but he did return her home. Once I got my daughter back, I left the state and went to California, and he accused me of kidnapping. It was almost a year before I ever spoke to him again. I was drained—totally emotionally bankrupt—with nothing to give to anyone, including my children, but mostly myself. That suicide spirit, the thoughts that had entered my being when my father sexually assaulted me, never left me. I wanted to die at the age of twenty-nine. Life felt over for me. I decided I would give my children to their fathers and kiss life goodbye. I entered a low place. I decided to try the drug crack cocaine and successfully became a drug addict before age thirty. I hoped the drugs would kill me, but they did not; they only left me with an addicted mindset chasing what was in my head. I spent two and a half years in California, suffered from burnout, and went back home to Arkansas. I spoke with my daughter's father, and he said he wanted to help me with the baby; I agreed and accepted the offer.

My life went from bad to worse, and I can remember it well as I look in my rearview mirror. It was 1992, and a transformation took place in my life, but not a good one. I had to let go of my children for their sake. I sent my twelve-year-old son to live with his father. My daughter spent a generous amount of time with her father and his new family. She had gone to visit him, so I left her there and gracefully bowed out of their lives. Letting go of my children was the saddest day of my life. The truth that I had to surrender my children because I had succumbed to drug addictions and depression broke my heart in a million pieces.

Doctors had previously told me I needed major surgery or I could die. At this point, death would be a welcome friend. The hospital continued to remind me of the necessity of the surgery. However, to undergo surgery, I could have no trace of drugs in my system. That was impossible for this addicted girl. I could no longer afford my apartment and became homeless. I eventually went into a shelter for women, and by some miracle, I became clean enough to have the surgery. I wanted to die, but I also wanted to live. Wouldn't you know it? I survived the surgery but not without complications. I had to undergo a second surgery to stop the hemorrhaging. I welcomed death, but it seemed to evade me. I was bedridden for months, and that was good for me. But as soon as I had mobility, I left the house where I was living, breaking the house rules.

The director had to maintain accountability and ask me to leave. I was homeless again, except that this time, I had nothing stable in my life. I went from one friend's house to the next; you soon wear out your welcome, especially when you can't contribute. My friends were crack addicts, and we were all homeless at one time or another. I resorted to living in abandoned houses. If we had enough money, we would rent a motel room. We would get one or two people to rent the room, and the rest of us would join them. I jumped from windows to avoid being caught by the manager or arrested by the "Po-Po," the title we called the police. Did I tell you my life went from bad to worse? Things that crawl from under rocks!

I desired my soul to be healed. My needs were significant; I needed forgiveness, and I needed to forgive others for what they had done to me, beginning with my father. I had reconnected with my old overseer's daughter, the child I cared for during my employment with the farm. She was now an adult with a baby of her own. At one time, she said she wanted to come and stay with me, but I wasn't in any condition to take on that responsibility. Sadly, I later learned that someone stabbed her to death after she became involved in prostitution. Such a beautiful, smart little girl swallowed up by this crazy world. I began attending church and was in and out of rehab centers; it wasn't working for me. It seemed the more I tried standing up and doing what was right, accepting my wrongs, and being accountable for my actions, the more I used crack. I stayed with friends when I could until one day the sun shined on me, and a friend referred me to an aunt of theirs who ran a rooming house. She gave me a room, and I also got a job and was able to pay my rent. But Mr. Crack Cocaine had a way of calling my name, and I felt powerless and had to answer him. I didn't have enough money for rent, and that could have placed my living arrangement in jeopardy. She was nice to me and allowed me to work off my debt. Thank God!

I infrequently called to check on my daughter. On one particular occasion, when I called, she told me her father was taking me to court to get full custody. She was eleven and sounded so afraid over the phone. I knew I had to do something. I was ordered to take random drug tests and failed every test. Somehow, by the grace of God, the state's attorney entered into the fight on behalf of my daughter. I was the girl who couldn't speak correct grammar or use correct pronunciation, I sounded ignorant, I had no strength to fight, and now I was addicted to crack cocaine. Other people, including me, repeatedly failed me. Every disappointment became a contributor to my suicidal delusions; my only thought was, will I ever be free?

In 1994, I received a call from my mom. She told me my dad was very sick and confined to his bed. I knew this was hard on my dad because he was a very active man. But it was also hard on me because I knew that he had not asked me for forgiveness for what he had done, and from the teaching I had received, repenting before dying was very important. I trusted God to grant us the time to make amends. I didn't want to go home as a drug addict; I wanted to be clean and sober. God was moving behind the scenes. A year later, I still hadn't gone home.

I was still fighting to get my daughter back. I had an interview for a job. I felt excited and had hope that things were about to change. I couldn't wait to get to my room and prepare for my interview. But breaking house rules was my specialty, and when I returned to the house, management had placed my items outside the door. The guy next door had witnessed the incident and talked to me. I told him I had a job interview the next day, and he paid for a motel room for me so I could make that appointment. I went to the interview, and I got the job. They didn't do a drug test on me. Herein lies a miracle: when I was twenty-nine, out of my mind, I was caught stealing at this same business and spent the night before my thirtieth birthday in jail. And they were now giving me a job without a drug test. Did I tell you this was a Fortune 500 company? Sometimes God causes something good to crawl from under the rocks.

God was moving behind the scenes. I was working as a cashier, and one day, a young lady came in to pay on her account. Without me asking questions, she told me she was once an addict, addicted to crack cocaine. She was so happy that she could pay her bill now because she wasn't buying drugs. She continuously spoke about different things that had happened in her life, and I thought, *Why is she telling me this?* I also thought I had seen her before. As she left the store, I made a mad dash to catch her before she exited, I had to ask her a question. I caught up to her and asked, "How did you stop smoking—not cigarettes, crack cocaine?" She answered me and gave me more information than I thought she would share. Later in the week, she came by and gave me her number and offered to take me to several rehab meetings. She told me all things were possible with God. She became my support person and kept me encouraged. We became knitted together; she was my accountability partner and held me responsible for everything. I remembered why she looked familiar to me; she was the receptionist at the clinic where I had my surgery. Now, two years later, she was my lifeline.

One day as I was working, a lady came into the store and began to talk to me differently, somewhat like my newfound friend. And she asked me a question: "Are you ready yet?" How did she know? Could she see the pain in my eyes? Yes, I was ready, so ready that I later spoke with my manager about my problem, and I wanted to follow through with the options given to me by my accountability partner. My boss was from my hometown, which made me feel a little comfortable, and I was ready to get help. I noticed connections with hometown folks were happening. I told her I wanted to check myself into a rehab center, and it was a twenty-eight-day program—seven days for detox, and the balance was rehab. She approved me for the program and told me my job would be there for me when I was done. She told me to take all the time I needed and not to worry. However, after completing the detox, I was told there was no bed for the program's rehab portion. I was to go home, stay clean, and call every week to see if a bed was available. During this time, I had friends and some family members at my apartment who were smoking dope. It was wearing me down, and I didn't have the strength to tell them to leave. I eventually gave in and used drugs, and the very next day, someone from the program called me. When I reported, they asked me if I had used drugs, and I told the truth. I broke my own heart. It was like I had open-heart surgery, and my chest was left open. How could I do this and continue to rob my children?

I contacted my accountability partner and told her what had happened, and she referred me to another program. She was resourceful and never gave up on me. She gave me the number, and I made the call. I started this journey to freedom. Shortly after Thanksgiving, I was so happy because they accepted me into the program. The only requirement was that I had to bring five changes of clothes and a King James Bible. God was moving in my favor. I went through the program, and the program plan worked for me. The program consisted of us attending religious services. God spoke to me one morning in the service, and He took me back in my mind to the place where I first encountered Him. He welcomed me back to Himself and reminded me that there was one step between me and death, and that was Him. And I am so grateful God took me back. This time, it was me crawling from under rocks.

The phone calls were still coming reminding my siblings and me of our dad's condition and that we needed to come home. I trusted God to get me clean before I went home so I could minister to my dad. I tried before to get him to confess what he had done to me, but he acted as if he hadn't done anything. He was now on his death bed, and he wasn't going to get another chance to repent. I went home to see my dad with a clean heart, a forgiving heart, and by God's grace, a drug-free life. I sat alone in the room with him, thanking God for all He had done for me and asking God for mercy. Strangely, this time, it was my dad who reminded me about what he tried to do to me, and he said, "When you said, 'You are my daddy,' that is what stopped me." My dad crawled from under his rocks that day.

Our rocks have names like guilt, shame, anger, hatred, bitterness, perversion, unforgiveness, and many more. It was March 6, 1996, my birthday. My daddy was gasping for breath, and as I prayed for him, I also thank my Heavenly Father for my birthday gift. God had reconciled the three of us. Dad had repented to both God and me, and in turn, God had forgiven my dad, and I had forgiven him. He allowed my father to live one day longer, and on March 7th, he took his last breath on this side. What a birthday gift to know my dad was ready to meet God! He got it right! Going to church didn't make him right; getting right with God enacted God's righteousness, given to us because of His Son, Jesus Christ. We have a new Rock; this Rock is called Jesus, the Forgiver of sins, Rock of Ages, and many more. I rest on this Rock, and yes, sometimes I even hide under this Rock!

> … and all drank the same spiritual drink. For they drank of that spiritual <u>Rock</u> that followed them, and <u>that Rock was Christ</u>. (1 Corinthians 10:4 NKJV)

> "Therefore whoever hears these sayings of Mine, and does them, I will liken him to a wise man who built his house on the <u>rock</u>: and the rain descended, the floods came, and the

winds blew and beat on that house; and it did not fall, for it
was founded on the <u>rock</u>. (Matthew 7:24 NKJV)

Today, my life is new, brand new. I have my wonderful son, daughter, and three grandchildren: two grandsons and one grand-daughter. My life is full; we're a family. God has embraced me and my children and grandchildren, and He has kissed us with the kiss of life, and I AM FREE!

Jesus answered them, … "Therefore if the Son makes you
free, you shall be free indeed." (John 8:34–36 NKJV)

Third Time the Charm

by Christine Love

Like most young girls, I dreamed of one day getting married and having a beautiful home and a beautiful family, yet I was not mature enough to define it.

Sometimes I wonder if I was absent when the class on choosing a mate was taught. Or was it ever taught? I think the latter. Even though I know I grew into having good sense and sound judgment in practical matters, which is what they call "common sense," everything I thought I knew on the subject matter of marriage was merely a theory, a myth, or from a fairytale I had read. The social norm concerning marriage had been established in society and in my head, and it had become imprinted on my emotional DNA. The mantra sounded like this:

Every girl should grow into a woman, and every woman should get married if she wants to be a "real woman" and be COMPLETE!

Looking back over my life, I became more and more confused about this subject matter. And when I discussed it with my peers, they were just as confused. My parents divorced, and subconsciously, I could have been affected by their divorce. And I never had a discussion with my father concerning what I should look for in a man. My maternal and paternal grandmothers, on the other hand, were married to their mates forever. I had the incredible pleasure to observe and be a part of the interactions between my mom's parents, Grandma Essie and Grandpa Willie. They seemed to drench each other in love; they were happy and hilarious!

As the years passed by, the thought of marriage lingered. It was not smothering—more like a nudge. And at sixteen, I was an employee! Everyone in my family got a job at sixteen, a requirement of our mom. At first my only form of transportation was my reliable bicycle, but soon my mom surprised me with a car she had purchased from a friend at work. She also had connections to a great mechanic, Raphael, who always kept us on the road. He was an extraordinary person, and so was his wife, Connie.

Along with school and work, I was a track and field kind of girl who loved throwing those heavy discs and shot puts. My sister and I were on the track team at school. She ran track and was great at it. She missed being chosen for the Olympics by a fingertip. My mom and grandma Essie were always proud of us and supported us by attending every game. School, work, and sports kept at bay any worry about boys and dating. I never felt like I lacked in that area; I just kept moving forward doing the things I loved doing. I managed to escape peer pressure because I was solid on what I wanted and could not tolerate. I made it through high school, studying hard and working hard.

Nonetheless, that unspoken desire lurked in the shadows of my mind.

After I graduated from high school, I worked even harder. My hard work paid off, and at the age of nineteen, I was promoted to manager of a well-known retail store. I never told the employees my age for fear that they would reject me because I was the youngest. I had become financially stable, and I moved into my apartment; my mom thought it would teach me to be more responsible and accountable for my well-being. It did! I was never that far from her, and she always kept the light on for me. I experienced more new changes in my life. I began going to church and developed lifelong friendships with three special young ladies in my new church. Yes, lifelong, and we are friends to this very day.

Life seemed a blur and was moving faster than I could keep up with it, but I was enjoying every moment. As they say, "time flies when you are having fun."

I kept placing one foot in front of the other and trusting God to keep moving me forward. I was living a productive life, singing in the choir, hanging out with my friends, laughing just to be laughing, not worried about a single thing. My church life kept me focused and balance, and it gave me peace. However, we never discussed those challenging subjects regarding our personal lives or how to be successful in daily living. You know, the things that can make you ask question after question, but only in your head. The girls and I would have deep conversations, but I am not sure if I would call them fully transparent. When I think of transparency, I think of me being able to express myself to the fullest, ask the most outrageous questions, and not be judged or made to feel condemned for asking. I had reservations about coming completely clean because I was pre-dressed in shame, guilt, and fear of not being accepted.

My mom would tell us how the military taught there was no such thing as a stupid question except the one not asked. I wonder why they developed that concept? Maybe because they understood that the one question not asked could cost the lives of many. Well, that same principle should apply to families, churches, and other institutions and organizations.

We should live life to its fullest potential, and this can only be accomplished if questions are asked freely and answers freely explored!

I have many questions. Why all the secrecy, why all the condemnation, and what is the solution?

I enjoyed this emotional high with God and my friends; indeed, I had my sisters with me, and we were having fun—good, clean fun. Noticeably, we were growing up and becoming interested in the next season of our lives. I believe the subject of our biological clock ticking came up a few times. The thought of meeting that special guy, getting married, and having a family began to dance in our heads.

It appeared that our lives were on hold until marriage; the princess was always looking for the prince to complete her. Vulnerable prey we were!

Finally, guys at church started to notice us. It appeared that I caught the attention of a particular guy, and I was intrigued and returned the compliment. I never inquired about him because I assumed that people who attended church were inherently good. He was in the church; therefore, he must be a good guy. I saw people as I saw myself.

We engaged in long and fast conversations, doing a hundred-yard dash on our journey to true love. The next stop should be "marriage," and hopefully, a family. At least, that was the expected end pinging around in my head. Remember that I said I escaped peer pressure because I knew what I wanted and could not tolerate the pressure? That was true with me dealing with just me, controlling myself and not others. But now I was inviting someone into my space without question and with blanket trust. Why?

We wanted some of the same things and had the same dreams and goals. He loved Gospel rap, and I loved singing. He wrote the songs and rapped, and I sang. We were both raised by single mothers. He was funny and would always make me laugh. We loved hanging out together and with our friends. We prayed together as a group; we were endeavoring to grow in grace!

This young man and I began to date seriously. I soon found out that he was thinking like me and wanted to have a family. The day had finally arrived when I could declare that I had found my first love; my prince had arrived.

I wanted to shout out, "Hey, look at me; I am on top of the world!"

But my mom was not in agreement with us becoming a unit. She did not think he was a "good fit." I was very much in love, and I believed that he had great potential and would be a "great fit." We had long conversations, and I could hear and even see his great possibilities because he vividly expressed them. We continued dating and discussing getting married, and eventually, we made that big decision. We proudly announced to all:

We are getting MARRIED!

He was working, and I was busier than ever, working two jobs and doing overtime. Thank God, a few friends became volunteer event planners. I love to shop, but shopping to purchase the necessary items to have a beautiful wedding was exhausting. My friends and family supported me, even my mom. I felt loved!

Our wedding day was fabulous. Even though we had a few missteps, we quickly overcame them. It was our day, and it was a beautiful day. I felt like a queen and was told a few times that I even looked like one. The wedding was a success; the reception was exceptional. Then it was on to life as husband and wife.

The song with the words "I am riding high on cloud nine!" explicitly described my feelings. For years I rode on this cloud. Still, after five years of praying and hoping that his many potentials would come to fruition, they only became a burden. I had to stop pretending and realize that those "potentials" were NEVER going to become a reality.

I had a beautiful olive tree with green leaves, but no olives.

What became a reality was emotional abuse over and over again. But I hung in there for five and a half years as though it was a badge of honor. I finally called it quits, and although my dignity was embattled, it was repairable.

The only thought that flooded my brain was getting free. I ran as hard and fast as I could, escaping the madness and mental cruelty. I was over-the-top excited about being free. Of course, I had my physical freedom, but there were strings attached that needed cutting. The divorce process was a time-consuming and painful one. But I was up for the fight because freedom felt good! You have probably heard the story of the fish that got away. Well, I was not a fish.

On second thought, maybe I was his fish—a meal ticket.

My good credit score and financial stability most certainly contributed to him having a healthy lifestyle, and he had no desire to let that go. One of those painful lessons of truth happened when he decided to take my car. I had forgotten about that extra key that was in his possession.

He actually stole my car. When I got it back, I had my locks changed and put an alarm on it. That only made him angry, and he came to my job with the police in tow to force me to give him a key to my car. I responded respectfully, as I have been taught to do, and said, "Okay." I then filed the necessary court paperwork to make my car legally mine. He had been the one to suggest I needed a car, not me, and together we car shopped and found one I liked. I paid the down payment, I paid the car payments, I paid for the insurance, and at no time did he spend a penny, but he wanted to take ownership of my car. The judge agreed with me and granted me my petition, and the car became my personal legal property.

Finally, when I could catch my breath, I asked myself, "What did I learn from this traumatic experience?" Honestly, I felt like a fool and was so embarrassed. How could I explain this mess, how did I get in it, and more importantly, why did I stay so long? What amazes me is that the church didn't encourage asking the hard questions, nor did it provide pre-marriage counseling. But now people in the church were discussing our failed marriage behind closed doors, determining, without facts, what went wrong and who was to blame.

To keep from becoming depressed, I decided to keep on living. I wasn't sure what that would look like, but I often heard my mom and grandmother say, "Just keep living!" That is what I did, I kept living, and I kept hoping that I would find Mr. Right one day—hoping that one day, I would eventually have that "happily ever after" testimony. You might say I grabbed my bifocals and started looking for him. I learned the hard way that a man in the church is not inherently good; therefore, a man who doesn't go to church might not be inherently bad.

As I said before, I enjoyed my girlfriends, and they were encouraging. Sometimes we walked a little too close to the edge, and I came close to falling off. I played around on the computer for a while and looked at online dating, and then this guy contacted me and got my attention. We would talk for hours, and his conversation was refreshing. He was intelligent and highly educated and would share incredible encounters with me. He would send me books to read about finance and other educational subjects. One thing he sincerely appreciated was his Blackness. It was not often that I found a man who was, without doubt, comfortable in his skin. He was happy to be who he was, and he had a wealth of knowledge about Blacks' contributions to this country and around the world. I never knew all that. He was a thinker, and listening to his thoughts encouraged me to think out loud. These long conversations continued for months. The beauty of it all was that I got to have great conversations without his physical presence. He was a hard worker; as a matter of fact, he worked two jobs. He didn't talk about his dreams and potentials; he was busy living them out daily. Yes, he was single, but he did have a child.

Time progressed, and so did our relationship. We took it relatively slowly, and I didn't feel rushed. However, from time to time, I would ask myself what I was doing. I was slipping away from my spiritual convictions for a romantic relationship. It weighed heavily on my mind from time to time. I was discarding the beliefs and practices that made me who I am, and that was scary. But somehow I found peace with my decision and felt safe, happy, and hopeful.

I brainwashed myself.

Eventually, our relationship reached a new level, and I had to decide if I was willing to relocate to San Diego, California, to be with the guy I loved. I was, and the relocation went smoothly, from the job reassignment to the physical move. I had never lived anywhere other than Sacramento, California. One can get a very narrow view of what the world is about being stuck in one town, but I had a narrow view of what my state had to offer. The change did me good. It stirred a sense of excitement in me. The only drawback was being away from my family. It would take longer than ten or fifteen minutes to get to my mom's house for the first time. But she still left the lights on for me.

I will pause here for a memory break! I cherish the memories of home, when we all lived together—my mom, two older sisters, and one younger brother. It was the simple things in life that I loved, like watching television on the weekend together, playing in the back yard, and squabbling. We fought, but we also defended each other from outside bullies. And school was the bullies' hangout. My deeply held belief and conviction was, "I am not a pushover." I was there to defend myself and my sisters if need be. Our mom was busy providing for us and endeavoring to give us the best possible chance of being successful.

We had excellent opportunities. We worked during the summer at our mom's job—what a blessing! That exposure did so much for my sister and me. Along with our mom, we also had Grandma Essie and Grandpa Willie; they were our backup. We loved our dad's parents but weren't as close to them. I can remember every home address, every school attended, and mostly all my teachers. I remember friendships developed on the way.

There is no place like home!

But I became well-adjusted in San Diego. I loved living there. There is something about the air and the people. Every day seemed like an adventure because there was so much to see and enjoy. It was different from Sacramento. I was enjoying my life with my new love. I had always dreamed of having children, but when I was younger, our family doctor told me that I had hormonal issues that may create a problem for me to conceive. After being married before and not getting pregnant, I assumed I would never be a mother. My boyfriend kept prodding me to get a pregnancy test and see because he believed

I was pregnant. Well, I got two, so I could show him twice, "I am not pregnant!" We had a roommate; she was the sweetest person you could ever meet. After I took the tests, she and I sat together to check them out. I asked her, "Okay, what does this mean?" She hesitantly answered me, "I think it means you are pregnant!" She was convinced that I was pregnant, but I wanted my confirmation to come from a doctor. The doctor confirmed that not only was I pregnant, but I was days from being three months pregnant. As a bonus, my doctor assured me that I no longer had hormone issues!

I enjoyed being pregnant. And before I knew it, nine months had passed, and I was giving birth to a handsome little boy. He was so cute and still is. He made me a mother, and I was determined to be a great mother. Eventually, my new love proposed to me, and we got married. It began to feel like we were a real family. Finally, we had some skin in the game, and I could call him my husband!

He decided that he wanted to join the Sacramento Police Department. He underwent all the testing, and it was a green light all the way. He was so excited as he prepared to attend the academy, but he became concerned that there would be no family support in San Diego. I had to relocate ahead of him. All went well, including the job reassignment back to Sacramento. We found a lovely house to rent and began the process of selling our home in San Diego. The light was still green, and the academy was near when the unforeseeable happened. He was in a bad car accident that caused significant injuries, rendering him unable to continue in this profession. It became a mess, a juggling act that even the best juggler couldn't manage.

He was stuck and had to stay with his current job in San Diego, and I had recently transferred my job, and there was no way I could undo that. We were separated and had to commute to see each other. The separation and commute continued for over four and a half years, and the strain became apparent; there was trouble in paradise. The distance and commuting stressed him out. It was evident by his weight loss. The time came when we could finally sell our property in San Diego, and he got a job in Sacramento. It was nice to be a family again.

I got pregnant with baby number two, and it was a boy—a cute bouncing little boy who is still bouncing around today. He is my energy bunny! But those four and half years of separation had done some irreparable damage; a lot had happened during this time. He did not tell me the truth; I saw the signs, and I did not like them. It was getting messy, and sooner or later, we needed to have a transparent conversation, which was not his norm. He was in denial and kept saying that everything was okay, but I knew better. One day, we did have that conversation, and it would be a decisive conversation to answer the question, Will we remain together or go our separate ways? Unfortunately, the latter was the decision. I heard the lies, and I recognized there would only be more lies. I didn't have time for that. I had two boys who needed my energy; I had none to waste on a marriage of deceit and going nowhere fast.

I know that life happens. I couldn't have predicted my past, and I cannot predict my future, but I can always learn from my past experiences. I did things that I should not have done; I made unwise decisions when contrary evidence was in plain sight. But I was blinded by ignorance and ensnared by my fleshly desires. Oh, wretched woman I am. Who will deliver me?

I finally stopped, sat down, and without fear of self-incrimination, took a good look at my life, past and present, and I began to note my "lessons learned."

Overall, the first thing I learned was that the image of marriage dancing in my young head was far different from marriage as I experienced it. Out with the theories, myths, and fairytales, and in with truth and reality.

Lessons Learned from Marriage Number ONE:

Painfully, I admitted that my husband did have dreams, but he saw me as the potential means to fulfill them. I also realized that I became a target because I didn't love and appreciate myself. I was overweight and thought I couldn't do any better. Therefore, I saw myself as the one who should tolerate shame while feeding his ego. I learn that you don't marry the person you hope someone will become; you marry who they are, as they are, and nothing is real until it's proven. Another fundamental lesson I learned was:

Just because you meet someone in a place called the House of God, that doesn't mean God lives in their house. They could be godless.

Lessons Learned from Marriage Number TWO:

I believe I learned the most from marriage number two. First and foremost, I learned I should have taken an intermission between marriages—a pause for the cause of ME! In a movie theater, an intermission between shows is very important for their business. It advertises the up-and-coming movies, enticing you to want to come back and watch another movie. It allows you time to get your snacks and settle in before the movie begins. If I had taken an intermission, I could have avoided the rerun.

I learned that everyone has flaws, but good intentions don't soften the impact of inflicted pain.

There were things hidden in my husband's closet that he dared not expose, and he was hoping, without telling me, that I would be that special someone to help him slay the dragon hiding in the closet. I failed to ask the right questions, but I didn't know the right questions to ask. Also, the long-distance conversations we had weren't conversations upon which to build a life. We should have conversed about our strengths, weaknesses, and expectations. After all, we had nothing to lose and everything to gain. Either we would grow into a healthy tree or realize that we were not a good fit and could have saved me the sacrifice of me.

My husband avoided decision-making conversations because he saw them as arguments. He lacked accountability and refused to see marriage as a union that requires, even demands, accountability. We weren't speaking the same language. We weren't transparent from the beginning. We only spoke dressed-up, feel-good, and stay-safe words to each other. Our marriage was built on sinking sand; the first rainstorm revealed the lies, and the lies destroyed the marriage. He was always quick to say, "Everything is okay."

I accept the truth of this matter. I didn't know what I didn't know, and unfortunately, at the time of my marriage explorations, there wasn't a handbook or a map I could follow.

Lessons Learned about ME:

I believe that it is an injustice to one's self always to look outward, never inward.

There is no way we can learn something about someone else and not learn something about ourselves. If we do, then that sounds like the worst kind of deceit, the deceit of one's self. William Shakespeare said it best, "This above all: to thine own self be true." I slowly began to change my old way of thinking, my self-destructive thoughts and behavior, and my habit of looking at myself through someone else's eyes and being defined by them.

I learned that I was valuable and so much more. It didn't happen overnight, but overnight, I experienced a sudden awakening. I realized there was a long road ahead of me, and I had better start moving my feet.

Third Time the CHARM:

But how do I move forward? The first thing I learned was, I had defined a lot of things wrong in my life. One example was the scripture repeated a lot in and out of the church, by both religious and nonreligious folks: Matthew 22:39 NKJV: "You shall love your neighbor <u>as yourself</u>." I strived to love my neighbor, but I had very little love for myself. My close friends and I never understood this scripture. So, you do what you think you know. I knew how to show love to others, but I didn't know how to show love to myself. What would that look like? It sounded selfish to me.

I understand that many of our church leaders were lacking in education and experience. My mom taught me to know what I believe and why I believe it; I needed to ask many questions of myself and others. I needed to pursue truth and embrace it. She told me she was disturbed because she had gathered from the church that one should not question pastoral leadership and dared not ask God questions. But she joyfully said she no longer believed that.

It is a hard-knock life, but pay attention; the lessons learned are priceless!

"The third time's the charm" implies that one has tried something at least twice, and it didn't work, and somehow, their third attempt has a high possibility of being a windfall.

My journey had started with my church girlfriends and me trying to maneuver our lives around a maze of "I think so, and I hope so." Well, you read how that turned out, not good, and yet, not totally a waste. I became the mother of two wonderful boys, still growing, and I smile every time I look at them or think of them, even when strangling them is on my mind. When we met, he had a child, and sometimes with a child, there usually comes some baby mama drama. We had our fair share, but that baby girl grew into a beautiful young lady. I gained a beautiful bonus daughter, whom I love dearly. Their father and I have an amicable relationship, and the boys haven't suffered any lasting damages. Sad as it may be, they are in the majority as being raised by a single parent. Although they are not tightly connected to their dad's family, I thank God that we have a village! The boys ask a lot of hard questions, and I pray they keep asking them.

I realized that this thing called life had to have a real purpose, and it had to be for something good. I got busy looking for the good. Then I came back to my starting point, the church. But not just the church this time—a deeper relationship with the One and Only who had created me and knew my purpose well, the Triune God. I needed to have my conversations with Him. I needed to get to know Him because I needed to know the truth in my inward parts—my soul. My "third time, the charm" is not about getting lucky. There is no such word in my vocabulary. It is about focusing on God; that is the windfall.

Older women in the church implied that the family didn't matter. The church culture seemed to have devalued family to the equivalent of a sideshow, coming in last. But God created man and woman, and God instituted marriage, not man. So, I went to the Creator and the Designer to understand the purpose of marriage, God's Word, and those who taught it well. God made the connection when He said it was not good for man to be alone (Genesis 2:18). Adam didn't appear in Scripture to be looking for a mate, and he didn't choose his mate; God did. God built a family before He formed the church. It was the perfect marriage, the perfect relationship, because God designed it.

I would agree with most traditions laid upon us if this was a perfect world, but I don't live in a perfect world.

It was the unspoken norm within the culture and embedded in our brain that marriage and children were the future of every young girl. And if we weren't married by a certain age, funny stares and accusations were released upon us: "What is wrong with you that you are not married?" The guys didn't get this type of pressure, nor did they have to be mindful of their behavior. It seems as though I had lived the majority of my life by manmade traditions defined as God's prescriptions for my life. I learned the roles and expectations placed upon me from those traditions.

This culture that taught me a man couldn't be a nurse also taught me that a woman couldn't be a doctor!

I had to take God out of the box where I had placed Him for Him to take me out of mine. My mom told me how God told her to stop acting like she wasn't human, but also to stop treating Him like He was! He wanted me to learn my real value as a stand-alone individual—not as a daughter, a girlfriend, a wife, or a mother, but as a person, His creation with His purpose living within me—and how to love myself. I had to allow the Holy Spirit to function as designed according to the Bible in the book of John, chapter 16. He is my comforter, my guide, my teacher, and He glorifies God within me.

God's Spirit began to teach me that I could still be a whole person, although I had come from broken relationships.

I also learned that I am to work *with* Him and not *alone*. I began to realize that He had taken all my pain, mixed it with His grace, and sternly reminded me that His grace is sufficient.

And He said to me, "My grace is sufficient for you, for My strength is made perfect in weakness." Therefore most gladly

I will rather boast in my infirmities, that the power of Christ may rest upon me. (2 Corinthians 12:9 NKJV)

I entered a new season on this journey of life, but with a new belief system. I now believe that God is enough and that I am not half of a person because I am single. Nor am I cursed because I am now twice divorced. I am not a failure, and I set out to identify myself correctly. I am getting from the "what I am" to the "who I am!" "What" refers to the identity of objects: gender, occupation, religion, nationality, political affiliation, personality, and the character attributes of an individual. I was always defined by the "what." False identification is not just a female issue; it is a human issue. I just so happen to be a female with a female's perspective and experience. Marriage was portrayed in the church and maybe outside the church as a woman's profession or occupation, not to be enjoyed but endured.

I am not an angry divorced woman who hates marriage; I am a single woman who is finally free and happy!

I agree with the Word of God that marriage is honorable, and I haven't taken it off the table, but I finally submitted to God's will. Marriage is the "what," not the "who." Jesus is always looking for the "who" in us first, because "who" identifies the person. It refers to the relationship, position, or status. I am a child of God. You have probably heard the introduction of a wife who is married to a famous guy; it usually goes as such: "This is Rob's wife." No name, just her title. I am sure it makes her feel a little less than valuable unless she values the title. It reminds me of the scripture Mark 8:27–29 NKJV:

Now Jesus and His disciples went out to the towns of Caesarea Philippi; and on the road He asked His disciples, saying to them, "<u>Who do men say that I am</u>?" So they

answered, "John the Baptist; but some say, Elijah; and
others, one of the prophets." He said to them, "<u>But who do</u>
<u>you say that I am</u>?" Peter answered and said to Him, "<u>You</u>
<u>are the Christ</u>."

I soon learned that Jesus asked a lot of questions; it was one of His teaching tools. My mom wasn't wrong, after all. Ask lots of questions until you know what you believe and why. Questions made Jesus's disciples stop in their tracks, scratch their heads, and wear a puzzled look on their faces. Questions made them think and, at the same time, created a hunger for the truth. No worries—Jesus would not leave them hanging; they just had to stay in the process. The answers were on the way. After others had defined what I was, I now knew it was time for me to understand how God defines "who I am," and it would be His definition that I would receive and declare forever.

I chose to agree with Him!

Earlier I asked, "Oh, wretched woman I am. Who will deliver me?" An apostle named Paul asked this same question, and then he answered it in Romans 7:21–4 NKJV:

I find then a law, that evil is present with me, the one who
wills to do good. For I delight in the law of God according
to the inward man. But I see another law in my members,
warring against the law of my mind, and bringing me
into captivity to the law of sin which is in my members. <u>O</u>
<u>wretched man that I am! Who will deliver me</u> from this
body of death? I thank God—<u>through Jesus Christ our Lord</u>!

I soon realized that I would get to know who I am as I got to know who Jesus was and is. The bottom line is, it doesn't matter who others say Jesus is, but rather who I say He is. And like Peter, I found Him to be "The Christ, the Son of The Living God"—hence "Third Time the Charm"—my game changer!

May I encourage you to CHOSE WELL!

God Had a Plan

by Tina Tranzor

"For I know the plans I have for you," declares the LORD, *"plans to prosper you and not to harm you, plans to give you hope and a future. Then you will call on me and come and pray to me, and I will listen to you. You will seek me and find me when you seek me with all your heart."* *(Jeremiah 29:11–13 NIV)*

The Beginning—Jeremiah 29:11

The disappointment I felt within was noticeable, thick, and heavy with every breath I inhaled, asking the big question, "How did this happen?" I exhaled, preparing to ask myself the next big question,

"What am I going to do?" I could barely catch my breath in between the questions that were racing in my mind. I began to feel nauseous, fighting with every ounce of strength to hold back the fountain of tears that were at the brink of overflow.

The dam was about to burst.

With my eyes wide open, all I could see was the shambles of my life stretched out before me like a canvas. How did I find myself here? I am a Christian woman. But there it was, no denying this: the plus sign on my store-bought pregnancy test delivered a damaging blow to my already complicated life. The little pink plus sign was bold, raging, and almost taunting me, creating a sense of dread. My thoughts shifted to my parents, who were pillars in the church. How would I tell them that I was pregnant outside of marriage?

In my opinion, I was the "screw-up" of this family pack. I was angry and hated myself for what I was doing with my life. The big question looming before me was, "What will I do? Will I accept and embrace this life, or will I terminate it? If I terminate, would I be able to live with having this on my record?" I wasn't a young kid, a teenager; I was a grown woman over thirty. We use the word "grown" when we want to emphasize who we are, attempting to state how qualified we are to do as we please, but it also means we must be accountable for what we do.

How did I find myself here? I was a Christian woman.

I had recently finished an intense Bible study at church to fulfill one of God's callings on my life. But, obviously, there was still a deep emotional void that I was seeking to fill, and now I was pregnant and single. The questions kept coming like rapid fire!

I tried to make sense of my life up to this point of being pregnant. It required me to look in my rearview mirror. I had to go back and take a long, hard look at my past to understand why I kept making irresponsible decisions. I remembered that when I was a little girl, I always sought validation. I wanted someone to tell me that I was "okay," that I was loved and accepted. Life had thrown me many hard balls. I knew my parents loved me, but I saw them as emotionally unavailable and not equipped to fill the void. There was a large gaping hole in my emotions. As I took my trip down memory lane, I remembered an old high school sweetheart who turned out not to be so sweet. And when in college, I was out of my league with the college boys. It was more like a free-for-all party. I felt like the guys could see my lack of confidence from afar and would take advantage of me over and over again.

I did not know how to read the road signs.

I was always hoping beyond hope that someone would help me to feel accepted without requiring my body as a sacrifice.

Then I remembered how I got married. I won't go into detail, but I will say this: I came to realize that my ex-husband had only attained husband status because that little girl in me was scared that no one else would ever ask her to be his bride. He proclaimed Christ but did not walk like Christ. He used his made-up position to capture me, and he used his fictitious background to inspire me and spoke the words I always wanted to hear. He lied with every word spoken. I opened myself and compromised in every area of the relationship imaginable.

It wasn't long before I could no longer live with this mistake. It was a very abusive marriage, and getting out was not going to be easy. I lived my days and nights in fear, but I finally got out. Thank God! But I remained broken, and I continued to do what broken people do—look for love in all the wrong places. My life was insignificant and one big compromise.

With that "compromise" mentality, I was awakened to the realization that I was pregnant. My doctor had told me there was a high possibility that I would not be able to get pregnant. I took it as meaning I would never get pregnant and lived likewise. I took five store-bought pregnancy tests, each time hoping the others were wrong; they weren't. I was approaching the age that pregnancy might not have been an option in the future. I had no plans to raise a child without a father. And I didn't think I could be successful as a single mom. The question of life again surfaced: Would I keep "it," or would I terminate "it"? I used the word "it" because it kept me unattached to what was growing in my body, and it would be easier to terminate.

As I pondered what to do, weighing my options, I knew that God knew. Somehow, I forced myself to believe that the Lord had a plan and a purpose. I was alone in my living room, in a quiet and calm moment; the sun was setting, darkness would soon appear, and I was enjoying the soft evening light, only to be interrupted by a ringing phone. Amid the twists and turns happening in my life, my dear sweet friend called me. I was in shock, wondering what our conversation would be. I had only told the father that I was pregnant. I wasn't sure if I would keep the child; I had to weigh all of my options first. My dear sweet sister-friend was busy chatting, and when she had finished her small talk, she dropped a bomb on me. As if she had been holding this in for this particular moment, she blurted out, without hesitation, "The Lord told me to tell you that you should keep the baby." At that moment, I no longer faintly thought God knew; I was sure He knew, and He had a plan for my baby. I praised God for her obedience; I praised God for caring enough about my unborn child and me to send a familiar and friendly voice so I could receive what He was saying to me. I praised God for showing me, and I decided to choose *life*!

For you created my inmost being; you knit me together in my mother's womb. I praise you because I am fearfully and wonderfully made; your works are wonderful, I know that full well. My frame was not hidden from you when I was made in the secret place, when I was woven together in the depths of the earth. Your eyes saw my unformed body; all the days ordained for me were written in your book before one of them came to be. (Psalms 139: 13–16 NIV)

The Pregnancy: God's Hand
Season 1—Decisions

The first phase of my pregnancy started with a flurry of decisions. I decided to keep the baby. I chose to consult with my son's father about his desired next steps. I decided to start prenatal care right away. I decided not to share my news with friends or family right away. My first visit to the obstetrician-gynecologist office was pivotal and emotional.

I completed my medical history information, and the magnitude of the path that I chose felt like a lead blanket. I had begun my journey as a single mama. I knew that to live this life, I would need to trust God and believe in his promises.

Standing on His promises was never needed more than when I began to show signs of pregnancy. As my body began to get bigger and change and develop, my circle of friends shrunk and got smaller and smaller. My church family was disappointed and pulled away. As I navigated my planning and preparing for my child, I was struck by how lonely the world became. I had one friend, Angie, who was not a church member, walking alongside me during this time. She would often drive me to work and meet me for a meal and provide encouragement. Angie was Christ in human form; she was the arms and hands of God with a great sense of humor. She was a single mom and knew how to prepare me for the road ahead. I continued to attend church but found myself sitting in the pew alone. No one would make eye contact with me or speak. In those moments, I trusted that the Lord had a plan. I had laid it all at the feet of Jesus and repented for my sins. I knew I could walk in forgiveness because of the grace and mercy of Christ. I was giving it my all.

Because my church family rejected me, I knew that having a personal relationship with Christ would have to become paramount. He was all I had, along with my angel, Angie. When I decided to move away, the women's ministry didn't give me a gift card. However, the pastor took me to lunch. She told me that they could not have a baby shower for me but that she wanted to give me something for the baby. I remember thinking how grateful I was for the gift. But I was disappointed that the church had no grace or mercy when I needed it most. I did not walk away from Christ, but the church's treatment shifted my thinking about the church. I resolved again that my hope and trust was in the Lord and not in man. That hope and faith have become my foundation.

Season 2—Impossible to Possible

The second phase of my pregnancy was the season of seeing the impossible become possible. I faced several challenges during the pregnancy that caused me to feel helpless, but I looked to Christ and trusted His plan. I had morning, noon, and night sickness and struggled daily to go to work. I was a schoolteacher, and every day I'd turn out the lights in the room and take a twenty-minute nap on the science table in my classroom during recess. Without that nap, I did not have enough energy to get through the day. Because the table was high and I'm short, I would climb on a chair with my travel pillow and blanket in tow and snuggle as best I could to get my daily needed nap. Somehow after twenty minutes and before the bell would ring, I would wake up in time to prepare for my students. To my knowledge, no one ever came into my room during recess, and I was always naturally awakened on time for work.

With the morning, noon, and night sickness, I figured out that junk food, dairy products, and sugar products increased nausea, so I almost immediately removed those items from my diet. I also developed the inability to eat raw vegetables, particularly lettuce, and fruits, especially citrus fruits. For survival, I removed those from my diet. I decided that God had created my body and that I had to trust my body and believe that the Lord would take what I was eating to nourish the baby and help him grow. I also limited wheat products to prevent allergies during the spring and summer seasons. I wanted to ensure I was doing all the right things for my baby. I did not want to take any medications that could harm him. Before pregnancy, I did not eat a great deal of meat. I didn't even like meat, but the baby wanted protein, so I ate meat, beans, and home-style meals, all the while trusting God's plan.

When I was about four months into the pregnancy, I received a layoff notice from my job. After I received the news, I pulled the covers over my head and cried. I cried out to the Lord because I did not know how much more I could handle, and I was unsure what His plan was for my life and my baby's life. I faced joblessness and no health-care coverage once the layoff took effect. I was four months pregnant, and who would hire a teacher who needed to leave the classroom for maternity leave at the beginning of the school year? I lived in a one-bedroom condo, which was limited in space, too small to raise a baby, and without employment to pay the mortgage, I would lose even that home. I could not see a path to a successful outcome. Before the layoff notice, I felt that I trusted God's plan with a strong faith and continued to hold my head high, knowing that I was forgiven and had chosen life. After the layoff notice, the magnitude of the circumstance weighed on me, and I called in sick and took four days to cry, sleep, wallow, ponder, and seek the Lord. I experienced every negative emotion possible. In those four days, I felt hopeless, lost, forgotten, defeated, sad, lonely, and desperate; my faith wavered a bit and shrank to the size of a mustard seed.

On that fourth day, the Lord began revealing his plan. He started planting seeds of hope for my next steps. My mustard seed–size faith was enough for God to move. The plan for the next part of my journey happened in the most unexpected ways. On that fourth night, I could not sleep and was up late watching TV. I did not have cable, and the small TV antenna could only get the signal of a few channels. That night a television evangelist was speaking from Memphis, Tennessee. First, I'm not sure how I could in California get a TV station from Memphis, Tennessee. And it was the only clear channel. Second, I was not in the habit of watching television evangelists because I never really liked their approach. This minister, however, was speaking words of life, hope, and wisdom. I was mesmerized. As he poured out the Word of God, I found healing, peace, and hope. Next, I drove to work and kept seeing Tennessee license plates on cars on the freeway. On my drive into work, I would spend time just talking with the Lord. I'd ask the Lord, "What is the plan?" and a car with a Tennessee license plate would drive by. I'd ask the Lord, "What is your will, and what are my next steps?" and a car with a Tennessee license plate would drive by. I cried out to the Lord and asked, "Where am I supposed to go?" and a car with a Tennessee license plate would drive by. Finally, I was stopped at a light at an intersection in Vallejo, California, and I was tired and weary and uncertain, and I cried out to the Lord and asked

Him what I was supposed to do with my life. I looked up, and to my amazement, there was a billboard advertisement for a particular tour site in Memphis, Tennessee. At that moment, I said to myself, "I think I'm supposed to move to Tennessee." I thought it was a little crazy, but I began to develop a plan with my mustard seed–size faith.

I reached out to my godmother, who lived in, yes, Memphis, Tennessee. I explained that I was pregnant and that I would be laid off from my job at the end of the school year. She shared that Memphis City Schools sought to hire over three hundred teachers and were looking for qualified, credentialed candidates. I had taught for four years in a private school and two years in a public school, and I was a fully credentialed teacher. I knew that to get a job as a teacher in Memphis, I would have to get licensed to teach in the state of Tennessee. I also knew that I would need to start the job search and interview process quickly. I knew that getting a job over the telephone was a long shot and that getting a credential processed in less than two months was almost impossible. With trust and blind faith, I submitted my documents and application for a license to the state of Tennessee. With just a glimmer of hope and not a clear understanding of how God was going to work things out, I submitted a general application for teaching positions with Memphis City Schools. I started this process at the beginning of April. By the end of April, I had a license to teach in the state of Tennessee and a job offer in hand.

The job offer came after a phone interview and a hearty recommendation by my godmother to the principal. The interview was by phone, and I had to be transparent with my prospective boss and tell him that I was pregnant. With the kindness of either a Christ-centered man who could hear God's voice or a desperate principal, he accepted the pregnancy and assured me that I could start the school year and have the six weeks of maternity leave, then resume the rest of the year.

We serve the God of the impossible. By May of that year, I had all of my worldly possession loaded onto a moving truck and transported to a storage unit in Memphis, Tennessee. In June of that year, I had my condo rented to a tenant, and I closed the door on my California life and began anew in Memphis, Tennessee. God had a plan!

Season 3—Blessings in Abundance

The third and last phase of my pregnancy was a season of abundant and overflowing blessings. On June 22nd, my sisters dropped me off in Tennessee and flew back to California. I was there to start my new beginning alone, with only God and my unborn baby. I didn't have my angel Angie to walk alongside me in person, but she remained close. My new job benefits wouldn't begin until October 1st, and my baby boy was due on September 1st. I seriously considered trying to keep him in utero for another thirty days by keeping my legs crossed, an impossible feat. As my due date approached, I realized I needed to plan for the medical cost of childbirth. I found a program at one of the hospitals in town that allowed mothers to pay in advance for their birth experience. Since I had a job, I did not qualify for government assistance for medical care. The out-of-pocket cost that I had to pay to give birth to my son was *five thousand dollars for a non-complicated delivery*—the no-frills birthing opportunity. My option was to pay upfront or after birth. I prayed and cried, and then I handed over my credit card to the hospital. It was the last bit of money for my "safety net."

I told the Lord that I would continue to trust Him and that I knew He would make a way for me to pay off this debt. I prayed that the Lord would give me an uncomplicated birth so that it wouldn't exceed the five thousand dollars charge. As I walked out of the hospital office, I was heartbroken. The hospital failed to meet my cleanliness standards. But I yet had a grateful heart!

That day, I also had to go to the human resource department for my new company to complete the paperwork for my upcoming unpaid leave. I talked to the lady in the department, and she explained and double-checked my eligibility for benefits. She pulled up my computerized information and confirmed that I did not qualify for benefits. She then looked at my very pregnant belly and asked when the baby was due and which hospital would I be using. I explained how I had just charged the five thousand dollars on my credit card to cover the cost of the birth of my son at this particular hospital. She frowned and continued to type into the computer. She peered over her glasses at me and frowned some more. She then looked up at me and declared that she could not let me go without medical benefits, especially since I recently started working. She stated that she had decided to retroactive my benefits to my employment start date and waived the waiting period. She looked at me sheepishly and shared that the one disappointment with this change of events was that the hospital where I was planning to have my son was not on my new insurance and that I would have to go to the brand new, state-of-the-art hospital that was across town to have my baby. I sat stunned in the chair. I asked her to repeat because my excitement had caused me to miss most of her presentation. She exercised great patience in explaining everything and assured me that when I left the human resources department that day, I would have benefits. The Lord had, in an instant, answered my prayers.

I thanked the human resources lady and ran-waddled out of her office. I immediately went back to the hospital to get a refund and then high-tailed it to the new hospital to take a tour of the facilities. Because of my "fallen" state, I often struggled to forgive myself for the sin I had committed. I would quickly fall prey to the thinking that I did not deserve good things because of my choice to have premarital sex. When I saw the first shabby hospital, I felt relegated to the shabbiness because I thought that was my lot in life and my penitence for my sin. I believed that those conditions were all I deserved. I temporarily forgot that Jesus paid for all my sins on the cross, past, present, and future.

When I walked into the new hospital to see the birthing room and met the nurses, I was shocked. There was a water fountain in the lobby that was sparkling and beautiful. There was beautiful artwork on the walls and lovely soothing music playing in the background. There were happy, warm, smiling faces at the entrance to greet me, and on the wall, a little off to the right, were written these words: "Be still and know that I am God." I began to cry. God is a God of mercy and grace, and He pours out His blessings to those who seek and trust Him.

God's grace, mercy, blessings, and miracles continued right up to the day I gave birth. When I moved to Tennessee, I was seven months pregnant in a city where I knew virtually no one other than my godparents. They were there and opened their home in my time of need, and they proved to be a great blessing since I lived with them for the first six weeks. Before I moved, I had saved a small amount of money and structured a budget for the move and our daily lives in our new city. Shortly after I arrived in Memphis, the Lord blessed my unborn son and me with a newly built three-bedroom and two-bathroom home. I had only hoped for a small two-bedroom, two-bath place with a small patio to enjoy. However, the Lord had other plans! He gave us a home and a yard that I could afford since the mortgage payment was less than renting. I closed escrow on our brand-new home on August 28th, and my son was born on August 31st. God provided and blessed us with the place that He wanted us to have, and it was beyond any measure I had asked.

The blessings continued during my maternity leave. Since I did not qualify for leave under the Family Medical Leave Act and did not have any sick leave accrued, I had to take my maternity leave as unpaid leave, and I had to pay for my medical benefits while on leave or they would lapse. I sat down and put together my budget, and it didn't look very promising. Although I had money in savings and lived frugally, it looked as though there would be a six-week deficit. In heaven, God had it all worked out. He supernaturally provided for my little family. I don't know how it worked out, but we did not miss a beat or a meal. He blessed us mightily. I did not live on credit, and I could pay all my bills, provide healthy nourishing meals, pay for my medical benefits while on unpaid maternity leave, and have a few "wants" met during that time. God showed up and showed out as He guided and blessed our lives. To the human mind and calculations, my financial circumstances were pretty dire, but to God's grace, He provided in a way that was beyond my imagination. I held on to faith, and I remember looking at my budget and saying out loud, "Only God!"

Moving Forward and Remembering: God's Plan

I gave birth to a handsome son, and I named him Aaron Jeremiah. His name was to remind me that God had a plan and a purpose for our lives. During his birth, God revealed once again that He had destined Aaron to be on the planet. After twelve hours of labor and within two minutes of preparing to push, Aaron's heart rate dropped, and they rushed me into the emergency room for an emergency cesarean section. This complication came unexpectedly, but God knew that if I had to birth Aaron at that first hospital, I would not have received the superior care necessary for his and my survival. Again, God had a plan that we both would live, and I would not incur a large medical bill because of the birth complications. God also allowed me to have one of the best doctors in Memphis as my obstetrician.

When I had first moved to Memphis, I was thirty-two weeks pregnant. Most doctors would not accept a new patient late in the pregnancy because of the liability related to the unknown prenatal care for the first thirty-two weeks. At my first appointment, I hand-carried all my medical records from California, outlining the prenatal care I had received from week four of the pregnancy. I was also in my mid-thirties and was considered a high-risk geriatric pregnancy. God knew that I needed this doctor with specialized knowledge to help me survive my son's birth.

As I think back on the first few hours after giving birth, I remember looking at my son and thinking, "Wait a minute, who has left me in charge of this little life?" I vowed at that moment that Aaron and I would walk this life together with an understanding that God was in control. Trusting God allowed me to rest in knowing that He knew what was ahead for our lives. Trusting God's plan provided blessing after blessing for my son and me from the start. The doctor knew that I was a single mom and would be leaving the hospital with just me and the baby. But my amazing parents had come to be with me for the birth. The doctor allowed me to stay in the hospital for four days rather than release me after two days so I could get a little extra rest in preparation for the next phase of my journey as a single mama.

When I walked into my new home, behold, I saw a miracle worked by my parents' hands. Unbeknownst to me, my parents decorated and purchased the necessary items for my son's room without a hint to me. They had purchased a crib, a glider rocker, a changing table, a dresser, and wall shelves with stuffed animals and toys lined up. My dad worked nonstop for three days to get everything set up so that I would be at peace when I got home with the baby. They were supportive, kind, and loving when I was most vulnerable. They were a blessing beyond measure. When it was time for them to leave town, four weeks after I gave birth, my parents stopped at the store to get a mobile for the crib just because they knew I wanted one for the baby. In those gestures, my parents assured me that they loved me and my son and would provide unconditional love, grace, and mercy; I felt forgiven, I felt loved, I felt healed, and I felt a peace that God had worked His plan.

My son is the absolute best thing that has happened to me outside of Jesus. He has helped me be my best self, my most healthy self, and my most happy self. God had a plan for our lives. He graciously walked with me every step of the way through the pregnancy and beyond. God forgave me, and amid my forgiveness, He blessed me greatly. God restored that which was lost and made me whole. In God's plan, I found that despite the church's response to my sin and pregnancy, I was able to find healing from the hurt and gain a new perspective on what the church should be to others. As I continue to work in the church, I strive to encourage others to have a personal relationship with Christ, and I desire to show grace, love, and mercy to all women and girls who walk through the doors. I endeavor to be the voice of grace and mercy as I walk out God's plan for my life. Herein lies my confidence:

> *And we know that in all things God works for the good of those who love him, who have been called according to his purpose. (Romans 8:28 NIV)*

It does not say that everything that happens to us is good. It merely reminds us that our God knows how to turn things around and make the not-so-nice things work for our good. What good? You may ask, Has it been worked out for good in my life as a result of this? I will tell you this:

In the broad details and the small details, He worked this pregnancy out for nothing but good as he worked His divine plan and divine placement in my life and my son's life. Today I am in right standing with my God. I have a healthy, happy son, with a calling and anointing on his life. I hope to impart to my son always to trust God's plan for him. I pray that this story will embrace him and show him just how important he is to God and me, and one day, he will pass this love on to others and to his family, should that be God's plan for his life.

And I pray that you, my precious readers, will know that God loves you and gave His Son, Jesus, for you because you matter to Him. And I pray you'll find the plan of God for your life, and walk therein!

Tracks of My Tears

by Bambi Ward

My parents were married in Virginia, where my father's family lived. My parents met in high school and stuck together. My parents lived in North Carolina until just before I was born. Strangely, my life on Planet Earth began when my mom and father decided to abruptly leave North Carolina, along with my other three siblings in tow, to embark upon a long train ride to Brooklyn, New York. Even stranger, my mom was nine months pregnant with me at the time of this long journey, and she probably didn't consult with a physician to determine if it was a safe thing to do. Why was it so urgent to get out of Dodge? you might ask. I later did, and my mom told me she had hoped to make it to their destination and then give birth, but I decided to make my grand escape and was born on the train bound for Brooklyn. My voice was first heard aboard that train. My mom told me it was a scream; I shed my first tear and fought my first battle for life onboard a fast-moving train. Little did I know that my life's pattern, on that day, was established. As abruptly as they had left North Carolina, we now suddenly had to exit this train at the next stop to seek proper medical treatment for both my mom and me. The next stop was Baltimore, Maryland, and we were admitted to a hospital and discharged three days later. Upon our release, my grandpa, my mom's dad, came to take us home with him. We stayed with my grandpa and step-grandmother for three or four months, and then we moved about two houses down from him; my mom insisted we stay close.

There we were in Brooklyn, but why had my parents taken such a risk to get there so quickly? A risk that was not measured very well, as it turned out. My father needed work badly, and my grandpa believed that he could find a job in New York and offered to house us until he did. So, like that popular movie back in the day, they loaded up all the belongings that could fit in their luggage, with me safely tucked in the womb, and boarded a train headed for Brooklyn. Finding a good job could be the equivalent of finding gold, and they were thankful when my dad found a job as a baker. He was a great baker.

It appeared that my parents were the last holdouts of our family clan to move to New York, except for one aunt who eventually followed us there. Once we arrived in New York, my mom's siblings would visit us often, and we became acquainted with her side of the family. My mom has three sisters and one brother. She is her mom's fourth child, and interestingly, I am her fourth child. But she wasn't born on a train.

I have never known my father's family, only his mother because we had spent a short stay with her, and he was her only child. Rumor has it that his father had many other children; we never got to know them. I later learned that my father's mom and dad never married, which was considered taboo and became a big scandal. Family members tended to not speak about such embarrassing situations.

His father never left North Carolina and died there, and I never got to meet him. I guess it had become rather difficult for my grandmother, who was a single mother. There was a big stink because my grandfather refused to marry her, and they both lived in the same town, probably the same neighborhood. I can only imagine the town gossip.

Mom discovered at her six-week checkup after giving birth to me that she was pregnant again; this would be baby number five. It was a boy, and he was born in 1958. Approximately two years later, in 1960, my mom gave birth to baby number six, another boy. Life became too much for my mom. What was it that caused this onset of distress? I don't believe that was ever made known to us, at least not to me. My mom had become too emotional to care for all of her children. She decided she needed help; she required caretakers for some of us to help make her life bearable. The way I saw it, she began to pawn us children off on anyone who would take us.

My mom kept the two oldest children, my brother and sister, and the two youngest boys. I guess my sister and I got the short end of the stick, and out of the house we went. She sent me to live with my grandpa and his wife, my step-grandmother, at four. My sister went to live with another family member. Four of my siblings remained with my mom and father, and two of us felt pawned off. Although my father was in the house, he was still an absent father because he was not emotionally equipped to care for us and obviously rendered no support to our mom. I loved my father; he was such a calm, soft-spoken man. I often wonder if it was passiveness that I was admiring in him because he was absent in plain sight; nevertheless, I loved him.

This might be an opportunity to share a little history with you. I have long since learned that this type of social behavior—having a large number of children and having them in succession—was the norm, even when it was a challenge to provide food for the family. Women would give birth to many children because they had no say on the subject, and birth control was either unheard-of or a well-kept secret. The first birth control, which was oral contraception, was approved in 1960. In 1965, the Supreme Court gave married couples the right to use birth control. Why didn't my mom use it? I do not know.

Many states denied birth control to unmarried women. This ineffective notion was that by not providing birth control to unmarried women, the denial in itself would act as birth control. I guess they didn't see the number of babies being born to unwed mothers; the theory was just that, a theory. It wasn't until 1972 that the Supreme Court legalized birth control for all U.S. citizens, including unmarried women. The fact it took the involvement of the Supreme Court tells us how intense the battle was. However, many women lost their lives seeking illegal and hazardous means of ridding themselves of unwanted pregnancies. They would drink turpentine, use coat hangers, or visiting the town abortion butcher who left women dying on his table or sent them home to bleed to death. The environment was not conducive for a woman to bring forth a child, knowing that she would have to go it alone even if the man was in the home; she struggled with provisions and rearing the children alone. Imagine giving birth to that many children. An older woman in the church had twenty-five children, and she had little to no social or emotional support. Don't even try to imagine that. The village ideology was alive and well, but it seemed that the village was missing in action. However, my father was always in the home. He worked and did what he had to do; he was not a drunkard and did not appear to be a skirt chaser, but he was absent emotionally. There were no hugs and kisses in our home, nor were the girls told how pretty they were or the boys told how handsome they looked. We were an emotionally bankrupt family.

Off I went to live with my grandpa. Because we had lived near his house, I had visited frequently and spent time with him, so it felt normal until the time came when I could no longer go home. At the age of four, I experienced separation from my mom. Imagine what it must have felt like to endure such a separation. As time went by, I enjoyed my grandpa because he would talk to me and spend time with me in the basement and let me play marbles and do treasure hunts. But my step-grandmother made it clear that she did not want me in her home, and she treated me accordingly. She had never had any children, but after I arrived she took control of a young lady's baby girl. The child's mother was a drug addict, and she knew she would not care about where her child was, so it didn't take much to convince the lady to give the child to her. She moved her in and gave her a private room even though I was there first. I had to sleep on the couch. The little girl was a year younger than me. She was a lighter-skinned Black child with curly hair, and she was, therefore, the goddess of the house. It would take another culture class to explain this, but I don't wish to share that at this time. She would get the first and maybe the last piece of the cake, and she most certainly got the best stuff; after all, she was a goddess. But at least I got to play and talk with my grandpa.

Of course, I am telling you this story as a much older woman, but I am also just beginning to allow myself to remember these stories. It took many years for my therapist to unbury many of these stories. These stories were painful and buried deep. I could verbally only tell my story in bite sizes—actually, more like a nibble. Like the one I am about to share, some of these stories didn't surface until I wrote this story. Our group of lady writers would meet monthly to pray and pray and allow the Spirit of God to minister to us. It was during one of those visitations that God revealed to a dear sister, friend, and fellow writer, Angelique, that I had spent a lot of time in a closet, and finally,

I could no longer keep it buried; it had to surface, and surface it did. I did not want to share this story because even now, it is painful. But in our circle of love and prayer, it was healing and yet a struggle at the same time. I remembered these things because my spirit had etched them in my soul.

My grandpa was a hard-working man. He was a maintenance guy for an apartment building in Brooklyn and had to ride public transportation. He worked in the white section of town, and yes, discrimination and segregation were real then, and they drew the separation lines on the maps. Sad to say, it appears to be somewhat the same today, but that is another social class I will pass for now. His commute was long and tiring. It seemed that no sooner had he closed the door behind him and walked a few steps away from the house than the witch would launch into action and lock me in the closet. The abuse I suffered at my step-grandmother's hands happened frequently and became more intense, and it would begin immediately after my grandpa left for work. The closet was dark; only a glimmer of light was visible from underneath the door.

Some stairs once led to the servant's room above the closet, but they had shut off the bedroom. The floor of the room above now became the ceiling for the closet. They left partial stairs in the closet, which was not very high. Locking me in a closet didn't make any sense; I couldn't understand why she did it. The closet smelled musty, and it was relatively small. It was a closet. I would stare at shoes all day because that is where the light would shine, and I would walk up and down the short stairs and sit on them. Why didn't I panic, scream, and yell? Because I knew the punishment would be severe. But on the inside, I was panicking, screaming, and crying. I spent hours in this closet only to be let out for a brief period to eat and to use the restroom—a very short time. If she had company over, I would get a reprieve and get to enjoy a little freedom. After all, the witch didn't want others to know she was a witch. I spent many months in that closet, and not only did my imagination expand, but I was continually asking why was I there; what had I done? It was in that closet that I, a little girl, learned to weep. I am sure if that house is still standing and the closet is still there, in it, you will find the tracks of my tears.

She seemed to know precisely when my grandpa would be returning home, or she stood close by the door listening for his footsteps, because before he would come walking through the door, she would remove me from the closet and act as though all was well. Of course, all was well for her, but not for me; it was a nightmare for me. Even though I had a reprieve from the closet since my grandpa was home, I wasn't necessarily safe. She would take every opportunity to remind me that she had the power. She would, without warning, slap me hard on my face just because she could. Of course, I dared not scream. Her eyes would torment me; I was a child on edge. The other girl in the house was always blaming me for doing things that I didn't do. She accused me of doing something to her, and my step-grandmother beat me so severely that standing up was a challenge. It appeared that for anything I would do to take any attention from the other girl in the house, I would immediately experience corporal punishment to the highest degree and be placed on what felt like death row.

She was always so kind to the other girl, and on one occasion, she had made her a nice cup of hot chocolate. I wanted some so badly, but she wouldn't give me any. Somehow it came to the attention of my grandpa, and he made her give me a cup. She boiled the water, made my hot chocolate, and placed the cup in front of me. I was sitting at the table on the edge of my chair, so excited to drink my hot chocolate. I grabbed it as I saw the other girl did, but my cup was so hot that I immediately let go, baptizing my chest with the hot chocolate. The pain from the burn was unbearable, and I can remember screaming in terror. It was the one time I couldn't hold the scream in. Sad to say, they didn't take me to the hospital because they didn't have any insurance, and my grandpa scurried about to get something to help relieve me of my pain. They applied a home remedy of urine and ice—yes, you read that correctly, urine and ice. It was nasty. And even worse, whose urine was it? Twice nasty! I suffered third-degree burns on my chest—a deep, painful burn that has left its scars as evidence to this very day. The scars are evidence of more than just being burned but also of being hated as a little girl by my elder, who should have protected me. Yes, here lie the tracks of my many tears.

After that incident, my grandpa started taking me to work with him, unknowingly saving me after a yearlong closet encampment. He was a very mild-mannered guy and seemed to go along to get along, but he appeared to be trying to save me in this instance because he knew she had purposely scalded me. After everything my grandpa did to keep me safe from the witch's hands, she managed to get her hands on me a few more times. As I said, the other girl in the house was always blaming me for doing things that I didn't do. One day she accused me of doing something to her that sent the witch into action again. My grandpa had left to go to the store, allowing her the opportunity to put her hands on me, and she beat me so badly I could barely breathe. From four to six, I endured such abuse that it left me speechless and very troubled. It seems like the trouble was stacking up, and the odds were against me, and I was only six years old. How many tracks of tears can be made by one so small?

At the age of six, I was returned home to my mom, battered, scarred, and defeated, but happy to be back home with my mom, dad, and siblings. It appeared that my mom had gotten better. She had begun to hang out with other ladies who offered her support, and most of the ladies had children around our ages. Hence, it also provided us children support with decent social interactions we had suffered without for so long. Mommy started going to church with these ladies, and she seemed to be better and happier. And we all had to go with her. She was a special usher to the pastor in this Pentecostal church. I had returned home just in time to start school, first grade, and I did not want to go to school. I didn't belong there, and I knew this at a young age. So, I would act out! Most of us were home by now, and the older ones would hang out only with each other, and it felt as though they weren't there. I had a smart sister, two years older than me, who had blazed the trail in school, and, oh, did she blaze the trail. I was the recipient of her old teacher who loved her and continuously bragged about her. I saw having her as my teacher as a curse.

I knew this teacher was wondering what was wrong with me. I was so opposite of my sister. The school had a rating system for students; a student would be ranked in the 2.1 group if they were smart, listened well, and followed instructions. I was moved to the 2.9 group. This group was titled "dummies, retards, and, basically, losers." I would fight, bite, or spit on others to get my negative attention. I gladly earned my rank with this group, and I didn't care. There were no expectations for this group, and I would be left alone. It worked for me.

I felt lost in the shuffle, and mom was still having children. Approximately two years later, in 1962, she was pregnant and gave birth to another baby boy, making the total of mouths to feed seven. There I was, trying to find my way in this jungle called my family and the world. School was beginning to take on a different look for me. With my new title, "the dummy and retard," things were changing; no one cared about this bunch of children. There were no expectations of us. As long as we didn't cause any problems or draw any attention to ourselves, everything would go well for us. They simply passed us from one grade to the next. But I was "good" with that! What I didn't know was that this title would follow me through high school and beyond. Even more significant and unbeknownst to me, this title, "the retard," was engraved on my soul, my inner identity.

In between this time and approximately two years later, in 1964, mom gave birth to another baby boy, baby number eight, and he was the last baby born. And there I sat, in the middle of the eight children. I was not the oldest nor the youngest; I was in the middle, where it seemed easy to get lost. I felt invisible, and only when I did bad things would I be noticed.

Along with the other women supporting my mom by helping out with us children, my mom's sister, our aunt, helped out. She had followed mom to Brooklyn from North Carolina, and she always depended on my mom to take care of her. She had one child, a girl, and she was the same age as my baby sister. Because my mom needed help, my aunt volunteered to press us girls' hair. Hair pressing was when one would use a hot iron that looked like a hair comb but was made out of metal, heated on a stove, and used to straighten Black hair. Today, the flat iron is the tool used. The straightening comb is much hotter and can cause much more damage, but they still exist today. Madam C.J. Walker developed hair products for use on Black hair in the early 1900s. She was the first Black woman millionaire. There is a movie inspired by her life called *Self Made*. Who actually invented the straightening or hot comb seems controversial, but the film is educational.

We would go to our aunt's house weekly to have our hair pressed. She burned both of us girls with that hot comb, but I was always the one she would burn the worst. First I was scarred by a hot chocolate baptism to the chest. Now I was being scarred intentionally on my face and neck, with a hot iron whirled by my aunt. What else was going to happen to me? Now I could maybe feel a little of what an animal feels when being branded. And I was always the one my mom would send to help her do her laundry, clean her house, and go grocery shopping with her. She would rudely call us nappy head and slap us on the side of heads and faces. Because she was a lighter-skinned Black woman, she thought of herself as the best of the best, but I thought she had the worst hair and wore a wig to hide it. This clash within the race over lighter-skinned Blacks versus darker skin and the nappy hair versus the good hair is all evident of self-hatred. But those of us of darker skin paid the highest price; remember the little girl that lived in the house with me? She got to sit, play, and watch television while I had to look at shoes in a locked closet.

This is not hurting as much as it might because I now know that everything God has made, He called "good"! You might call this behavior one of those sicknesses implanted within the race. It is all about color, texture, and shame over things out of our control, and it is *not* true. When she would do our hair, she would hold our head between her knees and dare us to move. The pressing iron was scorching hot, and she would leave sores in my head from the burns. She knew how I felt about her, and I was her punching bag; she was always hitting me. Every weekend or every other week was our schedule, but we tried so hard to find a way not to have to go back. I became desperate and learned how to braid our hair and make it look good enough that mom was pleased. Finally, saved from the wicked aunt!

As I have previously stated, my father was always in the home, and he was the calm that I so needed in my life. I watched him. I could always count on him being there even though he often seemed powerless. But just as I was entering my teenage years, our parents dropped a bomb on me. My mom and dad separated and later divorced after being together for at least sixteen years. I could not believe he left and later remarried. My heart received the final crack that broke it into small pieces when it became crystal clear that he had been having an affair for some time. It was evident because the daughter he had by his new wife was the same age as my baby sister. My dad was very special to me, and to have him out of the home under these circumstances was devasting. He just seemed to be so calm, and I needed that calmness. When he left, it broke my heart and left a gaping hole in our family— more tracks for my tears.

I looked around, and wow, I was fifteen, growing up fast in more ways than I should. My sister had a boyfriend who would come over to visit, and he would bring a friend. The friend and I started talking, and one thing led to another. He seemed like a very nice guy, but I was a very young, broken girl who needed healing, not engaging in an emotional relationship. But we did! And I soon found myself pregnant. I remember my mom's anger at finding out that I was pregnant; I could no longer hide the evidence because of the morning sickness. I recall the day when she told me to get ready because I was going somewhere with her. She took me to a clinic, and I assumed she was forcing me to see a doctor to make sure the baby and I were okay. Yes, I should have been under a doctor's care. They escorted us to a room. It was a bland room with no color, no emotional warmth, no pictures, just cold, and it made me feel hopeless. I was so afraid to be in this predicament of being pregnant, and now I had an angry mom growling, pulling, and directing me without any other emotion other than pure anger to see a doctor.

After escorting me into a room, the nurse told me to undress and lie on the table. And she added some extra words: "And remain there!" The room was cold to the eye as well as the soul, and the people were as well. I followed the instructions, and the next thing I knew, I was being strapped down like a prisoner and treated like one. Suddenly, I saw instruments that made me feel scared. It wasn't too long before, even without prior experience, I realized they were performing an abortion on me. How times had changed; not only was birth control now available to every woman, including girls or women like me—the unmarried kind—but abortion was now legal. I felt numb, and I knew that it was for my psychological protection. Afterward, my mom put me on birth control pills and ordered me to take them. In many ways, I believe she intended to prevent me from becoming like her with a boatload of children, a lot of stress, and no bright future. But sadly, I must report, it wasn't working. I refused to take the pills, and she couldn't force them down my throat. I was taking back my power, the power to say what I wanted to do or not do.

At the ripe young age of sixteen, whatever that means, I found myself pregnant again. I find it difficult to explain what was going on in my head or my emotions, but my very soul was in much turmoil. Within one month, I found myself having three to four different boyfriends, and I don't think "boyfriends" is the proper title for them. I knew who I was pregnant by and decided that he had made me angry and disappointed me; therefore, no baby by him would come forth from me. And this time, my mom didn't have to insist or trick me into having an abortion; it was my choice. Can you believe it? The thing that once scared me half to death, I now used as birth control. I refused the pill and chose abortion instead. Why? If only it were simple enough to understand and explain. It was far more profound and darker than the abortion itself. I was making companionship choices, and obviously, I thought that a baby would force a marriage. In hindsight, it was a sickness that had invaded my mind and the mind of other young ladies to disregard human life totally. Why? Because we disregarded our very own lives; at least, I know I did. It was as though someone had sent us a message by telepathy that this is how you get and keep a man: you get pregnant by him, and if he decides to stay with you, the baby stays safe; if not, then the baby's life is optional. I had an advanced case of this sickness because abortion by choice had entered the equation. What was once forbidden and only available in back allies or on the butcher's table, you could now do a walk-in and have it done on request. And although I was under eighteen, I could get an abortion without parental permission. With that power, I also realized that I could choose not to remain in a relationship; I took advantage of both.

With all this insanity going on, there was something inside of me that kept me in high school, endeavoring to graduate. But remember, I was in the 2.9 group, the special students, and no one seemed to care or notice us because we stayed out of the way. They passed us through the educational system like cattle heading for the slaughter. The agreement stood: I wasn't going to give them any problems, and I would get to graduate. I had so many problems donated to me, and many I gifted myself, all of which were far more than I could handle. Every step I took, I left teardrops. As I could see graduation approaching, I continued on that downward spiral of looking for love in all the wrong places. I know it sounds like a song or maybe a cliché, but this was my life. And, yes, once again, I was pregnant, at seventeen, and about to walk across the stage. With my child safely tucked away in my womb, we walked across that stage. After all, if my mom could board a train for a very long journey at nine months pregnant, I could surely walk across a stage to complete the graduation ceremony. Upon giving birth, I received the fantastic news that it was a boy. I was in a different mindset, and he had escaped abortion.

I had met his father after the second abortion. It seems that I always felt like I had to make sure I had closed all my loose ends before a new beginning. I knew how to close out an unwanted relationship or one that just stopped working as I had planned. If I became pregnant in a relationship that was no longer working, abortion became the period at the end of it. Or maybe it was an exclamation point; whatever it was, I had become good at calling it quits by tying it with the bow of an abortion. I didn't allow any grass to grow under my feet. I didn't let painful memories hang out in my mind; I would bury them in my heart, in my subconscious, and from time to time, they would surface and trouble me. I couldn't handle that, so off in a mad dash I went to find a new relationship. That never seemed hard to do; I could always find a willing partner who was just as broken as I was.

By now, my mom has embedded herself in the church. She was hitting me hard with her words, like, "You are in sin, and you are going to die and go to hell!" She preached that sermon until my boyfriend and I finally decided to get married, and my mom gladly signed the papers allowing me to marry at seventeen. Marriage was like a badge of honor, regardless of who you married, because being single, especially if you had a child, was a stigma. Being married was all that mattered. Even though there was physical and mental abuse, no one cared because at least you were married. Another sickness of that era, and I dare say it is alive and well today, was domestic violence. Although I did not tolerate physical abuse, I ate many hot, mentally abused meals served to me daily.

My husband's maternal grandmother wanted him to marry the girl he had been engaged to, and she hated me because I got pregnant by him. She preferred someone she felt was more prim and proper. You know, it always appears that when things go wrong, the fault is laid at the woman's feet, never the man's. Because I was pregnant, she saw me as the one who was destroying his life. Yes, it was yet another sickness of that era that is alive and well even to this day. We were married in the church and pursued a life together. How successful was that pursuit is telling! We didn't have the necessities to have a successful experience in life. The first year we lived with my mom, and afterward, we moved in with his paternal grandmother and then back to my mom's house, where we lived on the top floor. He was nineteen, and I had just turned eighteen. That was three moves within two years.

The houses in New York are rather steep and can go up to five stories. They are making the best use of their real estate. I know only too well about these buildings; I had spent a lot of time just looking around. From the time we were married until the time we separated and later divorced was almost seven years, and I was twenty-four years old. I was never happy. We moved over seven times and yet remained in Brooklyn. Those moves didn't happen because we were bored and moving on, nor were they a sign of upward mobility for us; no, landlords evicted us over and over again. After we separated, my life continued its downward spiral. I left teardrops in all seven of those places we lived. I cried so much that my tears had tears, leaving me dehydrated. Feeling somewhat inadequate and depressed because my marriage did not work, I didn't allow space to feel anymore; to do that would be dangerous because I was sure I could not deal with my feelings. Avoidance became my coping mechanism.

Ignoring them and burying them was the best thing for me to do, and that is precisely what I did. I hid my emotions, and I pushed forward, or so I thought. And then I would meet someone else, and the fling would begin again. You will not believe this, or maybe you will. Once again, I found myself pregnant, and I needed to make a decision. Because I knew it would not work between this new guy and me, the only thing I thought to do was, yes, have an abortion. I often wonder if my mom appreciated the door she had opened, although she appeared to want to close it by encouraging me to use birth control pills. I was in a cycle, choosing what seemed to me the easy way out. I didn't think about my behavior because I knew that abortion was always an option if I messed up. I exercised that option and chose to have another abortion. So, acting as the closer, I tidied it up with an abortion, and I packed everything up so I could move on.

Move on I did, off and running into another relationship. I couldn't stand being alone. Rather than marry this time, we had a common law marriage—living together without a marriage certificate, but the state recognizes it as a legal union. I called it the "no paper" marriage. But along with this relationship came another pregnancy. I chose this time to keep the man, and therefore, the child was safe as well. This beautiful child was a girl. We stayed in New York, but we moved twice in the short-lived relationship. Yes, short-lived! We stayed together for a little over four years, and once again, there was a separation that ended the common law marriage. Another relationship was dead, buried, and left behind. The only memories I have are the tracks of my tears! But I am a closer, remember: no grass grows under these feet, and I was ready to do something different but yet the same. I needed a new relationship, and I got just that.

Husband number three was in the forecast, but where was he? I had already met him before I closed out the last one. We connected, and we did something new and different. To celebrate my turning thirty, we got married and moved to Texas. After we had moved twice, I found out that, yes, I was pregnant again, and I gave birth to another baby girl. She was the last child I birthed. I was the mom of three aborted babies and three living, beautiful children, one boy and two girls. I wish I could say the marriage lasted, but it didn't.

We stayed together for approximately five years, and I was off and running again. All my relationships and marriages were jokes for several reasons. First of all, broken pieces don't make a whole person. It is incredible how quick we are to believe that someone else can heal us and make us better, but that is irritational. I could no longer take being the only one working two to three jobs trying to keep a roof over our head and food on the table while being mentally abused. These men were nothing but burdens, but I knew that when I met them. I guess I just wanted trophies, but all I got were burdens too heavy for me to carry. But this time and with this marriage, I was tired, completely burned out. I had moved more than thirty times within fifteen years between all my relationships and marriages. I was born on a moving train, and all I seemed to show for my life were constant movements and the tracks of my tears! Every place I have lived, I marked some part of it with my tears.

I was beyond fed up; I was choking on all of my life's repeated mistakes. By now, my son was all grown up and had joined the military. I was so proud of him, and he had been so kind and took on the responsibility of his little sister while I tried to figure things out with my oldest daughter. I rented a truck, loaded it up with most of my stuff and my daughter, and left Texas headed for North Carolina. Nothing like a long road trip to help clear your mind and give you the feeling of freedom. That is what I hoped I was doing—breaking free. We arrived safely in North Carolina, and I soon found a house to rent. I then drove to New York to move my mom to live with us in North Carolina. I knew the job would be tough when I took it, but that was my mom, and I had to try to live with her for her sake.

I could not seem to find a job, even with all of my qualifications and numerous searches. I found myself gleaning in the fields picking butter beans and being paid by the basket. You do what you have to do to take care of your family. But I never gave up, and I contacted my cousin, who lived in Richmond, Virginia, and was a public transit driver. I was a commercial licensed driver, and he helped me to get a job there. It was approximately an hour and a half's drive from North Carolina to Richmond, Virginia, and I would stay with him during the week and drive home on the weekend. I finally found an apartment in Virginia and moved there. I had one serious problem; my mom wasn't the best childcare provider for my daughter. She was heavy-handed and was not gentle in any way. I gave up the job, and we moved to Schenectady, New York. I had a sister who lived there and had a rental property she had rented to my other sister. We moved into her rental property, which was big enough for all of us. The houses in New York felt like apartments because they had so many floors. Eventually, my mom moved into a senior citizen's place, which made her happy, and I must say, a few other people were happy as well. I was introduced to this guy by my mom and his mother. They attended the same church and decided to play matchmakers. Well, I moved him and his daughter into my home. My daughter and his daughter became good friends. At the time, I struggled with disciplinary problems with my daughter and hoped this might have a calming effect. It did not work; she still wanted to do everything that displeased me. I felt like I was being paid back for all the times I gave my mom a hard time.

I found a job that pleased me, with working with the nurses' union, and the money was perfect. With the challenges I was having with my daughter and having to miss work or come in late due to conflicts, they asked me to resign, and I resigned. It was far better to resign than to be fired. I started a new job shortly afterward as a teacher's assistant. By then, I had earned my A A degree and added a few other recognitions to my resume. I was happy! I received a phone call from my son, who asked if I could come and spend some time there because his wife had given birth to their first child and my first grandchild. Of course I said yes, and off I went to California. I had become a grandmother to a beautiful baby girl. What a blessing from my son and his wife. This beautiful blessing gave me cause to pause and think hard about my actions. I spent my time there and returned home. What a joy—a grandmother!

I continued to enjoy my job with the school system and was still struggling with a teenage daughter until I eventually lost that battle, and she went to live with her boyfriend. Not too long after that, I received another call from my son asking me to come again to help with another childbirth. This time, the blessing was a handsome grandson. Life was getting a little sweeter until a few years later, my son asked me to help him with the children. Unfortunately, their marriage was in trouble and not working. After my arrival in California, the situation called for more permanent support. I returned to New York, sold some things in a few yard sales, and returned to live with my son to become the caretaker to my grandchildren. California became my home.

Then something happened. My oldest granddaughter was attending Harvest Church in Elk Grove, California, which had started with an invitation from one of her friends. She, in turn, invited me, and although I was somewhat hesitant, I attended. In reality, I was dropping off my grandchildren so they could enjoy church. But one day, as I was dropping them off, I was befriended by a sister named Val, and she was kind and invited me to stay. I felt compelled to do just that. It was an enjoyable experience, and I would come and hang out with my grandchildren in their classes. I hung out like this for a long time, and eventually, after a background check, I became a volunteer with the children's ministry because my grandson was one of the babies. Suddenly, I felt like my passion had met my purpose, and all of this was a calming and quiet experience. Imagine me finding solace in the nursery after having three abortions. Maybe this was God's way of beginning to walk me to my healing. And I felt it amongst the babies.

I continued to sit with my therapist, trying desperately to sort things out. It is essential to put things in their proper place and then try to sort it all out. It's like I do my laundry. My clothes go into one container, but when it is time to do laundry, they have to be washed separately according to color, texture, and other criteria. I was being pulled apart, and believe me, I was clawing hard not to let go. One example was the revelation of the time I spent in the closet. I often wondered why I was always looking down at people's feet; I had a shoe fetish because of all the time I spent in that closet with nothing but my imagination and shoes. I have lived a life filled with anxiety; now I know why. I continued to visit the church and hang out, and I also joined the women's mentoring group at the church. The books we read and discussed were tearing me apart and healing me at the same time. I had to do bite sizes. I cannot address all the abuse I suffered; there is far too much to name in this short story. Maybe I will have to write a book one day.

The girl, the teenager, and the graduating student in the 2.9 group labeled a retard, a dummy, and a loser has today managed to acquire an AA degree, has worked in law offices and schools, and now is partially retired as an educator—and for guess what group? Special students! Those twelve years in an educational system that labeled me as "special" were in the big picture, preparing me for my future. My passion and purpose collided, and I didn't even know it. It also became abundantly clear that all those years, I had been searching for that hard-working but calm man; I was trying to find my daddy.

Today, I can tell you I have found my daddy. Not my earthly dad, who has since passed away, but my heavenly Father, who has found me. I read many scriptures that tell me I am not an orphan; I have a Father:

*The Spirit you received does not make you slaves, so that
you live in fear again; rather, the Spirit you received brought
about your adoption to sonship. And by him we cry, "Abba,
Father." The Spirit himself testifies with our spirit that we
are God's children. Now if we are children, then we are
heirs—heirs of God and co-heirs with Christ, if indeed we
share in his sufferings in order that we may also share in his
glory. (Romans 8: 15–17 NIV)*

*But when the set time had fully come, God sent his Son,
born of a woman, born under the law, to redeem those
under the law, that we might receive adoption to sonship.
Because you are his sons, God sent the Spirit of his Son
into our hearts, the Spirit who calls out, "Abba, Father." So
you are no longer a slave, but God's child; and since you
are his child, God has made you also an heir. (Galatians 4:
4–7 NIV)*

It was as though He told me to stop laying tracks for more tears
to fall because suddenly, I felt hope. It is not that I do not cry—oh,
no, I cry and cry—but there are no more tracks of my tears being laid
down as though I am traveling to no place in particular, just going
down the track, hoping without hope. No, I have hope today, and my
tears are not dropping on the ground, but He, my heavenly Father,
places them in His bottle.

*You number my wanderings; <u>Put my tears into Your
bottle</u>; Are they not in Your book? When I cry out to You,
Then my enemies will turn back; This I know, because
God is for me. (Psalms 56:8–9 NKJV)*

One final blow struck my heart—not to break it, but to heal it. It happened when a dear sister said to me, "Bambi, isn't it going to be amazing when you are connected to those three aborted babies, and you will know they have been well cared for by your heavenly Father?" The burden lifted off my soul, and I could finally forgive myself. No more shame; no more guilt. I wept, and I finally knew—I WAS FREE!

And God has a bottle with your name on it that holds all your tears!

Acknowledgments

I begin first thanking God for entrusting me with this book. He stretched me beyond my comfort zone, assigned twenty-one women to my care, women who didn't need another voice of judgment but true love and appreciation. He provided the resources to make this book a reality, to God be the glory!

Thanks to my family for encouraging me once they knew this book was in the works. And then God appointed some of them to take this plunge with me. They dared to become vulnerable and transparent, sharing their stories with me for the first time.

I want to thank the twenty-one women who, without them, there would be no book. The long hours of workshops and traveling to various locations for video shoots, they did it with a smile and even laughter. A three-year journey and they never lost faith in me or doubted the publishing of this book. Thank you for sharing your pain and healing with me, and now you are sharing with the world.

Thanks to Mr. Frank J. Woods II, Executive Director of Future Development Youth Center, founded on March 28, 2014. We met in 2018, and he joined this venture as the Producer/Editor of each contributor and marketing videos. His patience has been incredible and much appreciated because we thought we knew what we didn't know. We have since learned that the process of taking a video from the basic to a well-produced short movie is daunting. Frank continues to work with youth. Thanks again, Frank!

I met this young man when he was twenty-one, and during our introduction, I learned he was a Film Producer. I wanted him on my team. He said yes, and the journey began. He never quit on me even when things became chaotic; his love overpowered his frustration. His name is Ashton Aspley, Co-Founder & Director of Production of Ubiquitous Pictures. He worked diligently to produce successful videos – He was our lights, camera, action man! As I was struggling to name this book, this 21-year-old looked at me with an intense look of surprise as if to say, "shame on you," don't you know, the title is 21. Thank you so much, Ashton. We all love and appreciate you!

Thanks to all who stood on the sideline, waving at me as I continued on this journey. Many took the time to review some of the stories. They provided valuable feedback, thanks to friends and family, Pastor Phyllis Towles, Shonet Brown, LiMetrias Daniels-Pierce, Betty Short-Sams, Patti Kremer, Dominique Bukasa, Sharon Lewis, LaQuesha Smith, Jasmine Duarte, Jason Perez, Lori Shimaski, even our director, Ashton Aspley.

Finally, but not least, I want to thank my girls, Elizabeth Brewer, Janice Palmer, and Shirley Redding, my special cheering squad. You all smiled at me every time this book was mentioned, and you immersed me in encouragement. Friends are gifts from God, and I thank God for you three wonderful gifts!

The Author

DOROTHY MARIE RIVERS-LOVE was born in the hills of Marvell, Arkansas. She lived in a two-room shack on what she calls a glorified plantation. When she should have been in school at ten years old, she had to chop and pick cotton, putting in a hard day's work. Poverty, racism, even border-line abuse could not sway her from believing there was something beautiful yet to be discovered on the other side of those hills.

She spent many hours lying on her back, staring into space, watching airplanes fly over, imagining where could they possibly be going since she had never left her small country town. She enjoyed writing at a young age and writing poetry was her favorite pastime. Dorothy finally left the hills of Arkansas and traveled to Sacramento, California when she was fifteen.

Her dreams materialized. She joined the military and served in uniform for thirty-one years. Some of her duties included Radio Operator, Military Police, Equal Opportunity Advisor and Diversity Coordinator. She received numerous awards and decorations.

During her military service, she graduated from law school, obtaining her Juris Doctor degree. She retired in 2013 as a Master Sergeant. Her new career is loving God and loving others. You will find her supporting women in becoming victorious and wrapping her arms around the youth. Dorothy considers this book a labor of love and a gift from God to her and the world.

I fought within myself to complete this book and publish it in 2019 and then 2020, the year of COVID-19, and as you can see, that didn't happen. As I was beginning to feel a little defeated, slothful, distressed, and a few other words, *God caused me to pause*. He said it was me who wanted 2019 and 2020; it was always His will that this book titled 21 be published in 2021. *The power of a pause!*

Our backs to the world; our eyes on the Cross…The Vantage Point!